MW00850255

Armed Groups

Armed Groups

The 21st Century Threat

Peter G. Thompson

ROWMAN & LITTLEFIELD
Lanham • Boulder • New York • London

Published by Rowman & Littlefield
A wholly owned subsidiary of The Rowman & Littlefield Publishing Group, Inc.
4501 Forbes Boulevard, Suite 200, Lanham, Maryland 20706
www.rowman.com

16 Carlisle Street, London W1D 3BT, United Kingdom

Copyright © 2014 by Rowman & Littlefield

All rights reserved. No part of this book may be reproduced in any form or by any electronic or mechanical means, including information storage and retrieval systems, without written permission from the publisher, except by a reviewer who may quote passages in a review.

British Library Cataloguing in Publication Information Available

Library of Congress Cataloging-in-Publication Data Available

978-1-4422-2652-4 (cloth : alk. paper)
978-1-4422-2653-1 (pbk. : alk. paper)
978-1-4422-2654-8 (electronic)

♾™ The paper used in this publication meets the minimum requirements of American National Standard for Information Sciences Permanence of Paper for Printed Library Materials, ANSI/NISO Z39.48-1992.

Printed in the United States of America

Contents

Acknowledgments

I wish to thank a number of people for their help in this journey. My department chair, Jay M. Parker, has provided mentorship and advice at every stage. My colleagues in the College of International Security Affairs have offered valuable assistance and professional guidance—thank you to Sean McFate, Alejandra Bolanos, Querine Hanlon, Geoffrey Gresh, Elena Pokalova, Rebecca Patterson, Andrew Novo, Jodi Vittori, Tom Marks, Heather Gregg, Brett Steele, and Tom Parker. In addition, I received research assistance from Lindsey Ohmit, Jon Edwards, Clayton Thomas, and Robert Solonick.

Thank you also to Mollie Murphy in the National Defense University Legal Affairs Division and Bill Eliason at National Defense University Press. Lastly, I wish to thank my editor at Rowman and Littlefield Marie-Claire Antoine for her assistance and guidance from beginning to end on this project.

I would also like to thank my family for their constant encouragement and support. And to my two daughters, who are convinced that Daddy's job is to "type and talk and read his books" . . . this book is dedicated to you.

DISCLAIMER: The opinions and statements expressed herein are the authors and do not represent the policy of the US National Defense University, the US Department of Defense, or any other US government agency.

Chapter One

Introduction

On Saturday, September 21, 2013, sixteen men from Harakat Shabaab al-Mujahidin, more commonly referred to as al-Shabaab ("Mujahidin Youth Movement"), entered the upscale Westgate Mall in Nairobi, Kenya. Over the course of the four-day standoff, the militants killed an estimated sixty-one civilians, including eighteen foreigners and six Kenyan military officers, and injured 175. In addition, the mall sustained massive structural damage, including the collapse of several floors. While live-tweeting the attack, al-Shabaab claimed that this was revenge for Kenya's invasion of Somalia as part of the African Union Mission in Somalia (AMISOM) forces that were sent to drive al-Shabaab out of the country and install the newly elected Somali Transitional Federal Government. Furthermore, they called for Kenya to withdraw from Somalia and to stop interfering in its affairs. The attack, purposely targeting an upscale shopping mall filled with affluent Kenyans and foreigners, surprised some analysts, given that al-Shabaab is a Somali insurgent group. Nevertheless, their previous attacks against two Ugandan venues demonstrated their strategy to pressure the population in countries invading Somalia. The attack raises the question of whether this is a signal that al-Shabaab is strengthening, or whether this was a last-gasp attack by a group that has lost its territory, support base, and external funding, and is succumbing to internal, factional squabbles. Only through a more in-depth examination of this armed group—its leadership, objectives, strategy, and strategic communications, among other characteristics—can we understand the motivation and purpose of such a heinous attack, one unfortunately emblematic of today's security landscape.

Armed groups are responsible for causing wars and political upheaval that affect nearly every state in the world. Despite his adherence to a "state-centric" theoretical perspective, Kenneth Waltz notes "states are not and never have been the only international actors . . . The importance of nonstate actors and the extent of transnational activities are obvious."[1] Whether it is the actions of insurgents challenging a state's legitimacy, pirates disrupting the world's sea lanes, or terrorists exporting their political grievances through violent actions, armed groups have long been a part of the security landscape. While they have not always been the center of focus for security studies, they have played a significant role in international relations, whether acknowledged or not. Historically, armed groups have sparked war and drawn larger political units into conflict, have been used by states to strike other states without involving official government actors, created financial ruin, or wielded power as security providers for states and city-states reaching back hundreds of years.

Today, armed groups frequently accompany any discussion of failed states, ungoverned spaces, economic development, human rights abuses, or political instability. Indeed, nongovernmental organizations, international organizations, and multinational corporations frequently—but quietly—hire armed groups to provide security and engage local armed groups to ensure they can effectively carry out their missions. Armed groups are international actors in that they constrain, and in some cases expand, state policies. They are also threats, challenging state legitimacy, killing or injuring a state's citizens, and preventing states from achieving their sought-after goals.

Armed groups play a major role in intrastate conflicts, which today account for nearly all active conflicts in the world.[2] However, little work has been done to assimilate armed groups into the broader field of international security studies. As the prime actors today in the origination of, prosecution of, and persistence of armed conflict, as well as the frequent targets of state militaries, armed groups should be integrated into a more comprehensive theoretical framework to understand their role in the international arena and the origins of conflict. This book points to the need to clarify the microfoundations of strategic interactions—namely, armed groups and their environment—while recognizing traditional distinctions are blurred in the current security environment. This will contribute to our understanding of the role that armed groups play as they use violence to vie for political power within states and across international borders.

This book does not purport to offer a new paradigm or "-ism" that will unify traditional state-centric, systemically-focused international relations (IR) theories with more domestic and individual-level analyses common in the intrastate war literature. Instead, this book is a call for a greater understanding of armed groups and their environment, and the degree to which potentially important aspects, relevant to the study of nontraditional security threats, have been marginalized within the current IR paradigms. This is combined with the desire to use existing methodological approaches to analyze areas that have remained separate within IR analyzes, despite their overlapping relevance and links. There should be a clear acknowledgment that contemporary conflicts greatly influence the international security studies field and that, in order to leverage the analytical tools available, the state-centric, military approach needs to be tempered given the relevant strategic actors.

There are two problems the study of armed groups has faced. First is that traditional international relations theories lacked clear, well-defined micro-foundations, primarily regarding the undertheorizing of armed groups and a lack of understanding of the international environment in the post-9/11 period. The second problem is the inherent blurring between traditional distinctions in security studies that arise when exploring transnational security threats. These crossovers include analyses across differing levels of analysis (to include state–nonstate actor relations), the increasingly hazy division between war and peace, and the overlap between the security and economic realms.[3] If current work in security studies cannot adequately explain or understand the prominent actors and their environment, including armed groups and the decline of the state and rise of overlapping networks of sovereignty, nor provide leverage to the academic or policy maker struggling to understand threat perception in a world where traditional distinctions across the security and economic realms, not to mention from differing levels of analysis, have been blurred and in some cases obliterated, then we need to start with a fundamental analysis of the main actors in today's security environment.

IMPORTANCE OF THE TOPIC

Armed groups are an important area of study because of the economic, social, and human costs of the conflicts they spawn. Multiple armed groups use child soldiers, employ mass rape as a weapon against whole villages, and commit other atrocities. There is a propensity for civil wars and other intrastate conflicts—which are distinguished by the presence of at least one armed group—to spawn interstate wars. Many indicators today signal a decrease in interstate war—nuclear deterrence, norms against aggression, or economic development are only a few of the factors theorists posit contribute to the increasingly rare phenomenon of interstate war. Intrastate conflicts remain deadly, destabilizing forces, fueled by armed groups and their erosion of state legitimacy.

Armed groups are not party to the common laws and norms of international society, nor are they signatories to treaties, international agreements, or international laws.[4] The common diplomatic tools and traditional instruments of statecraft states frequently employ in routine relations with other states may have little, or no effect, on armed groups. Armed groups are political entities, which constrain state policy choices at best, or pose existential security threats to weaker states at worst.

Academic-Policy Importance

IR theory—and its subfield of international security studies—has traditionally housed the study of war and conflict. While theoretical debates are of interest primarily to the academic, a history of crossover attempts to better integrate academia and policy making dot the landscape.[5] As Wolfers notes, "It is self-delusion on the part of the decision-maker to believe that he can get along without theoretical propositions."[6] Just as important from the academic's perspective is the intellectual rigor applied to these complicated and serious issues, keeping in mind Wolfers' admonition "Worthwhile general concepts and propositions emerge not from a static or dogmatic type of theory but from a live theorizing process, directed at modifying, qualifying, and enriching earlier formulations in the light of new facts and new experiences."[7]

For the policy maker, the implications of academic theory should become clear as it concerns fundamental issues such as threat perception and the use of military force. Policymakers, as part of devising foreign policy and state strategies, must have a theoretical understanding of the threats posed by various groups—whether a rising China, al-Qaeda, or transnational criminal organizations (TCOs)—as well as a method to compare the severity of those threats and the particular implications for their state and its allies. How can policy makers create a strategy—which by necessity involves prioritization—if academic theories do not fully understand the relevant actors or cannot model the strategic interactions between widely different actors?[8]

This textbook explores the most fundamental questions: who are the actors, what are their capabilities, what are their objectives, and what threat do they pose and to whom? Through an examination of numerous internally and externally oriented group characteristics, this text provides the student, analyst, and policy maker with the tools to analyze armed groups in the current and future geostrategic environment.

WHAT ARE "ARMED GROUPS"?

There is no universal definition of an armed group. Simply stated, armed groups are coherent, autonomous, nonstate actors that rely on the threat or use of force to achieve their objectives. This definition purposely does not spell out specific objectives, degree of autonomy or independence, function, purpose, size, or mode of operation of the group, as these may vary greatly. "Coherent" implies both a minimum group longevity and level of organizational sophistication. It does not imply that the group speaks with one voice or is free from factions, internal disagreements, or competing internal interests among and between its members and leadership. The definition carries with it the implicit argument that armed groups, by their very presence, challenge the state's monopoly of the legitimate use of force.

The United Nations Office for the Coordination of Humanitarian Affairs provides the following broad definition of an armed group: "groups that: have the potential to employ arms in the use of force to achieve political, ideological or economic objectives; are not within the formal military structures of States, State-alliances or intergovernmental organizations; and are not under the control of the State(s) in which they operate."[9] Chapter 3 will delve more deeply into the common characteristics of all armed groups and expand on the basic factors above. It is important to note here that armed groups use violence, are not under the control of states, and ultimately prove a security threat to the state, whether through violence, territorial acquisition, or simply through their existence challenging the legitimacy of the state.

Armed groups face five challenges: recruitment, control, governance, use of violence, and resilience.[10] These can be summed up as challenges during a group's formation, conducting their operations, and in perpetuating their organization. Their operations and perpetuation may be greatly overlapping, and their formation may constrain their later operations or perpetuation. The elements discussed here—leadership, organization, membership, ideology, objectives, strategy, tactics, strategic communication, external support, and linkages with other armed groups—correspond to one of these three basic actions. Formation draws from the ability to mobilize and create a cohesive, viable group, thus it draws on and shapes the "internal" components of a group. The group's operations draw from the "external" components of the group—the group's strategy and tactics, strategic communication, external support, and linkages to other armed groups. The group's perpetuation is a combination of the internal and external dimensions: to what degree has the group not only proven it is a viable, legitimate group or alternative, but also shown it can accomplish goals that build its legitimacy while undermining the state's?

Armed groups have played a secondary role in IR, in which threat perception is often viewed as a "zero-sum" game: if there are no great power threats, armed groups are seen as threats. But this belies the current period where threats from al-Qaeda coexist with US worries about China, Iran, or North Korea or state employment of armed groups; or nineteenth-century colonial competition and fighting with armed groups, while the Great Game in Central Asia ran its course; or armed-group threats during decolonization in the twentieth century, as the Cold War raged; or pirates in the seventeenth century, as Europe suffered through the Thirty Years War.

This section takes a closer look at armed groups to understand the threat they pose. This is not a threat traditionally measured or used in power comparisons between states. Stalin's exclamation "The Pope! How many divisions has *he* got?" is applicable in this analysis, with the same issues of how to incorporate ideological competition into a field predisposed to analyzing military contests where power capabilities were evident. Additionally, this section considers problems all armed groups face as they challenge the state.

Why Study Armed Groups

There is confusion given the multitude of labels applied to many current conflicts: intrastate conflicts, civil wars, low-intensity conflicts, armed conflicts, internationalized intrastate conflicts, hybrid conflicts, extra-systemic conflicts, insurgencies, guerrilla wars, and small wars, to name a few. This obfuscates the fact all of these conflicts involved armed groups. Many of these conflicts include states, but may also involve international organizations (IOs), nongovernmental organizations (NGOs), multinational corporations (MNCs), domestic and international activist groups, and well-resourced individuals. This demonstrates the true complexity of today's security milieu, but by focusing on the common element—armed groups—we can bring some clarity to these conflicts and those who fight them.

Each of the above conflict labels may not only bring added and unnecessary confusion to a situation, but also provide a pejorative label that masks the true nature of the conflict or brings emotional or ideological responses and presuppositions about the actors, their intentions, and their strategies that are unwarranted and potentially harmful to successful policy achievement.

If we do not understand armed groups, international actors may have a difficult time understanding conflict or understanding the main actors in them. In the fall of 2013, the United States was considering whether or not to intervene in the Syrian civil war. Previously, the Obama administration had to think about intervention in Libya, Egypt, Mali, and a host of other cases around the globe. Who are the actors? What do they want? How strong are they? Once they have secured their position in their country, what are they likely to do next? Are they likely to respect the rule of law, acknowledge international norms, and behave in a way conducive to positive relations with the United States and the country's neighbors? All of these questions can be better understood by a closer examination of the actors carrying out the fighting.

Whether or not all of the factors new war theorists discuss are occurring, whether or not interstate wars are becoming obsolete, there is at least one constant—armed groups have contended with government for influence over the population for centuries.[11] Their circumstances and their effects on international events may have ebbed and flowed, but they have long existed. Today, as noted at the outset of this chapter, conflict is characterized by intrastate wars, where armed groups are a key ingredient. This does not mean it will never change and that great power war is impossible, but even if great power war were to break out between the United States and China, for example, we should note two things. First, since 1945, intrastate war has been far more prevalent than other types of war. Conflicts distinguished by the presence of armed groups as one of the main actors is not likely to disappear any time soon, even if there is a great power war. Intrastate wars with no connection to great power war may be ongoing in various regions, they may use the international instability to press for their own localized or regional demands, or they may act during a great power war to attempt to escape notice by outside observers. Second, armed groups may play complimentary and complicating roles in conventional or "old wars," as a consequence of governments falling and governance disappearing, or they may bring states directly into conflict through their transnational challenges to state legitimacy and sovereignty. Armed groups play a role in postconflict and reconstruction settings, and understanding and engaging them is a key issue for the international community.[12]

Armed-Group Importance, Role, and Threat

It is paramount to understand and be familiar with the various definitions, criteria, typologies, and frameworks surrounding armed groups, as they are and remain an important aspect of the contemporary security environment. The discussion here aims to help the student, analyst, and policy maker in identifying possible threats before they are able to metastasize, understand the enemy the United States and its international partners are fighting, understand entities that may be future allies as the United States and other countries intervene in internal conflicts around the world, and create an addition to the military "order of battle" that has long defined strategic analysis. As interstate conflicts are currently on the wane and with the rise of intrastate conflicts, analysts need new tools to assess current security actors. The old framework of examining individual military units, their strengths and capabilities, their leadership, and the resources at their disposal is excellent for conventional military foes such as a state's armed forces. But these analyses break down when the enemy under examination does not adhere to an organizational structure, leadership structure, or contextual constraints that define state militaries. This is not to say that the traditional order of battle is no longer needed. It is simply to argue that in the current environment, where the majority of conflicts are intrastate conflicts characterized by the prevalence of nonstate actors, a new, additional method of analysis is needed to fully capture the security threats states face and will continue to face in the future.

Percy posits three broad questions surrounding armed groups. While there is much to be written on these topics, not all of which can be addressed here, they should be noted and followed for the directions they may lead the analyst and policy maker in thinking about the role of armed groups today. These boundaries include nonstate actors operating with state-like influence, armed groups with apolitical objectives (crime) possessing political impact, and the tendency for armed groups to provide security while also decreasing it. [13]

While conflict in the twenty-first century may be fundamentally different and represent a paradigm shift in warfare, it is clear it need not in order for a study of armed groups to remain practical, necessary, and in line with furthering our understanding of security studies and the modern use of force. States need to understand these potential enemies, allies, and spoilers in future conflicts and negotiations.

Armed groups have long been actors in the international arena, although security studies rarely views them holistically. Furthermore, any attention they receive has generally coincided with current affairs, only to be shunted aside when the next big event comes to light. What is apparent throughout history, however, is the prevalence and actions of these groups, waxing and waning in importance, but always ready to strike regimes, whether weak and crumbling or oppressive and divisive, or claim territory and sovereignty where state governance is remote. Even when armed groups are not the main focus of a state's security efforts, they may provide added complications to any situation.

Armed groups have a role to play in international politics today. While this does not mean they are the only actors, the need to understand and examine such a major presence and contributing force to conflicts in countries around the world is imperative. While IR scholars have long viewed the world through a state-centric lens, they have recognized the importance of other actors. From Waltz to Wolfers to today's discussions of transnational advocacy groups and terrorists, nonstate actors, to include armed groups, are seen as wielding a menacing and complicating force on the international stage. [14]

The security studies literature has struggled to define security threats and their referent objects—who is being threatened and in what way? [15] Armed groups pose a threat at all levels of security and even if their threat to the international system lessens in upcoming years, the threat remains to state governments and to individuals within those states and may threaten to spill over to neighboring and regional states. While this violence is not new in kind, it is new in the "global scale on which it takes place." [16]

Armed groups are international, national, and human security threats. [17] Armed groups may be international security threats because some groups threaten the very existence of the state system by advocating and fighting for the dissolution of the state system. They may threaten international institutions, seek to overthrow international norms, and provide a challenge to international stability due to their operations and transnational nature. Armed groups are a national security threat as they challenge the state's legitimacy and ability to govern, including through direct attacks on the government and the ruling elites, efforts to create domestic instability, and nonviolent actions that diminish the legitimacy of the state in the estimation of the population. Lastly, armed groups are threats to human security in the most fundamental way: they engage in an often violent contest for influence over the people. Armed groups also do not share many of the prohibitions on targeting individuals and engage in combat that blurs the line between the combatant and noncombatant.

Armed groups' amorphous and nontraditional threat—involving legitimacy, instability, and violent, direct challenges—is potentially a much more difficult threat for states to understand. Challenges to the legitimacy of a far-off, seemingly weak, nonstrategic state may be of limited concern for many of the great powers. But the armed group's ability to create regional instability and to operate across multiple borders creates concern for a great power. A group in northern Mali, southern Thailand, western China, or eastern Democratic Republic of the Congo may seem, on the surface, inconsequential to the United States, Western Europe, or Japan. But these groups may create instability among all of their bordering states, disrupt regional relations, and ultimately, use these areas as bases from which to strike out at targets that great powers consider strategic and within their national interest. Furthermore, as all states struggle to maintain and define their sovereignty in an era where multiple state and nonstate actors actively erode a state's governance within their borders, human security—the ability of people to satisfy their needs and feel safe from threats—is key to a state's legitimacy and "standing" in the international community. As more states are unable to provide human security, the "Responsibility to Protect" (R2P) doctrine has emerged, whereby some in the international community strive to intervene in states where human security is not addressed.[18] While controversial, the ability to provide for the people, and not just maintain a stable government or act internationally, is increasingly viewed as a norm that supersedes traditional state sovereignty.

Armed groups threaten states by both creating instability and directly challenging state governments. Instability within states drains state resources, weakens legitimacy, creates zones of impunity, and at its extreme, poses a direct threat to the downfall of the state or the overthrow of a regime. Armed groups also create instability regionally and globally, whether by disrupting commercial flows, creating lawless safe havens, instigating refugee flows, disrupting regional cooperation, spoiling peace processes, and overthrowing regimes, which may create larger zones of impunity that negatively affect neighboring, regional conflicts.

Instability overlaps with direct armed-group challenges to states, as instability can provide safe havens from which armed groups can launch attacks, regroup and train, and prepare and plan for new attacks. Instability within the state or on a state's borders drains a state's resources and legitimacy. More directly, many armed groups expropriate territory within the state, or seek the overthrow of state's government. To accomplish these goals, armed groups attack civilians and soldiers, as well as become service providers, alternative governing bodies, or prevent the government from operating in armed-group-held territory, depriving the people of all services.

States have also frequently relied on armed groups as tools. These groups provide a state with "plausible deniability," while not directly risking the state's population. In addition, states may employ armed groups to provide a military option when states do not possess military capabilities to strike rival or threatening states within or outside of their region. The costs, however, to using armed groups as tools of statecraft are lengthy. Outsourcing security to groups the state does not directly control risks losing even greater control of foreign policy outcomes in an anarchic international environment. Armed groups may perpetrate human rights abuses, dragging states into legal or political conflicts. Armed-group objectives may not align with the state's objectives, such that state support for armed groups may lead to unintended outcomes.

At another extreme, armed groups may control states, whether through corruption and subversion, or violent takeover, but due to their size and power relative to states, almost always accomplished through asymmetric strategies. The use of corruption and subversion, resulting in a "political-criminal nexus," is embodied in "narco-states" such as Guinea-Bissau, where many high-ranking state officials willingly cooperate with transnational criminal drug-trafficking organizations. Violent regime change may result in "neo-patrimonial" politics, as embodied by countries where former armed-group leaders have gained power, using their newly acquired access to natural resources and state coffers to extend their personal influence and power. In both cases, these states do not respond to their population's needs and further weaken whatever legitimacy remained in the state.

These goals and actions are fostered by the globalization of communications, information flows, and economic relations. Armed groups have access to communication and information technology, small-arm markets, and economic and social networks that allow them to bypass traditional markets. Armed groups, both those directly and indirectly challenging the state and those in control of states, have access to black markets for illicit goods and the ability to escape international attention, condemnation, and sanction; grey markets for small arms, information, food, communications, and natural resources; and white markets. State infrastructure may no longer be necessary to access these markets, as individuals, MNCs, NGOs, armed groups, and IOs may be willing and able to aid armed groups further their goals.

Overcoming Four Fundamental Problems

All armed groups, no matter their development stage, face four general problems: the collective action problem (free rider problem), the coordination problem, the time-consistency problem, and the principal-agent problem.[19] These problems arise not only from a study of the internal dynamics of an armed group, whether between members or between members and the leader, but also from the relationship between armed groups and external supporters. All of these issues relate to the difficulties groups have in overcoming various information asymmetries, whether it be about the members of the group, potential members from a given population, or the state against which they are fighting.

In many ways, an armed group's basic characteristics—the internal and external framework components outlined in chapters 5 and 6—shape the group's ability to address these four problems. A charismatic leader may maintain strict control of a group and encourage strong group cohesion; a flat, loosely organized group may encourage different cells to create their own ideological variants, objectives, or competing strategic communications; or the need to provide members with tangible goods now to maintain their loyalty may hinder the group's ability to achieve long-term objectives. Using these concepts derived from the political economy literature as methodological tools provides the analyst with the ability to rigorously analyze all aspects of an armed group. The next section briefly discusses each of these problems in turn, while chapters 5 and 6 demonstrate the problems in action by analyzing an armed group's characteristics.

Armed groups are both affected by these four problems, as well as motivated to attempt to prevent them from occurring. This occurs both knowingly or unknowingly through the various aspects of the framework presented here. While it is highly unlikely that the Lord's Resistance Army, a militia operating in the remotest corners of Uganda, Sudan, and the Central African Republic, critically analyzes the role that the principal-agent problem plays in their daily operations, they are well aware of the negative effects from their geographically splintered organization and may try to remedy the situation. As the student takes up the analysis in chapters 5 and 6, she should consider how each part of the armed group—the leadership, organization, or ideology, for example—affects, and is affected by, the problems presented below.

Furthermore, this text is not written as a normative analysis. That is, the text does not posit what the armed group *should* do, nor what is the *best* way for an armed group to address these problems. The text is written as a positive analysis, in that it seeks to address what *is* and create a foundation for knowledge aggregation and analysis. The lack of a normative discussion draws from the obvious bias that states may or may not want a particular armed group to be able to solve these four problems, as well as the fact that many different factors will come into play in addressing these four fundamental problems, making value judgments impossible to draw for every possible combination of variables. The student's role is to analyze how an armed group successfully or unsuccessfully solves these four problems at each stage of its existence.

Despite "borrowing" these four problems from the political economy literature, they are equally applicable across issues of economic, political, ethnic, and sectarian conflicts, as well as those motivated by primal blood lust. All organizations, no matter their motivations, objectives, ideologies, strategies, and tactics, must confront these generic problems. By understanding that all groups confront these problems, by seeking answers as to how groups do or do not attempt to solve them, and by analyzing various armed-group elements we gain a broader understanding of how all armed groups behave and move the literature beyond debates on specific groups or specific types of groups. In order to understand the security threats that states face from armed groups, the student, analyst, and policy maker need to be able to generalize the threats and conditions inherent in calculating balance of threat analyses.

Free-Riding and the Collective Action Problem

In its most basic form, "the argument of 'the logic of collective action' is that self-interest typically runs counter to group interest."[20] And because of this, the provision of public goods, or any goods where it is difficult to prevent those who did not contribute from reaping the rewards, is frequently underprovided. This is a fundamental problem in armed groups, as individuals may worry that the cost of joining an armed group may be too high—including imprisonment or death—and that it is better to let someone else accept the cost. By sitting on the sideline, the group may never form and the objective that the individual and group both seek remain unrealized.[21]

This simple, yet fundamental problem for states and armed groups alike can manifest itself in several ways. First, when forming an armed group, it might be difficult to not only find adherents but also those willing to fight or even contribute resources. Since one individual cannot engage the government alone, there is a need to confront the state collectively. But because of the costs of joining a group—and the potential to realize the benefits without joining—armed-group formation is a complicated affair. Armed groups face difficulty in carrying out operations, because group members face greater risks in carrying out violence than at any other time.[22] Lastly, the perpetuation of the group requires similar motivations and incentives to the original formation, especially as the achievement of the group's goals is pushed further into the future. Thus, the collective-action problem—an individual's incentive to not participate but to seek the rewards—is a fundamental problem that all armed groups must confront.

The armed group's ability to overcome collective-action problems is likely predicated on its ability to provide certain incentives to the member to not only join, but also remain a member. Olson argues that because members and nonmembers alike share collective goods, groups must offer some inducement to remaining committed to the group.[23] These incentives may be monetary, solidary ("'rewards created by the act of associating'"), and expressive ("'rewards that derive from a sense of satisfaction at having contributed to the attainment of a worthwhile cause'").[24] Solidary and expressive benefits are sometimes deemed luxury goods, although as we will see, the decision to join and remain with the group may be based on the assumption of the provision of these solidary and expressive incentives.

Second, people are more easily mobilized in response to threat, and more easily mobilized when the threat is couched in the prospect of averting losses, rather than making gains.[25] Similarly, member costs to joining or remaining part of a group can be expressed in monetary, solidary, or expressive ways, which are reinforced by the opportunity cost to joining a group.[26] All of this is context dependent and varies based on the individual's perspective and interaction with his or her environment.

The Coordination Problem

The pure coordination game involves two or more actors who agree that they want to coordinate on a common outcome, but may be unsure of which option to pick. They may stumble upon a solution seemingly at random, rely on a leader to provide the rallying point, or reach an agreement based on a norm.[27] Actors in a coordination game do not incur costs from their decisions, but the actors gain only when they act in concert.

Individuals attain greater power after coordinating to form a group or in starting a rebellion. The difficulty may be in the initial spark triggering the coordination. While charismatic leaders may provide this trigger, it may also be related to state action, such as harsh repression or radical policy change, state weakness following a war, or a leader's ouster or death. These "state-provided" opportunities create openings that either allow or push actors into action.

A second level of the coordination problem exists when individuals join an armed group but may suffer repression from the government. This moves the game away from a coordination game and toward the free-riding problem, discussed above. However, as Russell Hardin has argued, if groups are large enough, the costs for the individual may be so marginal that they are practically zero.[28]

Coordination is a means of creating power much greater than the individual. Nevertheless, most armed groups are not large enough to push the cost of joining the group—being targeted by state security forces—to zero. The state may thus try to impose costs on the individual, whether during the recruitment period or at any other time for joining the group, forcing the actor to consider free-riding, rather than joining the group. A state's use of varying degrees of repression in combating armed groups may relate to the degree to which the state believes imposing costs on individuals will prevent them from coordinating and push them to free-ride.

The Time-Consistency Problem

The time-consistency problem arises when actors make promises in the short term that they have no intention of keeping in the long term.[29] More broadly, individuals may worry that a state has an incentive to make promises or to enact policy measures now that they either have no intention of keeping in the long run or will face incentives in the long run to repeal. Individuals within an armed group may face similar problems, and negotiations or relationships between an armed group and the state face similar pressures. Neither side wants to act now, for fear that the other side will not deliver what it has promised.

Individuals in an armed group want to share the benefits from achieving the group's objectives. If the individual is barred from doing this—whether because of the risk of injury or death, the likelihood of dropping out of the group, risk that the group will not achieve its objectives, or the decades- or even centuries-long outlook for achieving the group's objectives—the individual may demand some short-term compensation for fear that the group will be unable, or unwilling, to deliver on its promised reward. This compensation can be monetary compensation for the individual, social advancement, education, training, or benefits given to the member's family.

Armed groups face pressure from their membership, prospective members, and the government to provide short-term, positive inducements as good-faith efforts. These could include the provision of services for members and the population in the territory the armed group controls, or confidence-building measures for the government that the armed group is attempting to negotiate or act in a "good-faith effort." Likewise, the armed group will be wary that the government will carry out their promises and will seek confidence-building measures of their own from the government, such as amnesty or prisoner releases. The armed group, as the materially weaker power, has an inherent concern that any peace agreement or call to lay down their arms will immediately lead to offensive action by the government. Ensuring this does not occur is difficult where incentives exist for both sides to make promises and pronouncements they have no intention, or ability, to keep.

The Principal–Agent Problem

The principal–agent problem exists in nearly every organization and in nearly every relationship between actors. It has at its base the problem of information asymmetry. That is, one side knows more than the other side. Furthermore, one side may have a reason to purposely withhold information from the other. The problem, then, is one of oversight: how does the principal make sure the agent, to whom the principal has given a task, has carried out the task in the manner in which the principal commanded?

Governing bodies face the principal–agent problem when they delegate authority to carry out laws to various bureaucratic organizations. How do they ensure that the bureaucracies are enforcing the regulations in a proper manner? They may wait for their constituents to tell them that a particular agency is not doing its job. Alternatively, the governing body may spend the time, money, and energy on closely monitoring the bureaucracy to ensure that the bureaucracy is properly executing the laws or enforcing the regulations the governing body has set.[30] Both practices come with basic costs. If the governing body waits for the constituents or others to report a lack of regulatory enforcement, there may be an underreporting of malfeasance. If instead the governing body pays close attention to the agency, they may spend incredible sums of money and human resources in overseeing the agency's every move. The desire, therefor, is for the governing body to find a middle ground—the most efficient way to oversee the agency, without missing fraud and abuse, and without wasting precious resources micromanaging the agency.

Principal–agent problems appear frequently between armed-group members, between leaders and members in an armed group, or between external supporters and the armed group itself. While an armed group's leadership may have difficulty monitoring its members, the leadership also has to worry whether the members are providing the leadership with accurate intelligence, reporting on political or strategic matters properly, or are turning over money raised for the group instead of lining their own pockets. Armed groups may be riven with principal–agent problems that threaten to tear them apart or prevent them from accomplishing their goals. For example, al-Qaeda in the Islamic Maghreb (AQIM) castigated Mokhtar Belmokhtar's group the "Masked Brigade" for its failure to carry out spectacular attacks, failure to file expense reports, and attempt to circumvent the local AQIM command structure.[31]

All armed groups need trust, which they achieve through shared ethnicity, kinship, and social networks, but they may also attempt to achieve this through ideological indoctrination and violence. Building trust, and the need for a reservoir of trust, is simply a manifestation of the degree to which armed groups attempt to overcome coordination problems, principal–agent problems, free-rider problems, and time-consistency problems. Trust among members of an armed group and between members of an armed group and the leadership will lead to greater information flows within organizations and a desire to see the successful completion of a group's goals. Groups that establish trust may be more likely to have members who carry out operations as directed, report information that may be important to those designing a group's strategy, choose not to defect to another group, or remain cohesive in their view of the group's objectives, strategy, and tactics. Trust is something that armed groups seek to foster in order to overcome the four problems presented here.

External vs. Internal Dimensions of Armed Groups

This text builds on the frameworks presented by Bard O'Neill and Richard Shultz, Douglas Farah, and Itamara Lochard.[32] O'Neill provides a framework of insurgent and terrorist groups by starting with their goals and strategies, and then examining the physical and human environment within which these groups operate, the amount and type of popular support for the group, external support, and government response, which he notes has a tremendous effect on how insurgents react and behave.[33] Following on these general themes, Shultz, Farah, and Lochard created a general framework that examines six main attributes: leadership, membership, organization, ideology and objectives, strategy and tactics, and links with states and nonstate actors.[34] These frameworks have been used as the basis for wide-ranging studies of insurgents, terrorists, militias, and criminal organizations.[35] This text aggregates these and other foundational works and more broadly divides the elements into internally and externally oriented characteristics.

Armed-group characteristics are internally and externally oriented. While a group's strategy and tactics may be internally deliberated and created, they are an externally oriented characteristic of the group that seeks to communicate, frequently through violence. This internal versus external division does not imply that these characteristics are isolated from each other. A group's strategy is most likely an internal creation, stemming from the leadership and shaped by the organizational and ideological constraints within the group. At the same time, armed groups are strategic actors—they factor the government's interests and presumed policies into their strategic calculations. Armed-group strategies, while internally constituted or externally directed, are a combination of internal deliberations and power struggles, as well as strategic reactions to the external environment and actors.

A second means of thinking about internal versus external dimensions of armed groups is to consider internal characteristics analogous to "private information" and external characteristics analogous to "public information." A group's strategy may be internally created and retain some measure of private information. Nevertheless, employing a variety of tactics to carry out that strategy and move the group toward its objective reveals information about the group that moves the group's strategy and tactics into the realm of public information. This division is not a clear line, as groups will find it difficult to keep all information private when they have an incentive to make some of the information public. Carrying out violent acts, negotiating with a government, seeking external financial support, or communicating in order to attract new members releases private information. There may be aspects of a group's strategy or ideology that remain private information, despite the government's best efforts to analyze the group. Nevertheless, the more externally oriented operations a group carries out, the more the group will reveal private information. Because of their fundamentally clandestine nature, armed groups maintain a constant tension between public and private information, with the tradeoff coming between security and successful completion of their goals. As external characteristics take precedence, internal characteristics—private information—will be exposed, potentially creating security tensions for the armed group.

BOOK OBJECTIVES

One aim of the research is to address the IR field's Western, great power bias.[36] This has meant that conflicts outside of great power and hegemonic wars in Europe have been given short shrift, unless Western great powers were fighting extrasystemic wars. Even then, analyses frequently focused on interstate conflicts and ignored nonstate actors.

This is surprising, given that intrastate wars have constituted the vast number of conflicts fought since 1945. In addition, states have used armed groups as proxies in various conflicts.[37] This research, however, has frequently sought to understand why and how states have used armed groups to accomplish their own objectives or integrated armed groups into state origin discussions, but rarely to understand armed groups on their own terms.

Second, there is a clear move to transcend the "-ism" debates in theorizing and incorporate widely held methodologies from other political science subfields.[38] This allows "cross-pollination" of new ideas and analysis frameworks.

Additionally, in order to accurately test our theories of war and peace, we need a more accurate accounting of the theoretical microfoundations of armed groups and their environment. Lastly, we need to gain not just a more complete understanding of the component parts, but how those parts—states, armed groups, and their environment—interact strategically. By focusing on armed groups, this book seeks to encourage debate, discussion, and understanding on a number of broader relevant and important topics. These include state threat perception of armed groups; armed groups' roles in creating instability, causing war, and expanding conflict in its scope or duration; and under what conditions states find it more or less challenging to confront armed-group threats.

This book is an attempt to provide an overarching framework for analyzing armed groups, by first examining possible broad categories of armed groups and the factors that separate them. The book then examines the various characteristics of armed groups, such as their leadership, organization, and strategies. While the discussion here focuses on armed nonstate actors, it applies as well to nonviolent nonstate actors.

This text does not argue that armed groups are the only threat or the only possible future risks the United States and other states face. The history of international relations is fraught with attempted predictions that were quickly dashed.[39] The point of this text is to prepare the student, analyst, and policy maker to take a more rigorous approach to analyzing armed groups, with the aim of understanding the real threats the United States and others do face and the way in which those threats manifest themselves. While intrastate conflicts are most prevalent today, and interstate wars have currently been resigned to the annals of diplomatic history, this could change tomorrow and by no means is a constraint on them rising again. What remains, however, are armed groups, which may be used as state proxies, to disrupt future diplomatic efforts or humanitarian interventions, or complicate any conflict through the imposition of their own preferences and interests through the use of violence to achieve their objectives.

This book makes no argument about how long intrastate wars will remain predominant, nor about the likelihood of the demise of interstate war, let alone great power war. Furthermore, many theorists in the "new war" camp have argued that the very nature of war has changed. Whether measured by the structure, methods, or motives of war, or a change in goals, methods, and funding,[40] new wars are frequently tied to changes in the international system, namely, the end of the Cold War, the decline of the state, and globalization. While this text examines the effects these systemic transformations may have on armed groups, it takes no position on the longevity or reversibility of these changes. In several places, the text notes that positive and negative outcomes are equally plausible from some of these structural shifts. And while it is entirely possible these changes may reverse course tomorrow, slow down, or accelerate, the focus here is on how these perceived changes create incentives and disincentives for the formation, operation, and perpetuation of armed groups.

In addition, focusing on structural attributes that are frequently held up by new war theorists as exemplifying why and how war has fundamentally changed does not further the argument that war has changed. The actors may change in relative importance—from state to armed groups—but the underlying goals and objectives that actors seek from using violence may, in most cases, remain the same. Likewise, the scale and scope of armed-group operations, or the threats and challenges that armed groups pose to states, may have increased, but this does not imply that why organized actors use violence or their objectives in using violence is something new or has fundamentally altered the institution of "war," as it has been understood. If war is "an act of force to compel our enemy to do our will," then war today, even when conducted between an armed group and the state, or even between two or more armed groups, is still the same.[41] Clausewitz's trinity of people, the state, and the military still exists, politics is still an overriding objective, and most aspects of conflict today would be recognizable to someone from the last several hundred years.

This text is aimed at understanding a discrete set of armed actors—all of whom are either purposefully seeking political objectives through the use of violence or have a political effect through their strategy of using force to achieve their ends. All of the armed groups discussed herein are political actors, whether they seek to depose the government or control de facto territory through their actions to secure profits. All of the groups analyzed here challenge the power, authority, and legitimacy of the state. Whether they succeed—and whether they change the nature of warfare—is not answered here, nor is an immediate or particularly gratifying answer possible. History will delineate phases and transformations; these are not our task. The goal here is to understand the environment within which armed groups operate today and how this may impact them; to understand how these groups differ from states, state militaries, and each other; and to provide an analytically and academically rigorous means of digging into these armed, nonstate actors.

In the end, this book accepts many of the structural changes and analyses of the world today, while seeking to understand what effects these have on armed groups. It makes no argument that these transformations are permanent, or always going to maintain their speed in their current direction. In addition, there is no argument that armed groups are new, that they are a part of a change in the character of war and the harbinger of "new war." Instead, this is an attempt at systematically and rigorously—from an academic and practitioners' perspective—to analyze these key actors involved in the predominant type of conflict and responsible for the majority of deaths therein. While states have been examined economically, organizationally, politically, electorally, legally, militarily, culturally, and so on, armed groups have been loosely bundled into sets and treated as inferior and homogenous units. There is no guarantee that armed groups will not recede into the shadows if great powers or hegemonic war breaks out. But even in the shadows, armed groups have complicating roles to play in modern conflicts, whether as the United States experienced in Iraq and Afghanistan or Mexico and Peru faced in networks of drug cartels and insurgents. Mali and the porous borders of the Sahel and Maghreb regions demonstrate the ease of transporting small arms, the scourge of ungoverned spaces, and the complex relationship between armed groups and globalization.

Even if interstate wars were to come roaring back into prominence, armed groups would still actively seek to upset the status quo. The Cold War era was replete with decolonization and independence movements and groups driven by ethnic, economic, and political grievances that were not addressed in post–World War II settlements. Even if a new bipolar system were to be established, the United States would still have to contend with armed groups—sometimes supporting their goals, sometimes supporting their adversary, and sometimes in it for themselves. In addition, weak states may depend on the use of armed groups to extend and bolster their power.[42] Understanding these groups, therefore, becomes a matter of understanding security threats today and for the foreseeable future, not due to the exclusive nature of the threat they pose, but because they are likely to remain as threats, no matter the future structure of international security and political relations.

Outline of the Book

The text proceeds by discussing a variety of factors most relevant to the academic and policy analyst examining armed groups. Chapter 1 provides an overview of several themes, notably that armed conflict has been and will remain intrastate in nature, armed groups blur traditional lines in security studies and international relations theory, and that an understanding of these actors is key to tackling the complex security environment. Lastly, it discusses four broadly applicable problems, which all armed groups confront during their formation, operations, and perpetuation: free-riding, the coordination problem, the time-consistency problem, and the principal–agent problem.

Chapter 2 provides an overview of the prevalence of intrastate conflict from 1945 to the present, with an emphasis on armed groups as the main security actors. Furthermore, this chapter examines why intrastate conflicts are likely to remain the most common form of conflict and therefore why armed groups will remain key security actors. The role of globalization in its multiple forms, the disappearance of superpower competition and global governance after the Cold War, and the profusion of weak, fragile, and failing states are key geopolitical factors in this analysis.

Chapter 3 provides a discussion of several points that help define what armed groups are and how they differ from official state militaries. This will include a discussion of how states employ, fund, or share objectives with armed groups, challenging the idea that armed groups are fundamentally "nonstate actors." Additionally, armed groups that may share some of these characteristics but not others, such as private military and private security companies, are examined.

Chapter 4, "Armed-Group Archetypes," provides a rundown of "insurgents," "terrorists," "militias," "transnational criminal organizations," and "private military and security companies." Furthermore, the trend toward hybridization of groups, and the evolution of groups as they take on characteristics of different archetypes over time, will be examined as key issues in understanding armed groups today.

Chapters 5 and 6 examine the internally and externally oriented elements that comprise an armed group, including leadership, organization, membership, objectives, ideology, strategy and tactics, strategic communication, and external support. A key point is these characteristics are interdependent with each other, as well as with the external environment. As leaders are imprisoned or killed, as the membership splinters into competing factions, as external sponsorship dries up, or as the government institutes a new policy to combat the group, all aspects of an armed group are challenged, forcing the group to evolve and adapt to the new context. State governments more easily exploit armed groups that cannot adapt, whether due to ideological constraints, organizational ineptitude, or poor strategic leadership. In addition, a group's characteristics may impinge on each other, constraining its ability to overcome the four problems identified in chapter 1, aiding the state's attempts at combating the group. In short, armed groups are part of a strategic and interactive environment whereby they are forced to anticipate, react, and learn from their interactions with other actors.

Chapter 7 emphasizes the need to analyze armed groups and exploit changes or look for opportunities to split groups as their internal and external elements change. Current decapitation strategies may not work on certain types of armed groups, while other groups require a concerted effort in multiple areas to combat. In addition, various facets of an armed group may come into conflict with each other, leaving them vulnerable to external exploitation. Lastly, armed groups' reliance on external support also leaves them vulnerable to isolation or changing state preferences, but this comes with the understanding that many armed groups today have the ability to leverage the multiple opportunities brought about through economic globalization. This creates a tension and challenge for states as they attempt to combat armed groups.

Chapter 8 reiterates key themes of the book, beginning with the key point that the future security environment will continue to exhibit the qualities that have driven armed-group expansion and threats. Furthermore, many armed groups today erase the boundaries between the archetypes, across divisions between combatants and noncombatants, and between economic and political objectives. Lastly, the individual factors and characteristics analyzed in the armed-group framework are constantly in flux and sometimes at odds with each other. Armed groups face the same dilemma surrounding misperception as states do in the international arena, namely that many of their characteristics and the factors discussed may not be perceived in the same way they are conceived, and may work at odds with the armed group's strategy and hinder its ability to achieve its objectives. While armed groups are likely to remain security threats well into the foreseeable future, they may be more limited in the threats they pose and their ability to present a coherent, and eventually persuasive, vision to the populations they seek to influence, given the increased complexity in the contemporary security environment.

Each chapter is intended to provide help in understanding armed groups as security actors in the international environment. The student or policy maker should quickly realize that, while many groups share common elements, there is a wide variation in armed groups. Common characteristics such as economic versus political goals or a group's ability to mobilize a mass base of support may help aggregate groups, but the boundaries, if they exist, between archetypes are quickly eroding. This is why it is important to look at the individual characteristics of armed groups. Understanding the specific armed group can remove potential mistakes that can accrue when groups are labeled with the broad brush of "terrorist" or "militia."

As we will discover in the chapter on combatting armed groups, however, labels matter. The political sphere may not see the similarities or differences across armed groups as the student or analyst. Indeed, it may be politically expedient to purposely label all armed groups as "terrorist." While there may be little the student can do about this, it is clear that despite broad political pronouncements, armed groups must be understood for what they are, and not for what policy makers may hastily assume them to be.

ARMED GROUPS AND INTERNATIONAL RELATIONS THEORY

IR theories have traditionally been state-centric and territorially biased, with military power the ultimate arbiter. Armed groups, by contrast, see the world comprised of overlapping networks, with influence their key weapon due to their relatively minimal military capabilities. Conventional IR theories have paid scant attention to these "outlier" threats. As Daniel Drezner, in the conclusion to his unconventional examination of nonstate actor threats in international relations, noted, "This sobering assessment highlights a flaw in the standard international relations paradigm—their eroding analytical leverage over the security problems of the twenty-first century."[43]

This need not be the case. Realism has frequently confronted states that have grown out of armed groups and revolutions, whether Mao's China, Bolsheviks in Russia, Fascists in Italy, or National Socialists in Germany. Constructivists and the Copenhagen School articulate the role of ideas and societal discourse in the process of securitization, while noting the plethora of new security actors.[44] Liberals have long examined the influence of nonstate actors in world politics, whether individuals or MNCs. It may be in the English school, however, where armed-group analyses find a theoretical foundation.

Hedley Bull discusses "a new medievalism" as a situation characterized by "a system of overlapping authority and multiple loyalty."[45] This overlapping authority might take the form of a regional, world, or even substate or subnational authority. Bull lists "five features of contemporary world politics which provide prima facie evidence of such a trend" toward neomedievalism, but states that whether or not it deprives the concept of "sovereignty of its utility and viability" is the key piece of evidence that the alternative neomedieval system is actually occurring.[46] These features include the regional integration of states, the disintegration of states, the restoration of private international violence, transnational organizations, and the technological unification of the world.[47]

The third feature, "the restoration of private international violence," is most germane to placing armed groups in an international context.[48] Here, Bull includes:

> the resort to violence by political groups which are not sovereign states, and which are only doubtfully public authorities at all, yet which . . . attack the territory of a foreign state, and its personnel and property in third countries, or seize the citizens of third countries as hostages; or which . . . use violence not only against the government they are seeking to overthrow, but kidnap the diplomats or private citizens of third countries in order to bring pressure to bear on the government with which they are in conflict.[49]

These actions are a blow to the "state's monopoly of legitimate international violence," but states have not organized against these actors because "a substantial proportion of international society" find these actions legitimate.[50] Bull believes that the nonstate groups that are exerting their violence are doing so in order to establish new states or to take over existing ones. This creates a paradox, whereby some states exert sympathy for armed-group objectives, which indirectly support actions that are undermining the state's privileged place in the international system.[51] As armed-group influence grows through tangled, international networks, states are trapped between supporting these actors and suffering from the instability they create.

CONCLUSION

Armed groups are an endemic feature of the international system and pose an ever-widening array of threats to the international system. They challenge a state's legitimacy, directly confront both human and national security through violent actions, and threaten greater regional instability. These actions frequently fall into the realm of "nontraditional" security threats, which academics and policy makers have been slow to understand and analyze.

Overlapping networked relationships, the decline in traditional conceptions of sovereignty, and the rise of a more globalized environment have created a more accommodating system for armed groups. The following chapter introduces the reader to the contemporary security environment, with a discussion of the contextual factors impacting the rise and importance of armed groups and the irregular conflicts of which they are a part.

DISCUSSION QUESTIONS

1. Do states lack the political will to label domestic groups "armed groups"?
2. What difficulties do states confront in explaining and analyzing armed-group threats?
3. Does the privatization of violence in Hedley Bull's model depend on the decline of the state, the increase in transnational organizations, and the technological unification of the globe? Are these trends reversible?
4. Have policy makers discounted armed groups because IR theories have relegated them as "outliers," or have IR theories followed policy makers in focusing on nuclear weapons and conventional warfare between states at the expense of understanding the role armed groups play?

RECOMMENDED READING

Mary Kaldor, *New and Old Wars: Organized Violence in a Global Era* (Stanford, CA: Stanford University Press, 2007).

Stathis N. Kalyvas, *The Logic of Violence in Civil War* (Cambridge: Cambridge University Press, 2006).

Douglas Lemke, "Power Politics and Wars without States," *American Journal of Political Science* 52, no. 4 (2008): 774–86.

National Intelligence Council, "Nonstate Actors: Impact on International Relations and Implications for the United States," August 23, 2007, http://www.fas.org/irp/nic/nonstate_actors_2007.pdf.

Ulrich Schneckener, "Fragile Statehood, Armed Non-State Actors and Security Governance," in *Private Actors and Security Governance*, ed. Alan Bryden and Marina Caparini (Geneva, Switzerland: Geneva Centre for the Democratic Control of Armed Forces, 2007), 23–38.

Richard H. Shultz and Andrea J. Dew, *Insurgents, Terrorists, and Militias: The Warriors of Contemporary Combat* (New York: Columbia University Press, 2006).

NOTES

1. Kenneth N. Waltz, *Theory of International Politics* (Reading, MA: Addison-Wesley, 1979), 93–94.

2. For simplicity, I use the term "armed groups" to include terrorists, insurgents, militias, warlords, pirates, and transnational criminal organizations, among others. On the frequency of interstate versus intrastate conflicts in the post-1945 period, see chapter 2.

3. For example, see Emile Simpson, *War from the Ground Up: Twenty-First-Century Combat as Politics* (New York: Columbia University Press, 2012).

4. Although they may be "bound" by the treaties ratified by the states in which they reside, most armed groups disregard international law and norms and for obvious reasons are not consulted in their adoption. See Zakaria Daboné, "International Law: Armed Groups in a State-Centric System," *International Review of the Red Cross* 93, no. 882 (2011).

5. For a starting point, see Alexander L. George, *Bridging the Gap: Theory and Practice in Foreign Policy* (Washington, DC: United States Institute of Peace, 1993).

6. Arnold Wolfers, *Discord and Collaboration: Essays on International Politics* (Baltimore, MD: The John Hopkins Press, 1962), xiv.

7. Ibid., xvii.

8. On creating strategy, see Terry L. Deibel, *Foreign Affairs Strategy: Logic for American Statecraft* (Cambridge: Cambridge University Press, 2007).

9. Gerard Mc Hugh and Manuel Bessler, *Humanitarian Negotiations with Armed Groups: A Manual for Practitioners* (New York: United Nations Office for the Coordination of Humanitarian Affairs, 2006), 6. This differs slightly from the 2003 OCHA Glossary of Humanitarian Terms definition of armed groups: "An armed non-state actor engaged in conflict and distinct from a governmental force, whose structure may range from that of a militia to rebel bandits." See ibid., 6n2.

10. See Jeremy M. Weinstein, *Inside Rebellion: The Politics of Insurgent Violence* (Cambridge: Cambridge University Press, 2007), 42–45. Although he applies them to "rebel organizations," these apply to all of the groups discussed here.

11. For historical overviews, see Max Boot, *Invisible Armies: An Epic History of Guerrilla Warfare from Ancient Times to the Present* (New York: Liveright, 2013).; and Robert B. Asprey, *War in the Shadows: The Guerrilla in History* (New York: William Morrow and Company, 1994).

12. Claudia Hofmann and Ulrich Schneckener, "Engaging Non-State Armed Actors in State- and Peace-Building: Options and Strategies," *International Review of the Red Cross* 93, no. 883 (2011): 603–21. See also Brian McQuinn, "Armed Groups in Libya: Typologies and Roles," *Small Arms Survey Research Notes*, no. 18 (2012): 1.

13. Sarah Percy, "Introduction," *Civil Wars* 11, no. 1 (2009): 1–3. See the other articles in this special issue addressing these questions.

14. See the discussion of Waltz below. Wolfers recognizes that when "nonstate entities are able on occasion to affect the course of international events," then they become "actors in the international arena and competitors of the nation-state." See Wolfers, *Discord and Collaboration: Essays on International Politics*, 23.

15. Helga Haftendorn, "The Security Puzzle: Theory-Building and Discipline-Building in International Security," *International Studies Quarterly* 35, no. 1 (1991): 3–17.

16. Hedley Bull, *The Anarchical Society: A Study of Order in World Politics* (New York: Columbia University Press, 1977), 259.

17. For a discussion of the different types of security, see Barry Buzan, *People, States, and Fear: An Agenda for International Security Studies in the Post-Cold War Era*, 2nd ed. (Colchester, UK: European Consortium for Political Research Press, 2008). See also Barry Buzan and Lene Hansen, *The Evolution of International Security Studies* (Cambridge: Cambridge Univeristy Press, 2009).

18. For the Responsibility to Protect, see "The Responsibility to Protect: Report of the International Commission on Intervention and State Sovereignty" (Ottawa, Canada: International Development Research Centre, 2001), http://responsibilitytoprotect.org/ICISS%20Report.pdf.

19. For example, see Paul Collier, "Doing Well out of War: An Economic Perspective," in *Greed and Grievance: Economic Agendas in Civil Wars*, ed. Mats Berdal and David M. Malone (Boulder, CO: Lynne Rienner, 2000) and Weinstein, *Inside Rebellion: The Politics of Insurgent Violence*. Despite the fact that Collier argues that greed-motivated conflicts are more likely to overcome these problems, these problems apply to all conflicts and all armed groups.

20. Russell Hardin, *One for All: The Logic of Group Conflict* (Princeton, NJ: Princeton University Press, 1995), 4.

21. Collier, "Doing Well out of War: An Economic Perspective."

22. See Rune Henriksen and Anthony Vinci, "Combat Motivation in Non-State Armed Groups," *Terrorism and Political Violence* 20, no. 1 (2007): 87–109.

23. Mancur Olson, *The Logic of Collective Action: Public Goods and the Theory of Groups* (Camrbidge, MA: Harvard University Press, 1965).

24. John Mark Hansen, "The Political Economy of Group Membership," *American Political Science Review* 79, no. 1 (1985): 79–80.

25. Ibid., 81. See also Barbara Farnham, ed. *Avoiding Losses, Taking Risks: Prospect Theory and International Conflict* (Ann Arbor: University of Michigan, 1994).

26. Hansen, "The Political Economy of Group Membership," 82.

27. Hardin, *One for All: The Logic of Group Conflict*, 27, 36.

28. Ibid., 40.

29. See Allan Drazen, *Political Economy in Macroeconomics* (Princeton, NJ: Princeton University Press, 2000), chap. 4.

30. These two methods are frequently referred to as, respectively, "fire alarm" and "police patrol." See Mathew D. McCubbins and Thomas Schwartz, "Congressional Oversight Overlooked: Police Patrols Versus Fire Alarms," *American Journal of Political Science* 28, no. 1 (1984).

31. See AQIM's letter to Belmokhtar translated and reprinted at Damien McElroy, "Al-Qaeda's Scathing Letter to Troublesome Employee Mokhtar Belmokhtar Reveals Inner Workings of Terrorist Group," *The Telegraph* (UK), May 29, 2013, http://www.telegraph.co.uk/news/worldnews/al-qaeda/10085716/Al-Qaedas-scathing-letter-to-troublesome-employee-Mokhtar-Belmokhtar-reveals-inner-workings-of-terrorist-group.html.

32. Bard E. O'Neill, *Insurgency and Terrorism: From Revolution to Apocalypse* (Washington, DC: Potomac Books, 2005). and Richard H. Shultz, Douglas Farah, and Itamara V. Lochard, *Armed Groups: A Tier-One Security Priority*, INSS Occasional Paper 57 (Colorado Springs, CO: USAF Institute for National Security Studies, 2004).

33. See O'Neill, *Insurgency and Terrorism: From Revolution to Apocalypse*.

34. Shultz, Farah, and Lochard, *Armed Groups: A Tier-One Security Priority*, 47.

35. A sample of other sources examining armed group characteristics in some manner include Anthony Vinci, "The 'Problems of Mobilization' and the Analysis of Armed Groups," *Parameters* 36, no. 1 (2006): 49–62; Chairman of the Joint Chiefs of Staff, *National Military Strategic Plan for the War on Terrorism*, February 1, 2006, http://www.defense.gov/pubs/pdfs/2006-01-25-Strategic-Plan.pdf, 14–19; Gerard Mc Hugh and Manuel Bessler, *Humanitarian Negotiations with Armed Groups: A Manual for Practitioners* (New York: United Nations Office for the Coordination of Humanitarian Affairs, 2006); Phil Williams, *Violent Non-State Actors and National and International Security* (Zurich, Switzerland: Swiss Federal Institute of Technology Zurich, International Relations and Security Network, 2008); Victor Asal and R. Karl Rethemeyer, "The Nature of the Beast: Organizational Structures and the Lethality of Terrorist Attacks," *Journal of Politics* 70, no. 2 (2008): 437–49; Thomas X. Hammes, "Armed Groups: Changing the Rules," in *Armed Groups: Studies in National Security, Counterterrorism, and Counterinsurgency*, ed. Jeffrey H. Norwitz (Newport, RI: US Naval War College Press, 2008); and CIA, *Guide to the Analysis of Insurgency* (Washington, DC: US Government, 2012), https://www.hsdl.org/?view&did=713599.

36. For example, see the critique in David C. Kang, "Getting Asia Wrong," *International Security* 27, no. 4 (2003): 57–85. See also Amitav Acharya and Barry Buzan, *Non-Western International Relations Theory: Perspectives on and Beyond Asia* (New York: Routledge, 2010).

37. Ariel I. Ahram, *Proxy Warriors: The Rise and Fall of State-Sponsored Militias* (Stanford, CA: Stanford University Press, 2011).

38. David A. Lake, "Why 'Isms' Are Evil: Theory, Epistemology, and Academic Sects as Impediments to Understanding and Progress," *International Studies Quarterly* 55, no. 2 (2011): 465–80.

39. On prediction, see Philip E. Tetlock, *Expert Political Judgement: How Good Is It? How Can We Know?* (Princeton, NJ: Princeton University Press, 2006). For an oft-misinterpreted example, see Norman Angell, *The Great Illusion: A Study of the Relation of Military Power to National Advantage* (New York: G. P. Putnam's Sons, 1913).

40. The first three are from Colin M. Fleming, "New or Old Wars? Debating a Clausewitzian Future," *Journal of Strategic Studies* 32, no. 2 (2009): 215, and the second are from Mary Kaldor, *New and Old Wars: Organized Violence in a Global Era* (Stanford, CA: Stanford University Press, 2007).

41. Carl von Clausewitz, *On War*, trans. Michael Howard and Peter Paret (Princeton, NJ: Princeton University Press, 1984), 75.

42. Ethan Corbin, "Principals and Agents: Syria and the Dilemma of Its Armed Groups Allies," *The Fletcher Forum of World Affairs* 35, no. 2 (2011): 25–46.

43. Daniel W. Drezner, *Theories of International Politics and Zombies* (Princeton, NJ: Princeton University Press, 2011), 112. For a laudable attempt to bring armed groups into international relations theory, see Anthony Vinci, *Armed Groups and the Balance of Power* (London: Routledge, 2008).

44. Barry Buzan, Ole Waever, and Jaap de Wilde, *Security: A New Framework for Analysis* (Boulder, CO: Lynne Rienner, 1998).

45. Bull, *The Anarchical Society: A Study of Order in World Politics*, 245. On "new medievalism," see also Wolfers, *Discord and Collaboration: Essays on International Politics*, 241–42; Stephen J. Kobrin, "Back to the Future: Neomedievalism and the Postmodern Digital World Economy," *The Journal of International Affairs* 51, no. 2 (1998): 361–86; and Philip G. Cerny, "Neomedievalism, Civil War and the New Security Dilemma: Globalisation as Durable Disorder," *Civil Wars* 1, no. 1 (1998): 36–64.

46. Bull, *The Anarchical Society: A Study of Order in World Politics*, 255.

47. Ibid., 255–66.

48. For one of the few comprehensive studies on this topic, see Sean McFate, *The Modern Mercenary: Private Armies and What They Mean for World Order* (Oxford: Oxford University Press, Forthcoming).

49. Bull, *The Anarchical Society: A Study of Order in World Politics*, 259.

50. Ibid.

51. Ibid., 260.

Chapter Two

Conflict in the Twenty-First Century

There were thirty-two armed conflicts recorded in 2012, with all but one of them intrastate in nature (classified as between the government and an internal opposition group).[1] The lone interstate conflict involved Sudan and South Sudan but was concluded with a peace agreement. Not all of the issues were finalized and some conflict continued between the states and their proxies. This marked a low level of conflict since World War II, with the fewest number of conflicts (thirty-one) occurring in 2003.[2] Since 1989–2012, Africa has seen the most conflicts, followed closely by Asia, with a sharp drop off to Europe, and the Middle East and Americas at the end of the list.[3]

Despite the decrease in the number of armed conflicts throughout the 2000s, several trends have occurred. Every year since 1945 has witnessed many more intrastate conflicts than interstate conflicts. Moreover, many more of those are internationalized today than ever before. Additionally, many of these conflicts are recurring, whether due to the lack of actors represented at the bargaining table, the emergence of spoilers, or the government's inability or unwillingness to adhere to their side of the agreement. One-quarter of "terminated conflicts" in the period 1950–1990 actually restarted, while nearly 45 percent of terminated conflicts since 1990 have restarted.[4]

Many of these conflicts are complex, with numerous countries experiencing conflict with multiple, unrelated armed groups. Lastly, the total number killed in these conflicts—37,941 battle-related deaths in 2012, by one estimate—does not fully capture the threat armed groups pose.[5] These conflicts lead to the erosion of state infrastructure, the rule of law, and the ability to provide services, which culminates in the government's overall loss of legitimacy. Some armed groups further erode the government through coercion and subversion, increase criminal activity, and create instability whether as a concerted policy or due to the aftereffects of their operations. The human toll is exacerbated by forced migration, the spread of disease, and the lack of development and growth. As armed groups' "battlespace" extends beyond the traditional battlefield, the consequences and spillover effects multiply exponentially.

Every year since 1945 has witnessed more intrastate than interstate conflicts. This does not always mean that intrastate conflicts are the most disastrous for human society, in terms of people killed, monetary losses, or material and/or infrastructure damage. But these conflicts are easily the most numerous and create further, systemic problems that states may be unable to escape in the future.

Terrorist attacks today are frequently pictured occurring in the Middle East, with stories of suicide bombings or insurgent groups using terrorist tactics in Iraq or Lebanon, for example. However, the "data strongly suggests that terrorism today is in large part a by-product of the war in Iraq, differing greatly from terrorism in the last quarter of the twentieth century."[6] This is reflected in the data in table 2.1, which shows the number of terrorist attacks and fatalities, by region, for the period 1970–2007. Despite the clarity of the rankings, there are some interesting findings buried in the data. Africa has almost half the number of attacks as the South Asian region, while North America has nearly half the number of attacks as Eastern Europe. East and Central Asia have nearly the same, small number of attacks as North America. The number of fatalities also carries some interesting figures. Africa has by far the highest fatality per attack ratio, with five deaths per attack. Western Europe has the lowest fatality-to-attack ratio, with only one death per every three attacks. North America has a high fatality-to-attack ratio, most likely owing to a few, high-profile attacks, including the 1995 bombing of the Alfred P. Murrah Federal building in Oklahoma City, Oklahoma and the 9/11 attacks. Additionally, the rankings are reordered (new rankings in brackets) if terrorism cases linked to the Iraq War are removed. In this case, the Middle East falls behind Western Europe for overall number of attacks (to third place) and falls behind South Asia for overall number of fatalities (to fourth place). While terrorism is frequently recognized as consisting of attacks against civilians or noncombatants, the Iraq War provided cover for multiple groups to seek revenge or push for their own political objectives, as well as adjust for some countings that include terrorist attacks against noncombatants in a conflict setting. This shows not only the growth in the use of terrorist tactics by a range of armed groups, but the outsized impact one case—the Iraq War—can have.

The number of terrorist attacks is less now than it was during the Cold War. "If Iraq and South Asia were to be removed from the data, a clear, steady downward trend would become apparent. There were 300 terrorist incidents worldwide in 1991, for instance, and 58 in 2005."[7]

Table 2.1. Regional Rankings of Terrorist Attacks and Fatalities, 1970–2007

Attacks	Fatalities
1. Latin America	Middle East
2. Middle East	Latin America
3. Western Europe [Middle East]	Africa
4. South Asia	South Asia [Middle East]
5. Africa	Southeast Asia and Oceania
6. Southeast Asia and Oceania	Western Europe
7. Eastern Europe	North America
8. North America	Eastern Europe
9. East and Central Asia	East and Central Asia

Note: Regions in brackets reflect new ranking after removal of Iraq War–related cases.
Source: J. Joseph Hewitt, Jonathan Wilkenfeld, and Ted Robert Gurr, *Peace and Conflict 2010* (Boulder, CO: Paradigm Publishers, 2010).

INTERSTATE CONFLICT DECREASING

Interstate conflicts are decreasing today, as intrastate conflicts remain active.[8] Different authors have pointed to the presence of nuclear weapons, economic interdependence, constraining effects of international law and norms, and casualty avoidance. These same factors that lead to a decrease in interstate conflicts simultaneously create space within which armed groups can flourish. As states leave the security arena, or are unwilling to actively engage in security issues, this provides space for armed groups, which in turn creates a greater number of complex problems for states to address.

Nuclear Weapons

Mearsheimer argues that nuclear weapons were a key component in keeping the peace in post-1945 Europe.[9] Others argue that nuclear weapons provide few, if any, political advantages to states.[10] Their effect was to "enforce caution and freeze existing borders," while "push[ing] conventional war into the nooks and crannies of the international system."[11] Nuclear weapons "sobered up" countries and prevented further escalation of conflicts.[12] So resilient has this constraint on conflict been that when the United States did use conventional force abroad, it was "for microscopic" stakes.[13] As nuclear weapons remain today, their constraining effects are still active.

States' use and support of armed-group proxies grew out of a desire to not escalate conflict with nuclear-armed adversaries. Nuclear weapons, as well as the most advanced and lethal military hardware, have little practical use in achieving a state's political objectives today.[14] Furthermore, this situation creates incentives for states to limit their conventional wars, opening space within which armed groups can operate. Ironically, it is "unconventional wars" that Hammes believes have been the source of a majority of significant political change. Indeed, he argues, "While most insurgencies fail, insurgency remains the only type of war that has defeated a superpower."[15]

Economic Interdependence

Some authors posit the international system is moving into a new period, where economic relations will overtake conflictual relationships and lead to greater peace.[16] Economic interdependence creates mutual vulnerabilities between states, conflict does not provide the economic goods and services states need, and the opportunity costs of conflict greatly outweigh any potential economic gains. As economic globalization increases and economies grow ever more interdependent and deeply enmeshed, the utility of military force declines for the most powerful of political entities. Economic globalization also offers greater opportunities for armed groups to expand and further their objectives.

International Norms

International norms, legal regulations, and treaties create a situation today where invasion and conquest are not only outlawed, but also actively proscribed through deterrence.[17] The United Nations was built on the fundamental premise of state sovereignty, where international intervention and war were legalized only in the cases of self-defense and when authorized by the UN Security Council.[18] Further norms and treaties against the use of chemical or biological weapons have arisen, as well as taboos against the use of nuclear weapons.[19] These constraints on state use of military force do not have the same impact on armed groups, which regularly flaunt international norms and are not a party to most international treaties.

Casualty Avoidance

Some theorists believe western societies are unwilling to accept causalities.[20] Constraints and pressures from domestic audiences, given the brutal nature of current conflicts, the level of economic misery, and lack of existential threat, lead some observers to question under what circumstances great powers would be willing to risk their soldiers' lives. Militaries today may use their forces to protect their forces, not to engage the enemy, further their political goals, or engage frequently misunderstood armed groups.

The decline in interstate conflicts does not point to the decreased relevance of armed groups. Intrastate conflicts remain the dominant type of conflict. Interstate conflicts, even if they were to suddenly increase in number, would still involve armed groups in various roles.

THE "NEW WAR" PARADIGM?

The decline in interstate wars, changes in the international system, and conflicts such as those surrounding Yugoslavia's disintegration in the 1980s and 1990s led to the rise of "new war" theorists. These journalists and academics argued war was undergoing a paradigm shift from "old" to "new war," as exemplified by changes in the means, methods, financing, and actors involved.[21] There are differences within the literature and questions revolving around whether these changes are new, as history is replete with examples of "irregular warfare." Furthermore, while changes in the international system create new incentives for actors, it is unclear whether these situations resemble incentives generated by previous systemic shifts. Lastly, is this move to new wars a permanent and unidirectional evolution toward a complete "transformation of war"?[22] Might future conditions reverse, halt, or alter these changes?

The "new war" arguments revolve around changes in the means, methods, financing, and actors of contemporary conflict. The actors are held to be nonstate actors, frequently organized around a unifying identity. These armed groups use irregular strategies and tactics, including attacking civilians, assassinations, bombings, and avoiding direct confrontations with state militaries. In order to carry out these operations, armed groups resort to illicit activities and exploitation of the increase in economic globalization, obscuring the boundaries between war and crime. These new wars stand in opposition to state-centric, ideologically motivated conflicts that mobilize the population to finance military-on-military clashes.

These factors, whether fundamentally new or a return to older forms of warfare, provide an opportunity to build a research program examining these factors in more depth. Kaldor has done a service in pointing out the blurring of lines and the reemergence of factors long-since left dormant and swept aside in political analysis. We do not need to believe that these conflicts are in some way different from any previous historical period, that they represent a paradigm shift in strategic thinking, or even that these conflicts represent an existential threat to all states or threaten to upend the international system. What we should acknowledge, as students, teachers, policy makers, and analysts, is that aspects of conflicts highlighted by this recent turn remain outside the standard course of study for many in security studies. Bringing a critical eye and theoretical focus to understudied, yet active and important issues in current political dialogues, helps minimize the gaps between the academic and policy communities confronted with these threats.

IRREGULAR WARFARE

Intrastate conflicts have adopted a multitude of monikers over the years, including hybrid wars, fourth-generation conflicts, low-intensity conflicts, small wars, and asymmetric conflicts.[23] What all of these permutations of "irregular warfare" have in common is the struggle over legitimacy (theirs and the government's), the battle for influence over a given population, and the role of nonstate actors—armed groups.

Irregular warfare is "a violent struggle among state and non-state actors for legitimacy and influence over the relevant populations . . . [which] favors indirect and asymmetric approaches, though it may employ the full range of military and other capabilities, in order to erode an adversary's power, influence, and will."[24] "Irregular" describes the nature of the threat, including actors who employ methods such as "guerilla warfare, terrorism, sabotage, subversion, criminal activities, and insurgency."[25] Success revolves around influencing populations and not outright military defeat of an opponent's armed forces and violence needs to be used sparingly or in very controlled ways, as it may negatively influence the target population.[26] More advanced weaponry, including many heavy weapons, may be discarded in favor of those that are small, simple, easy to maintain and cheap to acquire. The irregular battlefield may not allow for high-technology weapons, as armed groups may not have the skill or resources to repair, maintain, and upgrade advanced electronics, targeting systems, or complex weapon systems.[27]

Irregular warfare frequently creates indistinct divisions between civilian and combatant, blurs the line between war and crime and draws connections between the two, makes no distinction between public and private property, and attempts to wrestle control away from the state.[28]

War and crime have softened boundaries in today's environment.[29] Whether the focus is on individuals going to war to make a profit, armed groups using crime in order to further their political pursuits, or those authors who draw explicitly on market analogies in discussing force and the provision of security, armed-group economic activities further complicate an already complex battlespace.[30] The analysis of whether a situation is criminal or warfare determines what means and strategies are used to counter the activity. The blurring of distinctions creates problems for both law enforcement and military forces, which may be unprepared and unable to adequately address the challenges presented in such a hybrid environment. Armed groups may play off of this asymmetry between their tactics and strategies and the government's inability to adequately respond.

Both governments and nonstate actors can participate in irregular warfare, but we frequently assume nonstate actors are the ones perpetrating this. Most definitions usually indicate that at least one nonstate actor is present in the fighting, attempting to use irregular threats against states because armed groups may only be capable of irregular threats, while states feel more comfortable or able to respond in conventional ways. These armed groups do not have to be of any one type, thus irregular warfare is not only for insurgents. According to van Creveld, "War will not be waged by armies but by groups whom we today call terrorists, guerrillas, bandits, and robbers, but who will undoubtedly hit on more formal titles to describe themselves."[31]

Why Use Irregular Warfare?

In order to counter some of the irregular threats listed above, US policy applies some combination of "counterterrorism, unconventional warfare [using special operations forces in lieu of conventional, direct US military power project], foreign internal defense, counterinsurgency, and stability operations."[32] Given the uncertainty and increased complexity of irregular threats, current warfare often resembles humanitarian actions or incorporates aspects of humanitarian missions in conflict.[33] Actions such as development, state building, or counterinsurgent "hearts and minds" operations may, in many cases, take on hues of both military operations and humanitarian missions. This increased complexity and possible confusion is often accompanied by a diverse group of actors in a conflict zone, from traditional state military actors to armed groups to NGOs and IOs backing development or humanitarian interests. In some of these cases, humanitarian workers and civilians are directly targeted, bringing further complexity to the question of combatants, noncombatants, and the role different actors are playing in the battlespace. Often, humanitarian workers must cooperate with military or security forces in order to access the conflict area, further blurring distinctions between the groups.[34]

Why do states and armed groups engage in irregular warfare, instead of using conventional, direct military force to engage the enemy? Basic reasons include the lack of resources, including personnel, material, and a mass base from which to draw both manpower and economic support. This prevents the armed group from territorial occupation and force-on-force direct engagement. The group may have changing goals, whereby territory loses its importance, the ideological conversion or destruction of others gains in prominence, and identity and religious conflicts rise to the surface. These objectives may not be satisfied by direct military engagement, instead seeking to influence the population by demonstrating the group's increasing legitimacy and the government's decreasing legitimacy. Armed groups also infrequently adhere to traditional state norms, embracing chemical, biological, radiological, and nuclear (CBRN) weapons, seeking to violate and destroy state sovereignty, and building criminal and recruiting networks to accomplish their goals and finance their operations. These norm violations may preclude building mass support or widespread acceptance, forcing the armed groups to retreat to utilizing globalized communications, psychological operations, and information campaigns, along with indirect means, to remain clandestine and compensate for a lack of a mass base.

Irregular warfare allows armed groups to adapt to a variety of changes, including changes in the geostrategic environment, changes in government strategy and policy, and changes in demographic or economic conditions. The armed group is competing for influence over a population that may be shifting and changing in its acceptance of the armed group's narrative, moving away from the government, or retrenching back into the government's camp. Irregular warfare provides the tools and flexibility to adapt to this ever-changing and fluid environment.

In the end, irregular warfare uses violence as one tool in an attempt to influence the population. The psychological effects of violence—and the threat of violence—are important to spreading the armed group's narrative and in shaping the context within which the fight is occurring. While armed groups may use the latest technological advances to communicate this message, to recruit and communicate with members, and to transport illicit goods and fundraise, the group must still provide a compelling message that seeks to increase their legitimacy, while decreasing the government's legitimacy.

Irregular warfare may not have a clearly defined beginning or end. It may flare up, only to be quickly extinguished and retreat into safe havens, only to return once the conditions are ripe. One defining characteristic of many recent conflicts is the degree to which they recur and are extended for many years. The underlying grievances and inequalities that armed groups build upon—whether centered on political, economic, or identity issues—remain, while the groups strive to achieve their goals. Killing a leader, eradicating the members, or scattering an organization may not remove the grievance or discredit an ideology. Irregular conflicts, many of which are designed to be protracted and take advantage of the armed group's clandestine nature, may not end until the environment has been permanently altered, or at least the perception that it has been altered predominates.

Many of these conflicts frequently unfold in weak states that lack the ability to provide security in their borders and offer safe haven to armed groups. These are significant for weak states with frequently large civilian casualties since the conflicts are fought "amongst the people."[35] There is also the potential for spillover to neighboring states due to forced migration and refugee flows, armed-group safe havens, and porous borders due to neighboring state weakness, or neighboring state support for armed group. Although conflicts may spillover due to ethnic or religious groups spread between multiple states due to the whims of colonial mapmakers, many states might prefer to remain aloof from the conflict. States have an incentive to reinforce territorial integrity and sovereignty norms, meaning some states may not act unless circumstances force their hand. This may occur through domestic lobbying to intervene on the side of coreligionists or ethnic kin in a neighboring state. In other cases, the overwhelming burden that humanitarian crises place on the state makes nonintervention impossible.

ROLE OF GEOPOLITICAL AND GEOSTRATEGIC FACTORS

Decline of the State

IR theories and security studies have traditionally focused on the state. However, scholarship growing out of the 1970s has examined the theme of the loss of state power. Three broad issues have emerged. First, drawing from the international political economy literature, is the "erosion of the state" due to international institutions, multinational corporations, regional trade agreements, and other nonstate actors and supranational bodies. These challenges to the state either appropriated new powers for themselves, constrained state choices, or in other ways created strategic dilemmas for policy makers, such as through oil embargoes. Second is the large number of failed, weak, or fragile states and the accompanying ungoverned spaces and their attending consequences and implications. This erosion of state strength may be due to bad governance, armed conflict, loss of external support at the end of the Cold War, or internal state failings. While states have been defined by their position as the highest political actor and possessors of both legitimacy and sovereignty in the past, most states never possessed absolute sovereignty or legitimacy. In both legitimacy and sovereignty there have always been challenges to the state, whether from inside or outside, but as long as the concepts were recognized by other states in the system, the state could be assured of maintaining its legitimacy, in the eyes of other states. As other states recognized and acknowledged the declining legitimacy, states lost power and are even more susceptible to both internal and external challenges. The third issue is the decrease in state power due to systemic factors, namely globalization and the post–Cold War shift in polarity.

Despite the erosion of state power and demonstrated armed-group actions, security studies has not fully embraced the changes in states and armed groups. In security studies, armed groups of many stripes and varieties can carve out power for themselves, they can constrain state choices, they can create strategic dilemmas for policy makers, they can cause a state to reorient and rewrite its defense policies and posture, and reconsider its force makeup. But they do not have to overthrow the state or conquer the state to be a threat, in much the same way that MNCs have not overtaken states or supplanted state governments. There are varying degrees of threat and not everything has to be an existential threat to be important.

The shifts noted by the "new war" theorists and echoed by those studying current threats from al-Qaeda, insurgent groups in Southeast Asia, or the complex web of criminal, insurgent, and terrorist actors in the Sahel and Maghreb are driven in part by several contextual factors. These include the end of the Cold War, the many facets of globalization, and the growth in weak and failed states. These "preconditions" create an environment and opportunity within which armed groups are more likely to increase in importance, to operate, or to be able to strike more lethal blows at governments. Preconditions or permissive factors are differentiated from precipitating factors.[36] While the environment may be ideal for armed-group creation or operations, it may require charismatic leaders, aggressive strategies, or the right blend of ideological justification and external support to push a group into executing attacks and taking advantage of the permissive geopolitical context. This section analyzes recent shifts in the international environment that provide opportunities for armed groups.

End of the Cold War

The end of the Cold War and the disintegration of the Soviet Union have created both opportunities and challenges for armed groups. On the one hand, small arms have flowed into conflict zones as former Eastern bloc countries look to unload their armories and make a profit. Unburdened by the need to maintain large stockpiles for a superpower war that will never happen, governments and private actors with access to government stores have dumped inexpensive small arms in many of the world's hotspots. Additionally, superpower constraints on their client's actions have been removed. The United States and Soviet Union feared direct conflict and while each supported their own proxies, there was always the concern that even proxy conflicts would escalate to involve the superpower. These constraints are missing today, allowing conflict dynamics, including the seeming rebirth of ethnic conflicts and "ancient enmities" to return to disrupt the international system.

On the other side of the ledger, the Soviet Union has disintegrated, taking with it a major source of funding for ideological "wars of national liberation."[37] States and armed groups alike can no longer rely on superpower support, simply for agreeing to uphold one ideology over another. While some states, NGOs, and individuals have stepped in to help fund armed groups, the Cold War competition produced unrivaled access to funding, training, and even safe haven for many proto-insurgencies and was key to the success of many others. With these supporters sidelined by their own economic concerns and no overarching ideological battles, armed groups have been forced to seek their own sources of funding.

Armed groups sought funding from nonstate actors, creating further complexity in the international system reeling from the loss of "stability" and "predictability" of the Cold War. At the same time, regional, weak states, robbed of military aid by the end of superpower competition, sought military power and security from armed groups. These weak and fragile states are less able to control armed groups, however. These states face a greater principal–agent problem than the superpowers, as weak states lack the capacity to monitor armed groups. Simultaneously, armed groups undermine state legitimacy, which also contributed to weak states' inability to monitor and control armed groups. The end of the Cold War has thus created new incentives for previously excluded states to draw on armed group capabilities to further their own state policies, and introduced complexity due to the myriad motivations and targets behind the support of these armed groups, while removing some of the constraints that provided "governance" of armed group.

Globalization

Globalization—the second environmental factor—has been driven by technology, open economies, and greater communication.[38] The impact on states, according to Ripsman and Paul, has been to make the stronger states stronger and weaken weaker states.[39] The impact on armed groups has been to allow armed groups easier access to economic markets, remove the "stopping power of water," greatly enhance communication, as well as allow anonymous activity in many of the above areas. While this increased the speed, scope, and scale of armed-group attacks, organization, and recruitment, it has complicated the interaction between states and armed groups. Stronger states may have an easier time locating, tracking, or combating armed groups, while weaker states may be more susceptible. All of this is contingent on continued globalization in the international environment. None of the trends discussed above are inevitable, irreversible, or necessarily moving toward an ultimately "globalized world."

Globalization may bring unwanted elements to a state—whether people, ideas, or war materials, it may decrease the state's ability to determine its own policies, and it may decrease the state's ability to react to threats. By contrast, globalization increases the opportunities available to armed groups, including increased freedom to travel, communicate, and access markets.

Globalization is frequently posited to be a main driver of change in the international system and as such, has a strong effect on armed groups, as well as states.[40] The two most frequent topics for consideration are "what is globalization?" and "what form does globalization take?" A third question, specific to our undertaking, lurks within the first two questions: what effect do these systemic level dynamics have on armed groups?

What is Globalization?

Globalization has been conceptualized in many different ways. One of the most basic constructs is that globalization is an increased level of connections between all actors in the international system: states, international organizations, armed groups, NGOs, MNCs, and individuals. These interactions create mutual dependence between groups, increasing not just the breadth or number of interactions, but also the depth of interactions. States and others are more deeply interconnected with other actors, which reduces barriers to even further interaction and opens up new avenues of cooperation and possibly conflict.

A related idea proposes that these increasingly complex interactions between states are carried out across multiple domains, opening areas of interaction, and allowing access to actors and issues that were not considered in classical conceptions of diplomacy, cultural exchanges, or economic relationships. The depth and breadth of interconnections not only increases the issues and avenues of exchange, but also creates new systemic dynamics that further influence the actors.

States, in the traditional Westphalian model, are sovereign actors, where they not only have a monopoly over the legitimate use of force within their borders, but also are answerable to no other states concerning domestic matters. Conversely, each state respects the sovereignty of all other states, a construct that helped, by many accounts, to end religious wars in Europe.[41] Yet sovereignty is being eroded today, as globalization turns local issues into global issues, and global issues have potentially unmanageable effects locally. This conception of globalization posits that issues internal to the state are matters of national and potentially international importance. Discussions concerning intervention in civil wars today revolve around the role of respecting and protecting human rights, the international legal basis for intervention, and the rights of the regime to "internal sovereignty." These decisions place a state's internal politics at the mercy of international laws, norms, and power considerations. They also place neighboring states—affected by refugee flows or economic strains—at the mercy of local decisions, making the local regional or even global.

These interactions may be framed in a simpler manner: globalization is the increase in the scale, scope, and speed of interactions occurring today. Scale is the extent to which an actor produces a good, frequently with an eye toward an increase in production, which leads to a decreased cost per good. As states, MNCs, or armed groups produce goods or services—whether the classical "widget," stability, or security—an increase in their production may lead to the ease or decrease in costs to producing that good. For armed groups, a decrease in the cost of providing security within a sovereign state is directly correlated with a decrease in the state's sovereignty. Globalization may empower the armed group at the expense of the disintegration of the state.

Actors may also see a change in the scope of their production, such that international actors produce a wider range of goods and services. Some armed groups are able to marshal resources from international or globalized networks to produce not just brutal violence against the government, military, and uncooperative civilians, but also provide social services to the population under their control.

Lastly, globalization may also be considered as an increase in "systemic speed"—the flow of information, the transportation of people, the movement of goods, and the transfer of wealth occurs at ever-increasing speeds. Typical examples include the creation of jumbo jets that fly hundreds of passengers all over the globe within hours, the revolutionizing effect of the shipping container and super tankers, and nearly instantaneous communication over the Internet or cell phones. These advances demonstrate that what once took months, weeks, or days, is now measured in hours, minutes, or seconds. This speed in turn places pressures—whether real or imagined—on politicians, pundits, policy makers, and populations to increase the speed of their decision making. The consequences—from a government's overhasty reaction to an incident based on little more than gut-wrenching video, to an individual's economic decision to withdraw money from a bank based on rumor—are magnified and carried out by a system that does not so much create order or constraints, but imparts incentives to react with ever greater speed and haste. For armed groups, the ability to instantaneously transmit their narrative and message to hundreds, if not thousands of individuals, states, and organizations, as well as the ability to move and adapt quickly to a changing strategic environment, provides small, clandestine groups with an agility not previously enjoyed.

What Form Does Globalization Take?

Globalization can be broken down into four areas of analysis: science and technology, economic aspects, military issues, and culture and political aspects. Science and technology—the spread and advancement of scientific knowledge and research and its adaptation into technology innovations—are the foundation upon which much of globalization rests.[42] It provides the abilities inherent in the notion of the increased scale, scope, and speed of connections and relationships between actors. Science and technology advances impact three areas of importance to armed groups: communications, the information technology revolution, and the transportation revolution. The spread of global communications allows an armed group to decentralize, yet remain in contact to disseminate ideology, plan operations, and other factors important to the maintenance and operation of the group.[43] Armed groups benefit from the overwhelming number of tweets, emails, phone calls, webpages, blog posts, comments, and chat rooms that are proliferating at an increasing rate. This anonymity makes it easier for armed groups to remain clandestine as they communicate, plan, recruit, and fundraise in international markets.

Another aspect of science and technological innovations is the information revolution. States and nonstate actors are strongly affected by the information revolution, including telecommunications and computerization, which allows groups to operate on a global scale with a greater amount of local and specialized knowledge. This information can be communicated instantaneously and shared across a wide range of actors. Technology advances have greatly aided states, NGOs, and IOs, as well as armed groups. Issues concerning the rise of "big data" and the access to ever greater amounts of personal information, including the movements, thoughts, and strategies of key decision makers; scientific and technological data concerning bombs and other tools of violence; and the sharing of successful operations, strategies, and tactics, have the advantage of advancing armed group abilities much more so than would be capable in isolation.

The standardization and proliferation of shipping routes and air travel, as part of the transportation revolution, has had a great impact on the ability of armed groups to transport illicit products, whether for fundraising purposes or to supply insurgent or terrorist groups.[44] Armed groups are able to take advantage of all means of transportation to move in and out of multiple regions and markets, hiding in the vast scale of global transportation. Previously, it was distance that in many cases presented armed groups from bringing the conflict to colonial or Western powers.[45] Arguably no market or regions are off limits or beyond the reach of an armed group, which allows for safe havens, recruitment, or operations reaching all corners of the globe. When combined with the massive scale of the transportation of people and goods, this enables the armed group to remain anonymous in the face of government attempts at surveillance and monitoring.

Globalization's second form involves economic relations and covers some of the more frequently studied aspects of globalization—the spread of new markets, the openness and scale of capital markets, and the growth in foreign investment. The rise of multinational corporations demonstrates that if a firm can transfer money electronically, and is more likely to have safe, secure economic transactions, then it is more likely to expand overseas. The same is true for armed groups, who are able to transfer money and gain access to fundraising opportunities and target populations previously out of reach, whether through Internet-based strategies, wire transfers, or access to a diaspora. Additionally, formerly isolated state and regional markets now have access to international markets through enhanced communications and technology, which lead to worldwide integration and global production and distribution chains.

Armed groups are enabled by the increasing networks and economic ties, which allow a greater movement of goods and services and increases each one's ability to seek out additional sources of external support. Much as in the case of communications, the sheer scale and scope of global markets effectively hides illicit transactions and the transportation of those goods and services, allowing armed groups to remain concealed, while states must pour a greater amount of resources into monitoring and tracking armed groups. Armed groups are easily lost among the 1.5 billion passengers who passed through the world's twenty-five busiest airports in 2012, or among the 316 million twenty-foot equivalent units (TEUs) that traversed the top twenty-five container ports in the world.[46]

Increased access to regional and global markets brings with it complications. Both armed groups and states compete for funding, public recognition, diplomatic aid, and other types of support in the global marketplace with a plethora of new actors. This may hamper an armed group's ability to secure necessary financing or diplomatic recognition, as they may have difficulty distinguishing themselves from others in the global arena.

Military issues constitute another aspect of globalization. States benefit from transportation and communication in terms of power projection capabilities, overseas basing, operations outside of their local area in regard to antipiracy or counternarcotics efforts, as well as in greater ties between militaries, whether operationally, educationally, or strategically. At the same time, armed groups have been able to take advantage of a large, and in some cases, loosely regulated, international small-arms market.[47] Access to training and weaponry is one reason for the increased lethality of Tuareg insurgents in Mali. These insurgents returned from fighting in Libya with more lethal weapons and military experience, which greatly increased pressure on a weak Malian government.[48] Small-arms proliferation may not be the cause of armed-group grievances, but they provide the opportunity to not only resort to violence, but for that violence to overwhelm all but the best-equipped law enforcement and state militaries. It is more of an enabler of greater violence than has previously been available in such wide circulation.

Lastly, cultural and political aspects of globalization are inextricably linked and, given the degree to which global issues become local and vice versa, it should come as no surprise that local political leaders are under pressure from local and foreign sources of cultural influence. Whether due to the spread of American popular culture through Hollywood and the Internet, or progressive views on modernization that stress secular society, liberalism, or materialism, local leaders may be forced into taking steps to curtail outside influence or to protect identity groups that fear they are threatened by these outside forces. The fear of forced assimilation, of cultural homogeneity, and of the loss of identity, whether real or imagined, is frequently cited as a key factor in current conflicts.[49] Alternatively, the ability to see one's relative deprivation, as compared to a more economically advanced country, may create rising expectations that governments will address these issues. The gap between what is expected and what has been achieved may lead to political violence.[50] Increased interdependence means that policy making in other states or international bodies may constrain local policy options and resources. This further alienates individuals and groups from the political leadership in the country and may drive armed groups to seek redress of these conditions.

Globalization's benefits are not uniformly distributed among states.[51] State power can be reduced by international factors such as debt relief and loans provided by the World Bank or International Monetary Fund (IMF) that frequently come with conditions on desired domestic policy reforms. Both leaders and states' institutions are simultaneously constrained by international regulations and, in a global marketplace, the economic whims of other countries. At the same time, these states face pressure from their domestic constituencies to provide a buffer against negative external forces.

Technological advances make it easier for stronger, more developed states to monitor, police, and combat armed groups. They are also less frequently subjected to challenges to their authority. Armed groups may take advantage of many of the same technological innovations, however, potentially canceling out some of the advantages that strong states possess. Nevertheless, strong states can increase their power through beneficial economic and political relations, as well as stable, well-developed infrastructure.

Globalization may weaken fragile states. These states are unlikely to be able to counteract international economic swings or secure their borders. Many have a palpable sense of economic, cultural, political, and security disparity between haves and have-nots in society. This is amplified and reinforced by messages and narratives through satellite television, the Internet, and social media. Weak states have few resources at their disposal to combat these influences and many are made weaker by corruption. As globalization further weakens fragile states, the erosion and loss of state legitimacy provides fertile breeding ground for armed-group and internal conflict.

States in Transition and the Profusion of Weak, Fragile, and Failing States

States in transition, postconflict states, and weak, fragile, and failing states all face a combination of four broad concerns focused on issues of peace and stability, governance, territorial control, and economic sustainability.[52] A state's security may be hampered by weak institutions, demographic shifts, organized crime, or postconflict instability, all of which may combine to form a market for force within the country to provide the most basic of services. Force, and the stability that may accompany it, is a foundational good, without which a country cannot carry out any of its other pressing needs. Economic relationships, social equality, and political access are easily denied and grievously unequal in a state without internal security and stability. State institutions weakened by corruption, war, or lack of resources may be unable to enforce security or enforce it selectively and unequally. Shifting population and demographic trends may bring masses into newly urbanized areas, teaming with organized crime and few economic opportunities. And civil wars may leave societies awash in small arms, lacking basic services and political representation. All of these issues leave the state unable to provide security, which is taken up by private actors. Violence becomes a commodity, bought and sold and completely unregulated by the state. This further erodes what little legitimacy the state had.

Moreover, the state's ability to provide effective governance, a sometimes amorphous concept that variously incorporates adherence to the rule of law, improving the efficiency and responsiveness of the public sector, addressing corruption, while improving inclusiveness and transparency in all aspects of society is frequently hampered. Factors that negatively affect this include weak governmental institutions, organized crime, and socially fractured states. At the heart of this category are weak state institutions that are unable or unwilling to provide services and equal treatment to all groups in society. Elites may be corrupted by organized crime or under the control of one identity group, effectively disenfranchising certain groups within the state and even potentially providing safe havens for neighboring violent extremists. There may be a steady decrease in norm adherence within the state, as the rule of law is routinely flouted, creating incentives to work outside of legal channels and accepted standards. The lack of effective governance delegitimizes the government and provides opportunities for an armed group to seize the narrative, build their legitimacy, and ultimately to extract resources and recruit members to their cause.[53]

Porous borders and lack of internal sovereignty is a clear consequence of lack of control over security, weak institutions, and criminal activity. The proliferation of a market for force within the delegitimized state is another symptom of the lack of control over its territory. The loss of territorial control runs the gamut from porous borders and the inability to monitor armed groups due to a state's insufficient resources, lack of political will to enforce its borders, and corruption within law enforcement or internal security services, to the loss of the monopoly over the use of legitimate force within its borders.

The last concern is whether a state remains economically sustainable. Again, a key factor involved is efficient and effective state institutions. Governance plays a role, as does the security and stability of the state. States that are under economic sanctions or embargoes may resort to smuggling and other illegal means of securing basic goods. This creates incentives to import goods that will bring in the highest profits and that benefit elites and powerful interests, rather than the population at large. Alternatively, criminal organizations may corrupt elites, potentially leading down the road to state sponsorship of criminal behavior. Guinea-Bissau is a recent example, where TCOs have diverted drug-trafficking routes from South America to Europe. North Korea is also in the business of manufacturing and exporting illegal drugs.[54] This can effectively siphon off resources and funds that reduce the state's ability to provide for economic sustainability. Weak states may also suffer from the creation of rentier economies, where individuals use state infrastructure or goods for personal benefit. Frequent examples are state employees charging for licenses that should be free, requiring bribes in order to file paperwork, or in other ways abusing the employee's regulatory position to profit from state business.

Many armed groups create a self-reinforcing environment, as they take advantage of, and are born out of, a state's inability to provide even the most basic of services.[55] Their presence and actions further weaken the state, leading to the proliferation of armed groups and increasing the state's inability to respond. Weak and failing states, while not sufficient to explain armed-group actions, reduce an armed group's costs of formation, operations, and perpetuation. All four problems addressed in chapter 1—the free-rider problem, the coordination problem, the time-consistency problem, and the principal–agent problem—are frequently easier to overcome in a weak state environment.

It should be recognized that many armed groups need a basic level of development, infrastructure, stability, and government services in order to function. Too much state weakness can be detrimental to the armed group. Without basic electricity or the ability to power generators, armed groups cannot charge cell phones, satellite phones, or laptops. TCOs cannot function without a customer base that can afford their illicit products, cannot make a profit without access to natural resources, and cannot increase their organization and profits without an infrastructure to transport and deliver their products to market. Without even the most basic services, most armed groups will find it very difficult to operate.

US PARTICIPATION IN INTRASTATE CONFLICTS

The United States has engaged in intrastate conflicts from the very "beginning," as the American Revolution presented the United States with an early taste of "hybrid war."[56] Throughout its history, the United States has fought numerous armed groups. From the various American Indian Wars to Communist insurgents in Latin America and Africa during the Cold War, to struggles for "national liberation" in Southeast Asia, to terrorist groups in Central Asia, the United States has a long history fighting armed groups in intrastate conflicts.[57] As the post-1945 period makes clear, the worldwide prevalence of intrastate conflicts outweighed that of interstate conflicts. As great power conflicts—or any interstate conflicts—appear unlikely in the near future, it remains intrastate conflicts that dominate the headlines.

One account of US involvement in low-intensity conflicts—which included insurgencies, counterinsurgencies, coups d'état, transnational terrorism, combating terrorism, and "narco conflict," among others—notes that these conflicts are of the greatest frequency, with the most variety in their type, and they are the most complex in terms of causes and deterrence. The report further notes that it is imperative that the United States understand these conflicts, as failure might lead to destabilizing friendly governments, reducing US access to raw materials and sea lanes, and target US personal and property abroad.[58] Despite US involvement in Iraq coming to an official end and Afghanistan scheduled to come to an end in 2014, at least in terms of US military actions, the United States is still likely to have a military and irregular warfare contingent in place in support of the various missions outlined under the "irregular warfare" heading.

ARMED-GROUP THREATS TO THE UNITED STATES

Armed groups are a threat to the United States in several ways. First, as has been made clear by numerous instances, including the 1993 World Trade Center bombing, the 9/11 attacks, and numerous domestic armed-group attacks, the United States has been and will continue to be directly targeted by armed groups. Whether or not future attacks attain the scale of destruction of the 9/11 attacks, or opt for a greater scope in their geographic range or target selection, US civilians, the military, and government officials face direct attack at home. TCOs are also operating in the United States, trafficking in drugs, arms, or people, or in other criminal activities, including corruption.

Second, armed groups operate in the United States in ways that are not always violent, but nonetheless challenge US authorities and governance. Armed groups may carry out fundraising, whether through solicitation of donations from a diaspora, charitable organizations, or illicit activities. Instances include charges of fraud for charities sending funds to terrorist organizations to cigarette smuggling linked to Hezbollah.[59] Armed groups may also recruit members, whether in person or over the Internet, for combat in foreign theaters, such as Somalia.[60] Armed groups may also use the United States as a safe haven, in order to engage in planning or logistical operations. The United States has attempted to prevent these events from occurring, often to no avail.

Armed groups target US commercial and national interests abroad, including violence against US businesses engaged in natural-resource extraction, as well as through corruption and organized crime involving US officials, citizens, or business agents. Armed groups frequently act as spoilers in diplomatic negotiations in areas concerning US national interests and US allies. These groups may seek to draw US forces into intrastate conflicts to support their position, or to directly engage US forces in combat. On other occasions, US citizens are targeted in terrorist attacks abroad.

These attacks are not aberrations. They are instead logical extensions of the systemic and structural changes in the international environment combined with the accompanying changes in warfare discussed in this chapter. Armed groups pose a human security threat as they target the individual's ability to fulfill his basic physical, economic, and psychological needs. These groups pose a national security threat when they challenge the state's legitimacy through corruption, destroying the state's ability to provide services, adequate governance, and the ability to enforce its policies. Lastly, armed groups pose an international security threat by creating refugee and forced migration flows, by corrupting and destabilizing states through transnational operations, whether cross-border violence, multistate trafficking, or creating regional instability that involves IOs, NGOs, as well as regional and extraregional states.

DISCUSSION QUESTIONS

1. Do (some) armed groups need a basic level of state development?
2. Despite the definition given of irregular warfare, why might states not want to engage in it?
3. How might a shift in the international distribution of power change the prevalence of intrastate conflicts?
4. Would an increase in the number of democracies worldwide lead to a decrease in the number of armed groups?

RECOMMENDED READINGS

Arnaud Blin, "Armed Groups and Intra-State Conflicts: The Dawn of a New Era?" *International Review of the Red Cross* 93, no. 882 (2011): 287–310.

Jorge Heine and Ramesh Thakur, eds., *The Dark Side of Globalization* (New York: United Nations University Press, 2011).

Kalevi J. Holsti, *The State, War, and the State of War* (Cambridge: Cambridge University Press, 1996).

Mary Kaldor, *New and Old Wars: Organized Violence in a Global Era* (Stanford, CA: Stanford University Press, 2007).

Robert D. Kaplan, *The Coming Anarchy: Shattering the Dreams of the Post Cold War* (New York: Random House, 2001).

Norrin M. Ripsman and T. V. Paul, *Globalization and the National Security State* (Oxford: Oxford University Press, 2010).

Martin van Creveld, *The Transformation of War* (New York: Free Press, 1991).

Thomas X. Hammes, *The Sling and the Stone* (St. Paul, MN: Zenith Press, 2006).

NOTES

1. Lotta Themnér and Peter Wallensteen, "Armed Conflict, 1946–2012," *Journal of Peace Research* 50, no. 4 (2013): 509.

2. Ibid.

3. Ibid., table 2, p. 511.

4. J. Joseph Hewitt, "Trends in Global Conflict, 1946–2007," in *Peace and Conflict 2010*, ed. J. Joseph Hewitt, Jonathan Wilkenfeld, and Ted Robert Gurr (Boulder, CO: Paradigm Publishers, 2010), 31.

5. Themnér and Wallensteen, "Armed Conflict, 1946–2012," 510.

6. Gary LaFree, Laura Dugan, and R. Kim Cragin, "Trends in Global Terrorism, 1970–2007," in *Peace and Conflict 2010*, ed. J. Joseph Hewitt, Jonathan Wilkenfeld, and Ted Robert Gurr (Boulder, CO: Paradigm Publishers, 2010), 54.

7. Christopher J. Fettweis, *Dangerous Times?: The International Politics of Great Power Peace* (Washington, DC: Georgetown University Press, 2010), 85.

8. For general overviews, see ibid. and John Mueller, "War Has Almost Ceased to Exist: An Assessment," *Political Science Quarterly* 124, no. 2 (2009): 297–321.

9. John J. Mearsheimer, "Back to the Future: Instability in Europe after the Cold War," *International Security* 15, no. 1 (1990): 5–56.

10. See Martin van Creveld, *The Transformation of War* (New York: Free Press, 1991), 3; McGeorge Bundy, "The Unimpressive Record of Atomic Diplomacy," in *The Use of Force: Military Power and International Politics*, ed. Robert J. Art and Kenneth N. Waltz (Lanham, MD: Rowman and Littlefield, 2009) ; and John Mueller, *Atomic Obsession: Nuclear Alarmism from Hiroshima to Al-Qaeda* (Oxford: Oxford University Press, 2010).

11. van Creveld, *The Transformation of War*, 10, 11.

12. Scott D. Sagan and Kenneth N. Waltz, *The Spread of Nuclear Weapons: A Debate Renewed* (New York: Norton, 2003).

13. van Creveld, *The Transformation of War*, 14.

14. Rupert Smith, *The Utility of Force: The Art of War in the Modern World* (New York: Vintage Books, 2008).

15. Thomas X. Hammes, "Armed Groups: Changing the Rules," in *Armed Groups: Studies in National Security, Counterterrorism, and Counterinsurgency*, ed. Jeffrey H. Norwitz (Newport, RI: U.S. Naval War College Press, 2008), 449. He lists Soviet defeats in Afghanistan and Chechnya, as well as the US defeats in Vietnam, Lebanon, and Somalia. It is unknown how Hammes would view the US withdrawal from Iraq and scheduled 2014 withdrawal from Afghanistan.

16. For general arguments, see Richard Rosecrance, *The Rise of the Trading State: Commerce and Conquest in the Modern World* (New York: Basic Books, 1986) and Richard Rosecrance and Peter Thompson, "Trade, Foreign Investment, and Security, " *Annual Review of Political Science* 6, no. 1 (2003): 377–98.

17. For a general overview, see Carl Kaysen, "Is War Obsolete?: A Review Essay," *International Security* 14, no. 4 (1990): 42–64 and Mueller, "War Has Almost Ceased to Exist: An Assessment."

18. See the text of the "Charter of the United Nations," http://www.un.org/en/documents/charter/.

19. Peter J. Katzenstein, *The Culture of National Security* (New York: Columbia University Press, 1996) and Nina Tannenwald, *The Nuclear Taboo: The United States and the Non-Use of Nuclear Weapons since 1945* (Cambridge: Cambridge University Press, 2006).

20. For example, see Smith, *The Utility of Force: The Art of War in the Modern World.*

21. For example, see Mary Kaldor, *New and Old Wars: Organized Violence in a Global Era* (Stanford, CA: Stanford University Press, 2007); Herfried Münkler, *The New Wars* (Malden, MA: Polity Press, 2004); and Robert D. Kaplan, *The Coming Anarchy: Shattering the Dreams of the Post Cold War* (New York: Random House, 2001).

22. van Creveld, *The Transformation of War.*

23. See, for example, C. E. Callwell, *Small Wars: Their Principles and Practice*, 3rd ed. (Lincoln: University of Nebraska Press, 1996); John M. Collins, Frederick Hamerman, and James P. Seevers, *U.S. Low-Intensity Conficts: 1899–1990* (Washington, DC: Congressional Research Service, 1990); Thomas X. Hammes, *The Sling and the Stone* (St. Paul, MN: Zenith Press, 2006); Frank G. Hoffman, *Conflict in the 21st Century: The Rise of Hybrid Wars* (Arlington, VA: Potomac Institute for Policy Studies, 2007); and Williamson Murray and Peter R. Mansoor, eds., *Hybrid Warfare: Fighting Complex Opponents from the Ancient World to the Present* (Cambridge: Cambridge University Press, 2013).

24. United States Department of Defense, *Irregular Warfare: Countering Irregular Threats: Joint Operating Concept (IW JOC), V 2.0* (May 17, 2010), 9.

25. Ibid.

26. Eric V. Larson et al., *Assessing Irregular Warfare: A Framework for Intelligence Analysis* (Santa Monica, CA: RAND Corporation, 2008), 11.

27. Martin van Creveld, *The Rise and Decline of the State* (Cambridge: Cambridge University Press, 1999), 20.

28. United States Department of Defense, *Irregular Warfare: Countering Irregular Threats: Joint Operating Concept (IW JOC), V 2.0*, 9. These are frequently mentioned criteria for a range of civil war activity today. See Sarah Percy, "Introduction," *Civil Wars* 11, no. 1 (2009): 1–4.

29. See Douglas Farah, "Terrorist-Criminal Pipelines and Criminalized States: Emerging Alliances," *PRISM* 2, no. 3 (2011): 15–32 and Vanda Felbab-Brown, "The Crime-War Battlefields," *Survival* 55, no. 3 (2013): 147–66.

30. See generally David Keen, "The Economic Functions of Violence in Civil Wars," *Adelphi Paper*, no. 320 (1998); Paul Collier, "Doing Well out of War: An Economic Perspective," in *Greed and Grievance: Economic Agendas in Civil Wars*, ed. Mats Berdal and David M. Malone (Boulder, CO: Lynne Rienner, 2000); Deborah D. Avant, *The Market for Force: The Consequences of Privatizing Security* (Cambridge: Cambridge University Press, 2005); John Mueller, *The Remnants of War* (Ithaca, NY: Cornell University Press, 2007); and Steven Metz, *Rethinking Insurgency* (Carlisle, PA: Strategic Studies Institute, US Army War College, 2007); as well as the discussion in chapter 4.

31. van Creveld, *The Rise and Decline of the State*, 197.

32. United States Department of Defense, *Irregular Warfare: Countering Irregular Threats: Joint Operating Concept (IW JOC), V 2.0*, 16.

33. Gerard McHugh and Manuel Bessler, *Humanitarian Negotiations with Armed Groups: A Manual for Practitioners* (New York: United Nations Office for the Coordination of Humanitarian Affairs, 2006), 7.

34. Ibid., 8.

35. Smith, *The Utility of Force: The Art of War in the Modern World.*

36. See Darcy M. E. Noricks, "The Root Causes of Terrorism," in *Social Science for Counterterrorism: Putting the Pieces Together*, ed. Paul K. Davis and Kim Cragin (Santa Monica, CA: RAND, 2009). See also Gordon H. McCormick, "Terrorist Decision Making," *Annual Review of Political Science* 6 (2003): 480.

37. Ian Beckett, "The Future of Insurgency," *Small Wars and Insurgencies* 16, no. 1 (2005): 23.

38. For a good overview of globalization as it relates to armed groups, see Querine H. Hanlon, "Globalization and the Transformation of Armed Groups," in *Armed Groups: Studies in National Security, Counterterrorism, and Counterinsurgency* (Newport, RI: US Naval War College Press, 2008).

39. Norrin M. Ripsman and T. V. Paul, *Globalization and the National Security State* (New York: Oxford University Press, 2010).

40. For an excellent overview of globalization as it relates to security studies generally, see Victor D. Cha, "Globalization and the Study of International Security," *Journal of Peace Research* 37, no. 3 (2000): 391–403.

41. On sovereignty, see Hendrik Spruyt, *The Sovereign State and Its Competitors* (Princeton, NJ: Princeton University Press, 1994). For a challenge to the "traditional conception," see Stephen D. Krasner, *Sovereignty: Organized Hypocrisy* (Princeton, NJ: Princeton University Press, 1999).

42. For a broad survey of science and technology trends, see Richard Silberglitt et al., *The Global Technology Revolution 2020, In-Depth Analyses: Bio/Nano/Materials/Information Trends, Drivers, Barriers, and Social Implications* (Santa Monica, CA: RAND Corporation, 2006).

43. Cell phones decrease costs from collective action problems. See Jan H. Pierskalla and Florian M. Hollenbach, "Technology and Collective Action: The Effect of Cell Phone Coverage on Political Violence in Africa," *American Political Science Review* 107, no. 2 (2013): 207–24.

44. Hammes, "Armed Groups: Changing the Rules," 448.

45. van Creveld, *The Transformation of War*, 28.

46. For passenger data, see Airports Council International, "Preliminary 2012 World Airport Traffic and Rankings," March 26, 2013, http://www.aci.aero/media/afc782a2-a258-4c49-a700-fea9047d15fb/News/Releases/2013/PR_260313_Prelim_2012_World_Traffic_Rankings-final_pdf. "TEU" is a "twenty-foot equivalent unit," a standard shipping container size. See World Shipping Council, "Top 50 World Container Ports," http://www.worldshipping.org/about-the-industry/global-trade/top-50-world-container-ports. Both numbers are author's calculations.

47. Hammes, "Armed Groups: Changing the Rules," 448. See also Emile LeBrun et al., eds., *Small Arms Survey 2013: Everyday Dangers* (Cambridge: Cambridge University Press, 2013).

48. Ricardo Rene Laremont, "After the Fall of Qaddafi: Political, Economic, and Security Consequences for Libya, Mali, Niger, and Algeria," *Stability: International Journal of Security and Development* 2, no. 2 (2013): 1–8.

49. For example, see Kaldor, *New and Old Wars: Organized Violence in a Global Era*.

50. Ted Robert Gurr, *Why Men Rebel* (Princeton, NJ: Princeton University Press, 1970).

51. Ripsman and Paul, *Globalization and the National Security State*.

52. Liana Sun Wyler, *Weak and Failing States: Evolving Security Threats and U.S. Policy*, CRS Report RI34253 (Washington, DC: US Congressional Research Service, August 28, 2008), 4.

53. Belgin San Akca, "Supporting Non-State Armed Groups: A Resort to Illegality?," *The Journal of Strategic Studies* 32, no. 4 (2009): 589–613.

54. See Alexander Smoltczyk, "Africa's Cocaine Hub: Guinea-Bissau a 'Drug Trafficker's Dream,'" *SpiegelOnline International*, http://www.spiegel.de/international/world/violence-plagues-african-hub-of-cocaine-trafficking-a-887306.html and Max Fisher, "Report: North Korea Ordered Its Foreign Diplomats to Become Drug Dealers," *WorldViews—The Washington Post*, http://www.washingtonpost.com/blogs/worldviews/wp/2013/03/22/report-north-korea-ordered-its-foreign-diplomats-to-become-drug-dealers/.

55. Dietrich Jung, "A Political Economy of Intra-State War: Confronting a Paradox," in *Shadow Globalization, Ethnic Conflicts and New Wars: A Political Economy of Intra-State War* (New York: Routledge, 2003).

56. Williamson Murray, "The American Revolution: Hybrid War in America's Past," in *Hybrid Warfare: Fighting Complex Opponents from the Ancient World to the Present*, ed. Williamson Murray and Peter R. Mansoor (Cambridge: Cambridge University Press, 2013).

57. Max Boot, *Small Wars and the Rise of American Power* (New York: Basic Books, 2002). On American Indian Wars, see, for example, Robert Wooster, *The Military and United States Indian Policy, 1865–1903* (Lincoln: University of Nebraska Press, 1995).

58. Collins, Hamerman, and Seevers, *U.S. Low-Intensity Conflicts: 1899–1990*, 1–6.

59. Sari Horwitz, "Cigarette Smuggling Linked to Terrorism," *Washington Post*, June 8, 2004.

60. Steve Karnowski, "Somalis Still Leaving Minn. to Join Terror Group," *USA Today*, September 26, 2013.

Chapter Three

What Are Armed Groups?

There are many common labels given to the main focus of this book and a brief word about why the phrase "armed groups" is needed. Commonly used labels include "nonstate actor (NSA)," "armed nonstate actors (ANSA)," "violent nonstate actors (VNSA)," and "armed group (AG)." The phrase "nonstate actor" is a broad category that may include many groups that do not fit the characteristics discussed here. These may include NGOs, such as Doctors without Borders or the Red Cross; think tanks, such as RAND or the Brookings Institution, or MNCs such as ExxonMobil and General Electric. This is too broad of a category, and while armed groups are part of this category, a more specific label is needed.

The Federation of American Scientists (FAS) and others have used the phrase "para-state" to refer to organizations that contest the state's "legitimate monopoly on the use of violence within a specified geographical territory" through "direct action."[1] The list includes both "nasty and nice" organizations, with FAS making no judgment about the legitimacy of the group. The list also includes those who engage in terrorism, but is not a list of terrorist organizations per se.[2] Two problems emerge from the use of this term. The first is that despite the definition, "para-state" only appears to includes those groups seeking to overthrow the state, or that have created their own parallel or "shadow" state. Many terrorist groups may not desire to run the state or provide state-like services and may not seek to create an alternative version of the state. Second, TCOs are not included on the list, even though they directly contest the state's monopoly on violence but do not seek to govern. This phrase would appear to be limited to those with greater aspirations toward statehood.

All of the groups under consideration are "armed," but they also use violence as a distinguishing characteristic from other types of nonstate actors. While many observers use the phrase "violent nonstate actors," this might imply a particular level of violence that warrants a group's inclusion in the category. TCOs may not be as violent as insurgent groups, in some cases, while terrorist groups might be more violent than TCOs, in terms of casualties, but engage in fewer violent acts. While there appears little difference between "armed nonstate actors" and "armed groups," "armed groups" implies a greater sense of "acting on behalf of others" and touches upon the idea that irregular warfare is a competition for influence over a population. It also has the added benefit of being shorter. Although by no means a hard and fast rule, many in the United States may refer to "armed groups," while the convention in some European writings is "violent nonstate actors." This text uses the phrase "armed groups" as a short and easy phrase that does not imply any particular level of violence and reminds the reader of the collective nature of these organizations and that individuals act on behalf of others.

DISTINGUISHING BETWEEN ARMED GROUPS AND STATE MILITARIES

There are several notable differences between official state militaries and armed groups.[3] States control territory and the military exists to ensure the state's control over its borders. They repel enemy invasion, ensure domestic stability, and support the actions of the state. Armed groups by their nature challenge state legitimacy, they may likely have no territorially defined area within which they have authorization to operate, and they do not act on behalf of a separate, controlling political organization.

State militaries are generally hierarchically organized and cohesive institutions, but also very slow to change. They are marked by inflexibility and an inability to respond to rapid changes in the international environment. Armed groups, by contrast, are only able to survive and challenge the state through their adaptable nature and ability to remain flexible in the face of adversity. Lacking resources, they need to evolve in order to remain resilient.

States maintain clear oversight of their militaries, since states are held to specific standards proscribed by domestic and international norms and laws. States frequently abide by a constitution or similar legal foundation that provides for the role of the armed forces in the state. In addition, government leaders are subject to elections and other constraints from the population. States and their leaders have a clear incentive to reduce the principal–agent problem between the governing authority and the military, and states hold their militaries to account through legal statutes and normative constructs. This extends into the realm of strategy and tactics, such that states face the threat of sanction—legal, economic, political, or military—in the event of military atrocities, indiscriminate violence, or failure to adhere to a reciprocal level of violence.

Additionally, state militaries are not clandestine. The Geneva Accords outlines that soldiers are required to wear uniforms, have rank, be paid, remain under the command of the government, and abide by other rules, which help reduce the principal–agent problem by reducing information asymmetries, such as by distinguishing armed forces from civilians.[4] A state's armed forces may keep operations or membership secret and their special forces may operate without uniforms. Likewise, many armed groups may seek some semblance of a common uniform or mimic state military dress (or wear discarded military uniforms), whether for functionality or an attempt to maintain *esprit de corps*.[5] Nevertheless, armed groups strive to maintain their clandestine nature in order to avoid capture or escape the state's notice.

Finally, state militaries only operate on behalf of the state government and are not loaned out or placed under the command of another state. Only in special circumstances do states place their militaries under the control of the United Nations or a regional security institution. Armed groups, by contrast, receive support from states and may frequently acquiesce to their demands concerning objectives, strategy, tactics, or ideology. States occupy a privileged place in IR and international laws and treaties are designed to privilege states over nonstate actors, especially in the conduct of war.

COMMON ARMED-GROUP CHARACTERISTICS

All armed-group archetypes are assumed to have several basic characteristics. They are autonomous from the state but possibly receive state or other forms of external aid. Second, they are subnational, lacking legitimacy or sovereignty, but are transnational in their operations. Third, they pose a threat to the state most clearly through their use or threatened use of violence, but their very existence may threaten weak and failing states. Last, they are organized, rational, objective-seekers, who may nevertheless be opportunistic or rife with factions. These four broad categories are necessary to cover the vast spectrum of armed groups, while providing some organizational concepts on which to base future analyses. This section briefly unpacks each category to understand the dimensions on which armed groups may vary, as well as the broad similarities that make them a coherent unit of analysis.

Autonomous Actors

Armed groups are nongovernmental, nonstate actors. They are autonomous, exhibiting self-government and free from state control, and not officially a part of a state's armed forces, security services, or law-enforcement agencies.

Some armed groups are tied to a state tangentially through business contracts with firms operating from a particular home country. Armed groups may have unofficial "understandings," whereby the armed group and state are working toward common goals but do not officially ally. Armed groups may receive unintentional support from a state through the exploitation of ungoverned spaces, access to government documents through corruption, or illicit use of a state's infrastructure, such as the Internet or economic markets. Armed groups may receive active support, such as training, funding, or even safe haven from a state. Finally, a state may directly hire an armed group for security or other services.

An armed group's autonomous nature implies they act to fulfill their own objectives and are not directly controlled by a state or other political organization. Armed groups may not be fully independent of a state, however. Armed groups may be hired or receive direct support from a state, making them, to some degree, dependent on the state. An increase in state aid may create greater dependency on the state, decreasing the state's costs of monitoring the armed group. This increased oversight decreases the state's principal–agent problem. Nevertheless, the state may fear publicly exposing its connections to an armed group. Additionally, the armed group may lack territory or a headquarters that can be taxed, sued, or in some sense be held "hostage" in order to enforce government oversight. It is difficult to coerce an armed group into credibly committing to follow state policy, given the armed group's willingness to violate international laws or norms, even when they are provided support. Armed groups are autonomous in their objectives and not under state control, but may be influenced in their actions through state support. State-armed group relations may lack boundaries and clarity, further contributing to the difficulty in exerting pressure on an armed group.

A rough analogy with MNCs illustrates the point. MNCs are subject to laws in the countries in which they operate, but companies frequently break those laws and governments attempt to punish them. MNCs may be able to retreat to their home country to avoid litigation, or transfer costs between affiliates in order to avoid taxes in specific markets. They are autonomous— they make their own decisions about where to invest, how much to invest, and whether or not to abide by the host country's laws. MNCs, save for those directly operated as state-run entities, are autonomous from direct state control. But they are not independent from the state or state-system. They rely on international agreements such as bilateral investment treaties (BITs) negotiated between states and they rely on the state itself to grant access to a raw material or licenses to operate and produce in a given country. They may also receive generous subsidies from both the home and host governments in the form of tax breaks, incentives to invest, and removal of laws commonly levied on corporations.

Armed groups may act in ways that appear to violate their autonomy, especially in cases where the armed group and government's ideologies and goals coincide. Nevertheless, these situations can just as easily move in opposite directions. Armed groups may embrace a common cause with the government, but factors such as prior human rights violations or differing end goals may prevent the groups from cooperating and may even place them at odds, despite their apparent commonalities. In the end, because the armed group is not an official arm of the government, they pose a challenge to the state's legitimacy and sovereignty.

Substate Actors

Armed groups are substate actors, which means they frequently have small "populations" or membership numbers compared to states, they lack legitimacy and sovereignty, they are clandestine in nature, but they are also transnational in their operations and outlook.

Small Membership

Armed groups generally have small "populations" or memberships. Although states may vary in size and material power, from "micro" or "virtual" states to hegemons, they have a known population that lives within their borders, from whom states can extract various resources.[6] In addition to smaller "populations" than all but microstates, armed groups may not know who all of the members are. This may be due to network organization and unconnected cell structures, secretive ruling coalitions, their clandestine nature, or passive members who choose not to identify themselves. Armed groups are therefore unlikely to effectively extract resources from their membership.

Lack Legitimacy and Sovereignty

States, in Weber's language, possess a monopoly of the legitimate use of force, while armed groups do not.[7] The armed groups' leadership may not know its own membership. The inability to differentiate between members and nonmembers creates a serious principal–agent problem, which may lead armed groups to adopt a generally coercive extraction policy toward the population as a whole. This is unlikely to be a successful long-term strategy and may repel nonmembers and potential supporters alike, eroding the armed group's legitimacy. Secondly, armed groups lack sovereignty and as such compete with the state over the monopoly over the use of force. Despite the armed group's attempt at secession or to overthrow the government, they are still subject to law enforcement, internal security services, or other forms of armed violence the state is able to implement.

In this regard, while small states possess a monopoly over the legitimate use of force within their borders, albeit subject to the whims of more powerful states who may violate a small state's sovereignty, armed groups are always subject to "intervention" because their members are already members of and exist within states, whose own forces seek to prevent the creation of any other monopoly over violence within their territory. Within a country, the market for force may be a monopoly, oligopoly, or free market of violence. While states enjoy a monopoly over the violence market vis-à-vis external actors, due to the international norm of sovereignty, they may not enjoy one internally, due to the presence of armed groups. Armed groups lack both external and internal sovereignty, meaning they face constant encroachments on their sovereignty from the external states within which they exist or competing armed groups, as well as from within their own group through factional contests.

Armed groups lack international legitimacy due to the lack of recognition by the United Nations and other international organizations. While some armed groups may seek this legitimacy, in order to translate this legitimacy into material gain or moral support from potential donors, most groups do not receive legitimacy, let alone recognition. Recognition of international legitimacy has, in the Westphalian system, been withheld solely for states. [8]

Clandestine

Armed groups are clandestine by nature. States frequently operate clandestinely, whether through diplomacy, covert action, economic negotiations, or other activities that are not publicly revealed. States, however, are not themselves clandestine, as recognition by other states—and noninterference by other states—is a key characteristic of their existence. States are states because of the recognition of sovereignty they are afforded by other states. Armed groups, by contrast, may purposely shun recognition or simply not need recognition from states in order to possess legitimacy from a given population. Armed groups do not adhere to the same international norms of sovereignty and nonintervention as states.

Armed groups may have a spokesman who breaks the clandestine nature of the group to communicate with the authorities, the population, or foreign entities. The group also exposes itself through its use and threat of violence. These are dangerous times for the group, as its clandestine nature is one of its key means of survival and breaking that veil of secrecy can allow authorities to track it and gain an insight into various aspects of the group.

As discussed further in subsequent chapters, an armed group's clandestine nature is important to its longevity, but may have negative impacts on the group's ability to recruit new members, create and follow through on successful operations, and overcome common problems associated with groupthink. This key characteristic of an armed group, then, is also potentially one of its greatest liabilities.

Transnational

Lastly, armed groups operate not only within the state but also across state boundaries. Armed groups are aided in this endeavor by globalization and the prevalence of weak states. While armed groups are not a new phenomenon in international politics, their transnational nature—operating, recruiting, and generating support throughout multiple countries—translates into a greater threat to a greater range of actors than was previously possible. This is a violation of another state's sovereignty, as well as a violation of its monopoly over the legitimate use of force. Many armed groups are therefore serial abusers of both internal and external sovereignty, key norms for states.

Threat to the State

Threaten or Use Violence and Crime

The earlier discussion of the proper label for armed groups belies the fact that all of these groups threaten and use violence. The reasons for the threat or use of force may be to accomplish their broader political or economic goals. It is too limiting to add the qualifier that the violence is used to achieve "political goals," as this may exclude criminal organizations and some militias. Many argue that the political–economic nexus is a key characteristic of armed conflict today. No matter its intention, armed-group violence is sustained and exerted on a concerted basis. Violence is a reoccurring means of operating and goes beyond an individual using violence on select occasions.

Armed groups may use violence because they "possess interests that are not widely shared, especially by the target audience."[9] In addition, groups may use violence in order to credibly communicate their intentions, goals, and capabilities. Because armed groups are unable to demonstrate these things through more traditional means—policy documents and law creation, military parades or show of force, international inspection, or engaging in military-to-military diplomacy—they rely on the use of violence. This communication applies to the general population, group members, and state actors. This includes using violence to differentiate the group from rival armed groups. Furthermore, armed groups use violence for internal reasons, frequently to maintain discipline, enhance group cohesion, and eliminate leadership rivals. Armed groups may also use violence because the objects over which they are fighting are indivisible. Territory is frequently held up as an indivisible issue. Territory that a group regards as a physical or spiritual homeland, territory rich in natural resources, or territory holding major significance may be seen as indivisible and thus part of an all-out struggle with the state. Ideological control over a population may be viewed as a zero-sum game. Without the ability to muster support for a political solution, armed groups may resort to violence to gain political control in order to enforce their worldview over a given population.

This sustained violence is frequently used in asymmetric ways, as befits groups whose military capability is dwarfed by states' conventional military and law-enforcement power. These groups may use violence in smaller, more limited capacities than states on the battlefield, and they may use violence against noncombatants as a basic part of their strategies. Other groups, such as those in the latter stages of a Maoist-type insurgency, may have accumulated enough of a mass base and military capability that they seek to confront the state in conventional, or symmetric, warfare for control of the state. This is rare, given the nature of these groups and their inability to mobilize the manpower or material necessary for such actions.

The threat of violence is omnipresent from armed groups and may, in many cases, provide greater influence than the actual use of violence. Thomas Schelling argued nuclear weapons posed a psychological threat, as the state could always unleash yet more violence in ways that were unlikely to be countered.[10] States challenged by armed groups face the same type of psychological threat—the fear and uncertainty of more violence. The threat of greater or more widespread armed-group violence can fundamentally change state policies and condition security services that would not necessarily react to small-scale hit and run raids, hostage taking, or coordinated bomb blasts. Despite their small size, it is the unspecified threat of future violence that provides an armed group with their greatest leverage.

The group's existence is a threat, whether or not they are active in the country. A group may be using a state's ungoverned spaces as safe havens and fighting in a neighboring country. In this sense, they may not be a direct threat to the state in which they are seeking sanctuary, but that state is possibly threatened by the state the armed group is attacking. The neighboring state may not know whether a state is willingly or unwilling providing aid and safe haven to an armed group and may be forced to consider the sanctuary state as a threat. Additionally, just because the armed group is currently only finding safe haven in a state does not mean that the armed group will not turn on its host. The principal–agent problem, again, is active for states that have armed groups in their midst.

Criminal organizations may be armed and operating in a state, without using violence—they may be engaged in counterfeiting, smuggling, bribery, corruption, or money laundering, to name a few illicit activities. Nevertheless, TCOs frequently act violently against the police, security services, or other criminal organizations and involve government or civilians in the crossfire. Additionally, the police may be self-deterred—they may not want to take action against a criminal organization for fear of escalating violence, being outgunned, or because they have been bought off. In this case, even if the police have not been directly threatened or engaged in violent conflict with the armed group, the armed group is a threat to the state's legitimacy, governance, and use of force.

Threaten Legitimacy

Threats to a state's legitimacy differ from conventional military threats in armed conflict. States traditionally fight by attacking other armed forces and wearing down their opponent's military capabilities. Armed groups, unable in most cases to effectively target the state's military, attempt to erode the state's legitimacy and force the loss of popular support. By challenging the state's influence over the population, the armed group seeks the destruction of state capability not through the physical dismantling of its defensive capability, but through the psychological and political rending of the government from its base of support—the population. This may be accomplished in numerous ways, including demonstrating the government's inability to provide services, growing influence over the population, or control of territory.

Territorial control is an explicit challenge to the state's legitimacy, as the state clearly shows that it cannot provide services or advance its policies over all space within its borders. States are presumed to be "unified actors," in that the government speaks for the whole state, and maintain a monopoly over the legitimate use of force in its borders. An armed group's territorial control violates both of these factors.

Insurgents and militias frequently control territory to use as a safe haven and as a base from which to launch attacks. Controlling territory may also provide some measure of recognition that they deem vital to their operations and objectives. TCOs or terrorist groups may control no physical territory and may not seek to control territory. Terrorists may lack the capability to control territory or lack interest in providing services to the population, while TCOs are more concerned with economic profit than administering services or changing the political regime. All armed groups may control territory, whether through direct or indirect actions, so a brief discussion of how this occurs is warranted.

Territorial control may fall under the heading of either tangible or intangible control. In the tangible control of territory, an armed group physically occupies or controls a space. This is frequently a desired step or part of the group's strategy and can have beneficial consequences for the group. Insurgent groups, many following the Maoist model, may seek territorial control as they grow. This territory provides the insurgent with a base from which to plan, rest and recuperate, and launch attacks. If there is a town or village already occupying the territory this provides the insurgent with potential supporters who may provide resources, become members of the group, or remain passive supporters who provide intelligence or who turn a blind eye to armed-group activity.

Some armed groups, such as terrorists or TCOs, may either not be capable of physically controlling territory or may not seek to do so. These groups may still control territory, but they do so through intangible methods. TCOs, for example, may control territory through fear. Police or other criminal organizations may be deterred from a particular territory—"turf"—because they know a TCO controls those city blocks or neighborhoods. In other cases, the territory itself is "intangible," just as the means of controlling it is. This applies to trafficking routes, where highways and airports are tangible, but the actual driving routes, the officials bribed in select locations, or the knowledge that Los Zetas transport drugs through particular channels creates methods and avenues that can be considered "intangible." A roadblock on a key highway does not stop the flow of drugs, any more so than the removal of one corrupted official at the border. Drug cartels in Mexico control territory through a mixture of physical occupation of a space and corruption of officials or law enforcement, but also control territory or trafficking routes through fear.[11] The groups may not want to provide services to the local population, to engage in widespread governance, or even extract resources from the local population. Nevertheless, they control territory, posing another threat to the government.

A second form of intangible territory is cyberspace.[12] Armed groups use the Internet as a place to recruit, to spread ideology, to communicate, and to engage in attacks on governments and others. Armed groups may control their own websites, Facebook pages, Twitter accounts, or chat rooms. They may also deny authorities and unauthorized users access to these webpages, while attacking government webpages. Anonymous, a hacker collective, is a group that carries out attacks solely online.[13] While it is debatable as to whether it satisfies all of the armed-group criteria here or resembles a "traditional" armed group in very many ways, it is clear that they control—mainly through denial—government intangible territory in cyberspace. A group's ability to control small parts of online territory has greatly aided their ability to communicate, plan, operate, and find refuge and is a key component of any group's basic characteristics.

Rational Objective Seekers, Organizational Coherence, and Longevity

Armed groups seek to accomplish political and economic objectives. Most of the armed groups discussed have political objectives: they seek to overthrow an existing regime, gain autonomy for a region, change a policy, or gain greater access to the political system. TCOs, and increasingly other armed groups, have economic profit-maximization as their main objective. Some groups have overlapping political and economic goals. They may seek political power in order to gain greater access to economic resources. Alternatively, TCOs may seek economic profit and acquire de facto political control over a region or territory. Armed groups may also vacillate back and forth between economic and political objectives, depending the group's need and internal and external dynamics.

Armed groups are more than just violent mobs. They possess some amount of organizational coherence and longevity that mobs, spontaneous demonstrations, or riots lack. This is not to say that the Arab Spring could not have been partly organized or populated by armed groups, or that armed groups may not have taken great advantage of the situation in order to further their own goals. But the spontaneous eruption of violence at a street protest, or the organization of a flash mob through Twitter or Facebook—even though they are clearly organized ahead of time—are temporary and lack coherence. Longer-term demonstrations, such as the various and widespread "Occupy Movements," lack a coherence and clear objective that armed groups seek and attain.

Organized protests are not armed groups, unless they have a permanent organization that delineates tasks; draws up objectives, beliefs, tactics, or strategy; recruits and trains new members; and carries out additional functions that seek to achieve a coherent, recognized long-term objective. This does not mean that all armed groups have a clear objective or that they must exist for a certain number of months or years to be considered an "armed group." What it does imply is that an organized group, with some amount of internal cohesion, "sense," and understanding as to their purpose and objectives—however unattainable, "crazy," or far in the future they may appear to outside observers—that seeks to achieve those objectives, fits within the bounds of what is here considered to be an "armed group."

Rationality

The concept of rationality is frequently misunderstood or misapplied in analyses and deserves a brief mention here. Rationality implies that individuals or groups have various preferences, or interests, that are rank ordered. These can be formal, written interests, or simply within the minds of the leaders or members. Groups will act on the basis of these interests, frequently employing the strategy that best accomplishes whatever interest the group has. Rational armed groups do not attack a target "for no reason" and while their interests, motivations, or ultimate goals may appear "crazy" or "unreachable" to bystanders and analysts alike, the assumption here is that groups carry out violence with the purpose of achieving their goals.[14]

Outsiders may neither like, nor understand, the purpose of those actions, but if the policy maker simply labels the group "irrational," "crazy," or "out of touch," there are at least two fallacies that may be destructive for the state and society. The first is that groups labeled crazy or irrational cannot be stopped and the best one can hope for is that the state "lucks into" stopping them. If the policy maker or analyst cannot predict where or when a group will attack, or determines that what a group says has no bearing on its actual goals, actions, or strategy, then there is little point in studying any particular group. Nor would there be a point in investing in any means of combating armed groups save for defensive measures. Strategic communication by the armed group cannot be believed if they are irrational, as a leader may say one thing today and change his mind tomorrow. Thus, using law-enforcement tools of investigation, negotiation, or even preemption against an irrational armed group is a waste of time, effort, and material, since there is no "rhyme or reason" to what armed groups do. Since this is not the case for a large majority of groups, states have long chosen to assume armed groups were rational.

This is not to say that target selection for a terrorist group cannot be random. While some targets are carefully chosen as symbols of a country's wealth, power, or ideology, other targets are chosen for their ease of attack or based on what is closest to the attacker. Whether or not a terrorist group attacks a specific mall, movie theater, or other gathering of people may be completely random. Any undefended space with the opportunity to create fear among the population may be sufficient for a terrorist. Nevertheless, the end goal—create fear among the population in order to pressure the population to pressure the government into changing their policies—remains the same and thus the group can be said to rationally pursue its aims.

The second concern is that if armed groups do not act in accordance with international norms, or "Western" values, culture, or religious or political traditions, they will be dismissed, ignored, or again, labeled as irrational. An armed group's goals should not be disregarded simply because a state does not share similar goals with the armed group, or view the world through the same lens, or even understand what the group seeks. The US government does not want to see Western Europe under an Islamic caliphate, nor is the US government likely to believe that it is possible for al-Qaeda to achieve such a goal. Failing to act to prevent this stated goal because the United States does not think it possible or the United States does not understand why al-Qaeda would do this is not helpful in combating this group. Accepting that this is the group's goal and that this goal motivates the group's actions is necessary to understand, track down, and stop the group from carrying out attacks that seek to achieve that goal.

Factions, Rivalries, and Opportunism

Many armed groups are riven with factions and rivalries. Others may be much more cohesive and unified in their makeup. While some have argued that splits and factions are inevitable, these are not necessary to be considered an armed group. It is certainly the case, as discussed in chapter 5, that a group's members and leaders do not necessarily all agree on what a group's ideology, objectives, or tactics should be. Nor is it likely that the members themselves all agree on all fundamental points. The idea that armed groups possess different factions, however, may contribute to our understanding of the group and possible ways to combat a group, but is not necessary in order to be an armed group. It would be a mistake to assume *ex ante* that an armed group is a unitary actor, but it is not essential to being an armed group that the group be either perfectly unitary or split into any number of factions. The analyst with an eye on combating the group would be well advised to seek any splits among the membership or between the members and the leaders, so that factions may be enticed away for negotiations, or that the consequences of other strategies to combat the group take into account the likelihood of a group splitting into viable sections and not simply disintegrating.

Opportunism occupies a similar position to internal rivalries. Many armed groups may display opportunism in their alliances or actions, whereby groups make alliance decisions with an eye toward effectiveness at the expense of ethical or ideological principles. Other groups may strongly adhere to their basic principals and sacrifice expediency to "remain true to the cause." This can have a rational basis, in that the group calculates that by remaining faithful adherents to their ideology, for example, they may reap greater rewards in the future. Cutting deals with those the armed group opposes or seeking short-term gains at the expense of long-term objectives, may invite long-term complications or problems, from an inability to recruit, difficulty in maintaining members who disagree with the decision, or placing the armed group in a position of weakness vis-à-vis other armed groups or the government. It is thus important for the analyst to be aware of any opportunistic actions the armed group takes, but to not assume either way that the armed group will or will not seek short gains at the expense of their long-term goals.

What Is Missing?

Armed-group analysis is an ever-changing and evolving field. The hallmark of these groups—their ability to quickly adapt to their changing environment—means that new characteristics may emerge. Characteristics asserted today may not be apropos in future armed-group evolutions. Armed groups will not perfectly align to the standards listed here and some points may as yet be unidentified. The hacker group Anonymous is a case in point. While they may control intangible cyberspace through denial and they are clandestine, the violence they commit is online and does not, as far as is known, extend to controlling tangible territory or committing violence in the noncyber realm. Anonymous' degree of cohesion, objectives, longevity, and internal rivalries are unknown, but likely very scattered. While they attacked Israeli government websites on several occasions in 2013 to protest Israel's policies toward Palestinians, they did not do irreparable harm to Israeli capabilities.[15] This group is a threat to states, individuals, and MNCs, but it is unclear when and how they will mobilize their capabilities in the future. Is Anonymous an armed group, in the sense discussed so far? More research of this group and a greater understanding of armed groups may be necessary, both for the student and for the analyst addressing these groups through government policy.

ARMED-GROUP FORMATION

There are a multitude of reasons why individuals join an armed group and commit violence—economic motivation, political and social inequalities, social networks, protection from the government, forced by the armed group, urging of a charismatic leader, traumatic event, or fear of group extinction.[16] In doing so, armed groups must overcome the four basic problems discussed in chapter 1: the collective action problem, the coordination problem, the time-consistency problem, and the principal–agent problem.

The collective action problem prevents potential members from joining because they fear they will assume a variety of costs—imprisonment, injury, or death, to name a few—while the benefits will be widely distributed to the population. The individual has an incentive to free-ride by not joining the group and receiving the benefits when the armed group succeeds. The armed group, however, never forms because everybody free-rides.

The coordination problem posits that while individuals might want to join a group, there may be disagreement over the group's ideology, objectives, strategy, or tactics. Individuals, unable to coordinate their wide array of preferences, never form a group.

The time-consistency problem occurs when armed groups promise future benefits to individuals, whether economic profit, political positions in a new regime, or spiritual enlightenment or favor in the afterlife. The individual may not believe that the group will deliver on its promise. The group may be unable to credibly commit to providing the individual member with a future benefit, leaving the potential member to search for an alternative group.

Lastly, the principal–agent problem affects both potential leaders and potential followers. As discussed, the principal–agent problem is one of oversight. Leaders may be unwilling to admit members they do not already know or who do not have a similar cache of social capital, such as those belonging to the same religion, tribe, ethnic group, or other identity group. The member may also lack confidence in the leadership, not trusting or approving of the direction in which the group is going. Both sides suffer from incomplete information, leaving leaders unwilling to risk admitting potentially troublesome members—or worse, security service infiltrators—while members do not want to join a group whose leadership they cannot monitor.

There are three broad factors active in reducing the costs of group formation due to the fundamental problems above: social networks, context, and leadership. [17] First, individuals may join an armed group as part of their social network. Individuals belong to a wide array of potentially interconnected social networks. Friends, relatives, coworkers, coreligionists, tribe members, and ethnic kin are a few examples of these overlapping networks. Individuals may join an armed group because of identity connections and ties to these networks, regardless of whether they ultimately agree with the armed group's objectives, strategy, or tactics.

The costs of joining an armed group are reduced if the group shares a narrative, identity, or objectives with an existing social network. Perfect alignment of an armed group and social-network identities are not necessary for social networks to be used as recruiting tools. Many members may not have originally joined a terrorist or insurgent group because of their predilection to commit violence or their commitment to a particular ideological cause. They may instead have joined because others in their social network were joining. This reduced the costs to both sides, as potential members know and trust armed-group members in their social network and may find promises of future rewards or benefits credible. Additionally, social networks decrease monitoring costs on both sides related to the principal–agent problem, while costs associated with the coordination problem are decreased in an armed group built on a social network if individuals already know each other and have common values, backgrounds, ideologies, or objectives.

Contextual issues such as state repression, group survival, and resource availability impact the costs to joining an armed group. Political opportunity theories of insurgency, for example, emphasize state coercion as important for rebel group formation. State repression adds greater costs to armed-group formation, which exacerbates the collective action problem for armed groups. The more extreme the coercive power applied, however, including the real or perceived possibility of group extinction, the greater the incentive, and lower cost, to forming an armed group for group survival. Alternatively, if armed groups have space and opportunity, whether due to geography or weak state institutions, it becomes easier for them to form. Contextual factors that facilitate armed-group formation do so because they degrade the state's domestic coercive power, lowering collective action costs for the armed group.

The availability of resources may encourage armed-group formation and provide information as to a group's organizational structure and the likelihood of a group's use of indiscriminate violence.[18] Armed groups can extract resources from the local population or from natural resource deposits, MNC operations, or NGOs. External support in the form of military aid or training may ease armed group formation and perpetuation. Cross-border safe havens allow armed groups to evade state repression, to secure funding, to mobilize and recruit members, and to plan operations, among other activities.[19] Increased resource availability makes the armed group appear viable, decreases the coordination and collective action problems, and generally signals that the armed group has a greater change of achieving its objectives, which decreases the group's time-consistency problem. Evading state repression also allows easier mobilization, which helps overcome the collective action problem and the coordination problem.

Charismatic leaders and ethnic or political entrepreneurs play a role in armed-group formation. Leaders in this vein provide a rally point for potential group members, greatly decreasing the coordination problem. Leaders can provide an armed group with its ideology and objectives, as well as a strategy for achieving these goals. Leaders provide potential members a compelling narrative of the predicament they face: the problem a group confronts, who is to blame for this condition, and what the group can do to fix the problem. "Visionary" leaders provide a view of the "ideal" future environment and motivate people to work toward achieving that scenario. A charismatic leader may convince potential members of his trustworthiness in providing future benefits, decreasing the costs of the time-consistency problem. A charismatic leader may also decrease the costs of the principal–agent problem, as individuals may reciprocate what they view as the leader's personal forthrightness, moral standing, and exemplary behavior.

In the end, armed-group formation is accompanied by a new group identity, which separates members from their existing identities. The armed group provides goods, services, security, skills, and collective identity. It also provides values, entertainment, rules, norms, and a social life. In essence, it creates a new "family" or social network to replace, or augment, a previous social network. These rules, norms, and values may be enforced through harsh discipline.[20]

The creation of a new identity also aids in overcoming the collective action problem and the time-consistency problems. The group's identity differentiates the members from the general populace, providing a means to selectively supply benefits once the goals have been achieved. Because group membership is constrained, it is easier to restrict benefits, sending a more credible signal that the group can and will deliver on promised benefits in the future.

The formation process, whether based on social networks, context, or leadership, will impact all armed-group elements. Breaking an armed group down into its component parts and understanding the historical evolution of each aspect of the framework will highlight influential moments in a group's formation. The student and practitioner should understand the impact that solutions devised to overcome initial problems of group formation have on shaping long-term group strategies, objectives, and outcomes.

CHALLENGING THE "NONSTATE ACTOR" LABEL

Private military and security companies (PMSCs), progovernment militias, and a variety of other actors appear to challenge several of the armed-group characteristics discussed in this chapter. First, these groups are controlled by states as employees and part of the state's structure. Second, the progovernment militias or PMSCs do not pose a threat to the state and may be hired to protect or further the state's policies and power capabilities. Third, these groups do not violate the monopoly over the legitimate use of force as they are employed and authorized to act by the state. Fourth, these groups possess legitimacy, given their contracts with or creation by the state.

These "nonstate" actors appear to violate the most basic condition of armed groups: they are not autonomous from the state. The United Nations Office for the Coordination of Humanitarian Affairs (UNOCHA) notes that a key characteristic of armed groups is that they "are not under the command or control of the State(s) in which they operate."[21] This implies that not only are armed groups under a different legal code than state armed forces, but that private military and security companies violate this key consideration and should not be considered along with more "traditional" armed groups.[22] A key question, however, is how tightly states control groups they employ, given that the environment in which they are operating may provide a myriad number of opportunities to further their profit at the expense of their employer. Conflict zones decrease or remove constraints on resource extraction, markets, and business transactions. PMSCs may find it easier to engage in illicit business transactions or create their own legal business enterprises, which removes the connection and control from a state employer. The UNOCHA report also notes that armed groups "may receive direct/indirect support of the host government or other States, or may be provided with a safe haven in certain countries."[23] If armed groups may receive outside, direct funding, as well as safe haven, then there would appear to be little separating a PMSC from a "traditional" armed group, save its original motivation. Both PMSCs and TCOs are motivated by economic profit, removing distinction based on motivation. PMSCs that have both political and economic ideologies and objectives—those seeking profit but only working for states, against enemies of "the West," or in service to another cause—can find an analogous insurgent, militia, or terrorist group that combines political and economic objectives. The argument that PMSCs are not armed groups because they are controlled by the state or possess economic objectives does not differentiate them from other armed groups.

These groups act on behalf of a state and may be either directly employed by the state to carry out its policy, or they may act on behalf of the state in lieu of, or in addition to, a state's armed forces, without the state employing them directly. States' use of nonstate actors to further their policy goals may be conscience decisions based on economic efficiency, a desire to operate clandestinely in a conflict zone or other setting, or as a means to project power, whether clandestinely or openly, in ways that the state's military and diplomatic power are unable to exert power.

Another area where progovernment militias may differ from traditional conception is the view that they are state creations and not autonomous, and thus do not challenge the state's legitimacy. Since these groups were created or hired to fight on behalf of the state and to help the state project power, they are not a threat. In short, they will not "bite the hand that feeds." Nevertheless, states face a principal–agent problem in hiring or working with any nonstate actor, even if the state is responsible for its creation. Many countries have witnessed the evolution of the "sobel"—soldier by day, rebel by night. Members of the state armed forces put aside their uniform at night in order to further a political cause or simply line their pockets with extra income. There is little reason to think progovernment militias or PMSCs hired by the state could not act in a similar manner.

The government's use of proxies, progovernment militias, or PMSCs implies that these groups do not violate the state's monopoly over the legitimate use of force, as they are employed and authorized to act on behalf of the state. As expressed above, even state militaries have incentives, given weak state institutions, to engage in insurgent or criminal behavior to supplement their income or fight for a political cause. While the government may originally confer some degree of legitimacy on the progovernment group's use of force, the state can very quickly lose control of the group and lack the ability to monitor and sanction its behavior.

Moreover, these groups may possess some sense of legitimacy, given their contracts with or creation by the state. These groups are still not a part of the regular armed forces of a country, but may nonetheless be recognized as semiofficial military units within the country.[24] However, given that the state is unlikely to claim a progovernment armed group as an official state actor if there are legal or human rights violations, nor even to acknowledge that there is any connection between the armed group and the state, any sense of legitimacy is very constrained and unlikely to provide much benefit if the group attempts to parley the legitimacy into external aid or support. Furthermore, while a modicum of legitimacy may aid the group in garnering greater domestic influence, these groups are unlikely to be recognized under international treaties or laws.

States employing nonstate actors directly or indirectly must be wary of the principal–agent problem.[25] Despite the fact that states have hired PMSCs or created progovernment militias, the state has no guarantee that these groups will remain "loyal" to the state or see its mission through to the end. The state also has no guarantee that the group will not seek additional, outside employment, possibly playing one side off another. There is also no guarantee that the groups will not turn on the states that have hired them, transitioning from "hired gun" to challenging a state if their revenue stream dries up, the regime in power changes, or the leadership in the armed group changes. In short, as the principal–agent problem describes the dilemmas that principals have in maintaining satisfactory oversight of their various agents, states will have a difficult time maintaining control over their proxies, potentially with catastrophic consequences for the state.

PMSCs and progovernment militias may thus be considered armed groups in that, while they are directly tied to the government that hired them, there is no guarantee that this will not change in the future. They are, in the eyes of many other states, armed groups with varying degrees of legitimacy based on the alignment of their preferences with neighboring states. But these armed groups can be just as fickle as insurgents or terrorists and have none of the legitimacy bestowed on states by the international community through membership in the United Nations.

In its most extreme form, the issues raised here are exemplified by the question of whether any state would willingly deliver a CBRN device to an armed group.[26] One of the reasons many are skeptical that this might occur is that states would fear that, once a group has possession of such a destructive weapon, there is no guarantee that the weapon will not be used on the regime itself or any other inopportune targets. This possibility is discussed further in chapter 6.

Most of the arguments against including private military or security companies and progovernment militias alongside "traditional" armed-group categories boil down to the level of state control. In essence, PMSCs are held to a higher standard than "traditional" armed groups, due to their state links. This belies two crucial issues. One, that nearly all successful armed groups receive external support, calling into question how much external support is necessary before an armed group is classified as a "semiofficial state entity" or simply member of a state's armed forces. In the contemporary security environment, this dividing line may be impossibly blurred.

Second, the principal–agent problem demonstrates that all armed groups, to include PMSCs and ostensibly progovernment militias, have an opportunity to act in their best interest and, in a conflict zone, both an opportunity and incentive, given the lack of constraints and economic and political opportunities. It appears unreasonable that groups directly employed or created by the state will not pose a security threat to the state in the future, any less than a "traditional" armed group not supported by the state yet working from a shared perspective. History is replete with groups breaking oaths, promises, contracts, and treaties, all in the name of securing greater financial and political opportunities. We should expect no less from today's "progovernment" nonstate actors.

DISCUSSION QUESTIONS

1. Are PMSCs armed groups?
2. Would a criminal organization, such as a money-laundering group, that is not armed and does not have an intention of committing violent acts be considered an "armed group"? What factors does the above analysis leave out?
3. Do all armed groups attempt to control or deny access to territory to the government?
4. What other factors differentiate armed groups from state militaries?

RECOMMENDED READINGS

Ulrich Schneckener, "Armed Non-State Actors and the Monopoly of Force." In *Revisiting the Monopoly of Force*, edited by Alyson Bailes, Ulrich Schneckener and Herbert Wulf. Geneva Centre for the Democratic Control of Armed Forces (DCAF) Policy Paper No. 24. Geneva, Switzerland: Geneva Centre for the Democratic Control of Armed Forces, 2007.

Richard H. Shultz, Douglas Farah, and Itamara V. Lochard, *Armed Groups: A Tier-One Security Priority*. INSS Occasional Paper 57. Colorado Springs, CO: USAF Institute for National Security Studies, 2004.

P. W. Singer, *Corporate Warriors: The Rise of the Privatized Military Industry*. Ithaca, NY: Cornell University Press, 2007.

Phil Williams, *Violent Non-State Actors and National and International Security*. Zurich, Switzerland: Swiss Federal Institute of Technology Zurich, International Relations and Security Network, 2008.

NOTES

1. John Pike, "Para-States—Scope Note," FAS Intelligence Resource Program, accessed July 15, 2013, last updated Saturday, May 20, 2000, https://www.fas.org/irp/world/para/scope.htm.

2. Ibid. For the list, see John Pike, "Liberation Movements, Terrorist Organizations, Substance Cartels, and Other Para-State Entities," FAS Intelligence Resource Program, accessed

July 15, 2013, last updated May 4, 2006 by Steven Aftergood, https://www.fas.org/irp/world/para/.

3. For a general discussion, see Richard H. Shultz and Andrea J. Dew, *Insurgents, Terrorists, and Militias: The Warriors of Contemporary Combat* (New York: Columbia University Press, 2006).

4. Toni Pfanner, "Military Uniforms and the Law of War," *International Review of the Red Cross* 86, no. 853 (2004): 102–04.

5. Ibid., 102.

6. Richard Rosecrance, *The Rise of the Virtual State: Wealth and Power in the Coming Century* (New York: Basic Books, 1999).

7. Max Weber, "Politics as a Vocation," in *From Max Weber: Essays in Sociology*, ed. H. H. Gerth and C. Wright Mills (New York: Oxford University Press, 1958).

8. The Westphalian system recognizes state legitimacy at the expense of other political organizations. See Hendrik Spruyt, *The Sovereign State and Its Competitors* (Princeton, NJ: Princeton University Press, 1994).

9. Jeffry A. Frieden, David A. Lake, and Kenneth A. Schultz, *World Politics: Interests, Interactions, Institutions* (New York: Norton, 2010), 382.

10. Thomas C. Schelling, *Arms and Influence* (New Haven, CT: Yale University Press, 1966).

11. For a general overview, see June S. Beittel, *Mexico's Drug Trafficking Organizations: Source and Scope of the Violence*, CRS Report R41576 (Washington, DC: U.S. Congressional Research Service, April 15, 2013).

12. See chapter 6 for how groups use the Internet.

13. See Parmy Olson, *We Are Anonymous: Inside the Hacker World of Lulzsec, Anonymous, and the Global Cyber Insurgency* (New York: Back Bay Books, 2013).

14. As Carlos Marighella warns: "The seventh sin of the urban guerrilla is to fail to plan things, and to act spontaneously." See "The Seven Sins of the Urban Guerrilla," *Minimanual of the Urban Guerrilla*, http://www.marxists.org/archive/marighella-carlos/1969/06/minimanual-urban-guerrilla/ch37.htm.

15. For example, see Steven Musil, "Anonymous Targets Israel in Another Cyberattack," CNET.com, http://news.cnet.com/8301-1009_3-57578331-83/anonymous-targets-israel-in-another-cyberattack/.

16. For a discussion on the origin and adoption of violence among social movements, see, for example, Donatella della Porta, *Social Movements, Political Violence, and the State: A Comparative Analysis of Italy and Germany* (Cambridge: Cambridge University Press, 1995).

17. This borrows from Charles Tilly, *The Politics of Collective Violence* (Cambridge: Cambridge University Press, 2003), 119–20.

18. See Jeremy M. Weinstein, *Inside Rebellion: The Politics of Insurgent Violence* (Cambridge: Cambridge University Press, 2007).

19. For example, see Idean Salehyan, "Transnational Rebels: Neighboring States as Sanctuary for Rebel Groups," *World Politics* 59, no. 2 (2007): 217–42.

20. This echoes the discussion on gang formation in chapter 4. See also DCAF and Geneva Call, *Armed Non-State Actors: Current Trends and Future Challenges*, DCAF Horizon 2015 Working Paper No. 5 (Geneva, Switzerland: Geneva Centre for the Democratic Control of Armed Forces (DCAF), 2011), 10–11.

21. Gerard McHugh and Manuel Bessler, *Humanitarian Negotiations with Armed Groups: A Manual for Practitioners* (New York: United Nations Office for the Coordination of Humanitarian Affairs, 2006), table 1.

22. Ibid.

23. Ibid.

24. Sabine C. Carey, Neil J. Mitchell, and Will Lowe, "States, the Security Sector, and the Monopoly of Violence: A New Database on Pro-Government Militias," *Journal of Peace Research* 50, no. 2 (2013): 251.

25. For an overview of states, nonstate actors, and the principal–agent problem, see Janice E. Thomson, *Mercenaries, Pirates, and Sovereigns* (Princeton, NJ: Princeton University Press, 1994).

26. On the low probability of this occurring, see John Mueller, *Atomic Obsession: Nuclear Alarmism from Hiroshima to Al-Qaeda* (Oxford: Oxford University Press, 2010).

Chapter Four

Armed-Group Archetypes

While creating archetypes may seem an unnecessary step in seeking to more fully understand armed groups, these broad contours help decipher the nature of the group, provide heuristics for further analysis, and bring clarity to elusive concepts that populate policy documents, popular press accounts, and scholarly discussions.

Some states will reject labeling armed groups because they prefer a more politically beneficial term, given a particular audience. As Michael Bhatia notes, the labels states use for armed groups may speak more to the state's preferences than the actual group itself.[1] Governments may purposely label groups "terrorists" in order to gain domestic and international support, while "self-defense organizations" is used to garner an air of legitimacy.[2] The issue of politically motivated labeling is addressed in chapter 7, but the likelihood of this occurring should be acknowledged at the outset as an obvious, but unfortunate, aspect of politics. Politically motivated naming, however, should not detract from the idea that there are real differences between armed groups with consequences for not just how states perceive them, but how they combat them.[3] Failing to acknowledge the true "sense" of a group may lead to the inappropriate, inefficient, or insufficient application of scarce resources to combat a problem. The worst outcome of misidentifying a threat could be the downfall of the government.

Armed groups are greater than the sum of their collected characteristics. Gaining a sense of a terrorist group may require understanding the role that a terrorist group sees itself as playing, along with the reaction to a group labeled or identified as a terrorist group. Multiple armed groups are led by charismatic individuals or seek political regime change. These individual characteristics do not necessarily confer a broader understanding of the armed group and its place in the international environment. Likewise, examining a group's individual characteristics is necessary to fully understand the armed group's importance, role, and place in a state's threat matrix.

There are several negative aspects to creating archetypes, which this text addresses in building a useful framework for analysis. The first problem with creating labels or archetypes for armed groups is the reality that labeling is politically driven. Due to their pejorative connotations, a regime may refer to opposition figures as "terrorists" or "criminals." While this is unlikely to stop, this book tries to refine and clarify archetypes to improve future policy and legal decisions.

Second, archetypes may create intellectual "stove-piping," as terrorism, insurgency, and organized crime may be studied in different forums. This stymies the dissemination of important information throughout the academic community and leads to potentially misleading guidelines and polices as politicians and practitioners construct overly simplistic and incomplete narrative frames based on these erroneous binary distinctions.[4]

Third, the conceptual lines between armed group types are blurring. This does not mean that archetypes are useless, as we must understand the "ideal" form of a group before understanding how today's armed groups are blurring the lines with other groups. While there is no basic set of criteria that differentiate one armed group from another, several authors provide what they believe are foundational variables differentiating armed groups.

Armed-group analyses are frequently case studies, examining one group in detail. Others compare broadly constructed archetypes and delineate the difference between them without analyzing specific armed-group characteristics. Furthermore, some analyze specific armed-group characteristics or highlight several factors common to all armed groups that should be considered, such as the armed group's relationship to the people and how armed groups motivate individuals to fight.[5]

Several authors use their foundational variables to create archetypes, such as by positing that a "terrorist group" may not follow territorial tactics but does seek political or ideological objectives. This book distills each archetype down to its basic components in order to understand how each archetype differs from the others. There are two further important qualifications, however. All armed groups, as elaborated in chapter 1, must overcome four fundamental problems that are common to all aspects of an armed group's activity, from formation to perpetuation to executing its operations. Each armed group must overcome these problems in each of its characteristics. Understanding how an armed group overcomes the free-rider problem in its strategy and tactics, or analyzing the role the principal–agent problem plays in an armed group's organizational structure is key to a successful analysis of any armed group.[6] Second, due to the "evolution" and "hybridization" examined later in the chapter, armed groups today are apt to exhibit fewer "standard" archetypical traits and instead flow freely across archetypes. This points to the need to generalize the analysis. If armed groups are becoming such broad mixtures and no longer adhere to specific traits, the answer to analyzing and modeling these groups is to use tools that are fundamental no matter the armed group under consideration. Analyzing the role the collective action problem, the coordination problem, the time-consistency problem, and the principal–agent problem play in an armed group's formation, perpetuation, and operations entails understanding all basic characteristics of a particular group, without the constraint of rigid labels and variables.

Understanding armed-group archetypes is necessary because states, politicians, and policy makers label groups with broad strokes of the brush, so the student, analyst, and policy maker need to understand what it means when we say that an armed group is a "terrorist" or "insurgent." While the word "terrorist" may be fraught with political tinges and used against political enemies, there is something objectively behind this term. As words are used and adopted through societal discourse, they can alter understanding, behavior, and ultimately statements of policy.[7]

The next two chapters delve into specific factors fundamental to each armed group, such as leadership, organizational structure, or goals. Therefore, while the analysis of a group's framework is key to understanding and combating armed groups, examining the archetypes first provides some level of understanding the group as a whole, complex unit that is not necessarily captured by examining its individual, component parts. It is also important to understand how armed groups deal with four basic problems—the principal–agent problem, time-consistency problem, free-riders, and the coordination problem—during their formation, operations, and perpetuation.

There are a vast array of archetypes considered in the literature—from pirates and marauders to rebels and clan chiefs. There are as many archetypes as authors. But they have overlapping names—"rebels" and "guerrillas" may both be "insurgents"—and what is a "militia" for one author may not fit the definition of a "militia" for another author. The analysis here will focus on four main archetypes, following the example of Shultz, Farah, and Lochard: insurgents, terrorists, TCOs, and militias.[8] Any further specification may lead to a break down into too many categories, where each category and armed group appears *sui generis* and so specifically tailored as to leave the analyst with little material for a comparative analysis.

INSURGENTS

Insurgents may represent the prototypical armed group for several reasons. As with all of the armed groups under discussion here, insurgents are a threat and challenge to a state's legitimacy, whether due to a break down in the rule of law or an inability to provide governance to areas under insurgent control.

Insurgent and other armed groups create conditions of weakness and expand on existing instability and weakness created by globalization and the state's inability to provide services to the population. Insurgents hasten the state's disintegration, thus inviting further problems for the state and opening the door for additional armed groups to take root in the state, especially in ungoverned spaces.[9]

Insurgents also have political objectives, such as overthrowing a regime, redressing political inequalities, or exerting political control over part of a state's territory. While insurgents may at times exhibit behavior similar to terrorist groups or TCOs—attacking the population or pursuing economic profit—their ultimate goals are political in nature. As such, their protracted struggles combine political, psychological, and military operations in order to increase their legitimacy at the expense of the state's legitimacy. These political and information operations may be amplified by technology, globalization, or a global diaspora.

Furthermore, the group seeks parity with the government through the use and communication of information, as they lack the conventional military power to directly overthrow the state directly.[10] This communication often takes the form of protracted violence, which demonstrates that the state is not fully in control and that the insurgent has not been defeated. Insurgents may also broadcast information related to political or economic inequalities, government repression, or other messages through a variety of media. The spread of advanced information technology has greatly increased insurgents' ability to quickly disseminate their message, while providing an avenue to directly address the population. The nearly instantaneous global diffusion of a group's narrative magnifies the armed group's psychological impact.

Insurgents use violence in widely varying forms against government or regime-specific targets and, to a lesser degree, against various groups within the state population. Insurgents are much less predatory against local populations than militias, terrorists, or TCOs, as they frequently seek a mass base of support for their cause. The indiscriminate use of violence risks alienating potential supporters and active members alike. Nevertheless, they may use their local knowledge to threaten and intimidate individuals with violence in order to ensure the group is not "denounced."[11]

Fourth, insurgents seek physical control over a population, a territory, and its resources in order to affect political change, extract resources, and demonstrate the state's weakness.[12] Insurgents do not only vie for regime change, but may also seek more limited objectives in the form of political reform, secession of a region, or autonomy for a minority group.[13] This is frequently complicated by the fact that borders in many parts of the world are artificial and do not reflect political, economic, or social realities of those who live in them or are dissected by them.

The insurgent's inherent weakness relative to the state means that insurgents are most likely to engage in protracted conflicts as they cannot force a decisive military outcome. Protracted struggles increase the psychological impact of conflict and erode the state's and population's will. This is crucial in conflicts that seek influence over populations and not conventional battlefield attrition. By one estimate, insurgent campaigns have increased in duration, lasting well over a decade by the late 1990s. [14]

Insurgents need to find self-financing opportunities, as the end of the Cold War removed funding inherent in the superpower competition. There are also greater financing opportunities afforded by globalization, coupled with the loss of state control over economic infrastructure processes, networks, and raw materials. Given the weak state setting for many insurgent groups, it is debatable whether the state had control over these economic factors in the first place. As insurgents move to increase financial linkages with external groups, they may reduce the need for a base of support linked to their territorial ambitions. Insurgents can draw on foreign states, diasporas, armed groups, international organizations, MNCs, and corrupt individuals and side-step the need for dedicated policies designed to attract domestic population groups. [15]

These self-financing opportunities create further linkages with other groups, creating an ever more complex security environment. Steven Metz argues that the threat from insurgencies today is not that they will overthrow the state, but that they will create prolonged, unstable, and complex security environments with regional and potentially global implications. Insurgencies create areas of ungoverned spaces, which transnational terrorists exploit. There is also a general disregard for law and order, which organized crime leverages through corruption. Insurgencies create, and exacerbate, governance issues and state weakness that spur further deterioration in the state and surrounding regions. [16]

Insurgent groups do not exhibit a standard set of characteristics. For example, they may take on many different organizational forms. These can include creating complex shadow governments that provide services to a population and are ready to assume power, or small, loosely organized cells that are fighting for survival amidst harsh government repression. The traditional Maoist model of insurgency contains three phases. In the first phase, the group is a loosely organized collection of cells with no base and little formal organization. In the second phase, the group gains more organization, fighting a more coordinated and sustained guerrilla warfare campaign against government forces. The insurgents may establish rural bases, which are key to creating the conditions for an insurgent group to hide. [17] In the third phase, the group aims to directly challenge and overthrow the government through conventional warfare. This necessitates the creation of a large, complex shadow government ready to assume power and governing roles. [18] Consequently,

Bard O'Neill argues that group organization is a reflection of their goals and strategies, with groups increasing in size and complexity as their goals and strategies become more complex.[19] In the case of an insurgency, this complex organizational structure reduces the principal–agent problem through increased oversight. In order to attract the population and build legitimacy, the insurgency needs to prevent indiscriminate violence against civilians. A large, complex organization may be more capable of fulfilling this role than a loosely connected, decentralized network.

Insurgent groups also exemplify many different leadership types, ideologies, strategies, and tactics. They may attempt to build a base of support and engage the government directly, as in Mao's model. Whether or not an insurgent reaches Mao's third phase, generating a mass base may be the insurgent's attempt to overcome the collective action problem, the coordination problem, and the time-consistency problem. Demonstrating popular backing signals to the population, the government, and eternal supporters a greater likelihood of success. There may be initial difficulties in attaining popular support, but by doing so, the insurgent communicates a powerful psychological message.

Lastly, in many cases, insurgents are unlikely to reach conventional military parity with the state and seek instead to create a stalemate and avoid outright defeat. This is characteristic of early-stage Maoist insurgencies, many of which do not make it to the third stage of direct conventional confrontation against the government. Long-term existence can create *de facto* insurgent control, new norms, and stronger bargaining chips in the political arena. Psychological factors also play a role, as the group's continued existence and protracted conflict degrades the government's will to continue fighting. It also decreases the government's legitimacy, as the population sees that the government cannot defeat the insurgency.

The Taliban (Pashto for "students") controlled Afghanistan from 1996–2001, ruling by religious fiat and officially recognized by only Pakistan, Saudi Arabia, and the United Arab Emirates. With the US invasion and subsequent Taliban ouster, the group was cast into the role of insurgent, utilizing asymmetric attacks including improvised explosive devices (IEDs) and suicide bombings, providing "shadow government institutions," and protecting civilian populations, all while relying on safe havens across the border in Pakistan.[20] Although some in Pakistan may see the group as a potential strategic asset to constrain Indian influence, build a friendly neighbor, and satisfy domestic Pakistan opinion, the insurgency fuels regional tensions and instability on Pakistan's border. The Taliban largely targets the Afghanistan National Security Forces, as well as government workers and progovernment civilians. Civilian casualties are increasing in Afghanistan in general, some of which is blamed on more indiscriminate uses of violent tactics and civilians caught in the crossfire.[21]

TERRORISTS

Modern terrorist groups are likely to refer to themselves as something other than "terrorists," whether it be "insurgent," "freedom fighter," or simply "soldier."[22] Because of its near universal pejorative connotation, terrorist groups may be unwilling to use the name because of the possible negative impact, or because they do not see themselves as terrorists.[23] States have argued groups could not be "terrorist organizations" if they were fighting government oppression, colonialism, or occupation.[24] They said that all governments call the opposition groups "terrorists" and what matters are underlying causes. Despite the political nature of this debate, terrorists demonstrate several common features.

Terrorist-Group Commonalities

Definitions of terrorism are notably difficult to pin down. As multiple authors have noted, there are over one hundred different definitions of terrorism in the scholarly literature alone.[25] We will take the US definition as our starting point, as it highlights several key points. The United States defines terrorism as the use or threatened use of "premeditated, politically motivated violence perpetrated against noncombatant targets by subnational groups or clandestine agents."[26] There are several additional issues to consider as we seek to draw boundaries around this type of armed group.

Terrorist groups have political objectives. Similar to insurgents, political objectives may include regime change, policy reform, or greater access to the political process for minority groups. This leads to the question of whether al-Qaeda is seeking political or religious objectives and should be classified as a terrorist group. First, it should be noted that many definitions include the qualifier that terrorist groups seek political, religious, or ideological objectives. By most definitions, religious motivation is a terrorist characteristic. Second, any terrorist group that seeks to control territory, overthrow a government, change a policy, or protect the rights of a minority group is propagating their ideology—whether religious, economic, or political—in a profoundly political act. Any group that attempts to alter the rules and laws by which people are governed and by which power is distributed in a system is engaging in a political act. Al-Qaeda's goal may be to reinstate the caliphate in order to implement Islamic law over much of Europe and North Africa. Despite the role of religious ideology, this action would dismantle states, redistribute political power, and create a new type of political organization. Removing individual state boundaries and the concept of sovereignty from these states is to seek a fundamental change in how people are organized politically. Instituting a caliphate over parts of the Middle East, North Africa, and Western Europe would presumably remove boundaries between states, do away with the notion of sovereignty, and would reorganize the inhabitants of these regions in new political structures. This is the basis for grouping terrorist goals under the general rubric of "political" motivations.

Terrorism targets noncombatants. This is not confined to women and children, although the violence perpetrated against these groups may be different from that perpetrated against general civilian targets. [27] "Combatants," by some accounts, include those not fighting and those out of uniform and off-duty. The question then arises as to whether violence carried out against military targets classifies as terrorism. Groups that solely attack military targets are grouped into the classification of insurgent. Nevertheless, terrorist groups may commit acts against both combatant and noncombatant targets. But it is the terrorist's primary focus on noncombatant targets, a presumably more easily terrorized group, that generates the greatest pressure on policy makers. Al-Qaeda's attack against the USS *Cole* in Aden, Yemen, in 2000 highlights this dilemma. The purpose of the attack was not to seriously degrade the military capability of the United States. Instead, it was to generate a broader, psychological message aimed at influencing the US and Yemeni populations. While the physical target of the attack was military, the intended targets were noncombatants. Terrorist groups attack noncombatants, as they frequently lack the capabilities to engage the military and because it is easier to spread fear, uncertainty, and a sense of vulnerability among civilians than trained members of a state's armed forces.

The previous point demonstrates terrorism is designed to influence an audience beyond that targeted by an individual attack. While chapter 6 more fully discusses the instrumental versus expressive roles violence plays, the common assumption is terrorists are rational and intend to influence policy makers. Rational actors rank order their preferences or interests, and act according to these interests whenever possible. This does not mean that terrorist groups are always able to achieve their goals, or that they perceive their interests, the context, or other's actions correctly. Terrorist groups suffer from the same myopia and dysfunction as any other group, which may be compounded by their ideological worldview and groupthink. The implication is terrorist groups use violence as an instrument to achieve their objectives.

There may be a difference between the target and the audience. These groups may be the same—the population within the state—but a terrorist attack is designed to not just kill or injure a group of people, but to make a broader statement to a diverse group of actors. This includes the targeted group supporters and nonsupporters and the government and regime in power. Terrorists, by attacking noncombatants and civilians, aim to transcend the specific target of their operation and reach a broader audience. Most armed-group actions are confined to specific targets in a confined environment.

Terrorist groups do not have a large mass base of support. While they may be fighting for a cause they believe is beneficial for the community within which they are operating, their core beliefs or actions may be rejected by the local population, as was the case among many Sunnis in Anbar Province in Iraq.[28] They are thus weak relative to the state, in that they lack the numbers to wage conventional warfare directly against the state, as well as to marshal the population to vote for peaceful policy change.[29]

Terrorists demonstrate the state's inability to protect its citizens by attacking the population. The population, in response to this violence, pressures the government to change its policies to accommodate the terrorists. Terrorist groups may be less affected by the principal–agent problem as far as operations are concerned, because civilian casualties are expected and necessary for a successful attack. An attack that triggers a government overreaction may be part of an armed group's strategy of provocation, discussed in chapter 6. Additionally, because terrorist groups frequently lack a mass base of support and the need for a large, complex organizational structure, they may not suffer form collective action problems. Lastly, a terrorist group's small size may hinder its ability to attract members and signal the likelihood the group will not succeed. This increases the group's time-consistency, coordination, and collective action problems. It should come as little surprise that terrorist groups employ social networks, ideological fervor, and charismatic leaders to overcome fundamental problems associated with group perpetuation.

Boko Haram, roughly translated as "western education is forbidden," grew out of various movements in northern Nigeria. The group gained strength in 2009, sparked in part by government repression. The US Department of State designated Boko Haram a Foreign Terrorist Organization in 2013.[30] Seeking to create an Islamic state in Nigeria, they have perpetrated widespread attacks on civilians across northern Nigeria. They carried out a suicide bombing against a UN building in 2011, assassinated government officials, and killed scores of civilians, including women and children, in attacks against colleges and schools. Their April 2014 kidnapping of over 250 girls from a school in Chibok led to international condemnation and offers of aid to the Nigerian government. While the government has initiated a coordinated campaign against the group, pushing the group out of urban areas, the group has formed networks with AQIM, al-Qaeda in the Arabian Peninsula (AQAP), and al-Shabaab.[31]

Old vs. New Terrorism

There is a debate over whether terrorism has changed and if so, whether this "new" terrorism is a more intractable challenge than previous iterations of terrorism.[32] Russell D. Howard and Margaret Nencheck elaborate several ways in which the "new terrorism" differs from "old terrorism." New terrorist groups place the US homeland at risk; instigate greater levels of violence and seek to destroy the West and secular Islamic states; act as globally active, transnational, nonstate actors; are better financed; are more difficult to penetrate due to their decentralized structure and religious extremism; desire to obtain and use weapons of mass destruction; and create an ambiguous security situation where victory is elusive and possibly unachievable.[33] While al-Qaeda is held up as the model for this new terrorism, the general profile of a "new terrorist" group appears limited to large, well-funded, Islamic groups with global objectives. It is unclear whether any other groups fit the description.

By contrast, Martha Crenshaw argues that those arguing for a "new terrorism" do not fully appreciate the historical context of terrorism; do not currently possess the empirical evidence to support their notions that groups today are more lethal; cannot adequately discern religious from nationalist motivations among many terrorist groups; and conflate religious motivations for increased lethality with advances in technology, as well as overlooking evidence concerning current and historical nonreligious groups.[34] She further argues practitioners and policy makers today have a political and monetary incentive to hype the possible threats from "new terrorism." Creating a new archetype of "new terrorism" oversimplifies the situation and may mislead the student, analyst, and policy maker.[35] Understanding that nineteenth-century Russian anarchists exhibited similar traits to al-Qaeda in their organization and leadership by inspiration is more helpful than labeling one of the groups "new" and one of the groups "old."

Difference between Terrorists and Insurgents

Insurgents and terrorists appear similar in nature: both possess political objectives, both seek to influence the population in order to affect political change, both engage in asymmetric warfare given their initial lack of resources, and both target a state's legitimacy. Nevertheless, there are some factors that enable the analyst to differentiate between the two groups.

First, insurgents create a base of support while terrorists generally do not. Terrorists may suffer from an inability to control operations, leading to civilian deaths, or begin their campaigns with fewer resources and fewer benefits to offer prospective members. Terrorist groups may also be disconnected from the population due to their extremist views.

Second, insurgents may use "terrorist tactics"—indiscriminate attacks against civilians, such as bombings—but also use more conventional, guerrilla tactics of raiding and ambushing a state's military forces.[36] Terrorists almost exclusively focus on noncombatants. As previously mentioned, there may be isolated cases where terrorist groups attack military and government targets. The terrorist's benefit from these attacks pails in comparison to the utility achieved from operations against softer targets more capable of generating fear and uncertainty.

Terrorist groups may be smaller than insurgent groups.[37] This may be due to the need for less complicated or less hierarchical organizational structures given their operations and objectives. Insurgent groups create "shadow" governing structures to replace the ruling regime after it is overthrown, as well as to provide oversight of its members to prevent indiscriminate violence.

Insurgent groups are more focused on controlling territory than terrorist groups. Terrorists may be supporting an ideological cause that is less focused on a specific territory than on achieving results geared toward removal of a particular regime or protection of a particular people, no matter their location. In addition, given their potentially smaller size and lack of resources, they may lack the capability to control territory. Lastly, a small number of terrorists may be focused on expressive violence and not instrumental violence. This is not to argue that insurgent groups are nonideological, but to say that terrorist groups may have more of a focus on instituting an ideology than in controlling a state or other region.

TRANSNATIONAL CRIMINAL ORGANIZATIONS

TCOs, while not new, are differentiated from previous incarnations by their transnational reach and threat to states. The United States defines TCOs as transnational in both their operations and organizational structure, engaging in illegal activities frequently using illegal means, which use corruption and violence to further their objectives and protect their operations. Underpinning all of this is their ability to harness the globalization factors discussed in chapter 2.[38] TCOs can be differentiated from other groups by their primarily economic motivation—TCOs seek to maximize profit through criminal activities. The archetypical TCO does not seek political objectives, uses violence as a tool of business, and while they are willing to take greater risks for greater profit, they generally do not use violence to communicate with the broader population as terrorists do. The more clandestine they can remain in most cases, the better.

Economic profit is not the only motivation listed for these groups, but is labeled as the "primary goal" in subsequent sections of the definitions.[39] TCOs, by default, may control territory as a means to control market share. Other groups provide economic or social welfare benefits to the population living within their area of control. Additionally, TCOs may seek political representation with the goal of reducing the government's overview and constraints on the group. While individual members and group leaders may have political grievances against the state and are likely to see the state as lacking legitimacy, these groups are formed with, and maintain as their ultimate objective, profit maximization. De facto territorial or political control is either incidental—control of a market may mean control of the illicit activity within a physically defined territory—or a strategy to achieving their ultimate objectives.

All TCOs seek to maintain some form of anonymity and clandestine nature, in keeping with general armed-group characteristics. At the most basic level, keeping a low profile prevents the state from focusing on the TCO. The more publicity the TCO generates—whether through spectacularly violent operations, large-scale or relatively high-visibility illicit activities such as human trafficking, or prominent strategic communication campaigns—the more likely the state will face pressure from lawmakers, the domestic population, and international observers to crack down on the illicit behaviors and the groups that perpetuate them.

The US TCO definition further notes, "There is no single structure under which transnational organized criminals operate" and that these groups may change and evolve between organizational structures.[40] Traditionally, TCOs were viewed as hierarchical organizations with "mob bosses" and the "heads of the mafia families" resembling a firm's CEO. The consequence of having a clear leadership structure was assumed to be that law enforcement could remove the leadership and the group would fall apart. But in many cases, TCOs have proven much more resilient for three main reasons. First, hierarchical TCOs had clear lines of succession. Second, TCOs proved adaptable and flexible in the face of increased government pressure, engaging in new illicit activities and transferring assets or wealth to new markets or regions. Third, any one TCO is less important than the market. After Colombian forces killed Medellín cartel leader Pablo Escobar in 1993, other cartels were able to supply the cocaine market.

Two important TCO organizational features emerge. First, TCOs may have originally been flatter than commonly attributed, "with no independent institutional identity."[41] In essence, TCOs were loosely connected producers and distributors, who appeared as a coherent group because they were all market-oriented actors with profit-maximizing interests.[42] Second, illicit markets do not depend on provision by one TCO. Instead, market demand is met by numerous TCOs from multiple regions, operating in concert, alone, or in multiple markets simultaneously. TCOs are the outward manifestation of deeper political, social, and economic problems.

TCOs thrive in weak states, which are unable to provide adequate governance but maintain some vestiges of basic economic infrastructure and an exploitable labor force.[43] TCOs have a vested interest in perpetuating state weakness, but little interest in state collapse.[44] They are, in many ways, conservative, status quo groups, as sudden changes may disrupt markets and threaten profits.[45]

Armed conflict decreases the state's ability to enforce laws within their borders, decreasing the barriers to TCO operations in these areas. In addition, the need for both military and basic goods is in greater demand in conflict zones because regular business operations have been curtailed. TCOs are aided in satisfying this demand by the influx of humanitarian aid, which TCOs may capture and resell to refugees, internally displaced persons (IDPs), and the population at large.

TCOs use violence in order to protect their turf and markets and to intimidate and deter both rivals and the government. They also use violence to maintain internal discipline and prevent "defections." The level of violence varies based on expected government and rival actions, as well as the TCO's objectives and organizational structure. TCOs may constrain excessive violence, which invites greater government scrutiny. Furthermore, levels of violence may not accurately indicate criminal activity, as "the better organized the crime, the less violence associated with it."[46]

Many TCOs were originally created as "protective-benevolent societies" for minority groups that did not receive state protection. These "societies" later grew into criminal organizations that do not necessarily provide community services.[47] These ethnic- and family-based identities play an important role in providing trust within the organization. Criminal groups need to maintain trust between their members to prevent defection to law enforcement, as well as to keep out government infiltrators. Ethnic- or family-based TCOs help overcome principal–agent, time-consistency, and coordination problems. Leaders know they can trust family members to keep secrets and carry out operations, the time-consistency problem is solved by the fact that future generations will inherit family-based TCOs, and kinship or ethnic communities share common socioeconomic and political backgrounds that overcome coordination problems. Lastly, TCOs provide "quasipublic goods"—profits accessible only to group members—which enable these groups to overcome free rider problems.[48]

The changes wrought by globalization discussed in chapter 2 have greatly aided TCOs in all aspects of their operations. TCOs are able to take advantage of new commercial networks with the massive flows in goods, people, and capital. In the United States, illicit goods are easily lost among the 8.1 million TEUs that passed through the Port of Los Angeles in 2012, while criminals may skirt unnoticed among the 95.5 million passengers traveling through the Hartsfield-Jackson Atlanta International Airport.[49] The enormity of global capital markets is an ideal place to launder illegally obtained profits.[50]

TCO size and threats have increased in their scale and scope. Some of the drug cartels in Mexico, for example, have reached the size where their military power rivals law-enforcement and military capability.[51] The Naxalites in India claim tens of thousands of members and sympathizers. Along with this increase in organizational size comes an increase in the threats these groups pose. TCOs use many different tactics in pursuing profits. Bribery, subversion, and general corruption are frequently used to maintain a low-risk, highly permissive environment in which the TCO may flourish.[52] TCOs use violence to secure their turf, discipline members, commit crimes, and counter law enforcement. Nevertheless, many TCOs avoid large-scale or indiscriminate violence for fear of drawing unwanted government attention.

TCOs may engage in any number of illegal economic activities, which could broadly be considered under the headings "predatory," "market-based," and "commercial crimes."[53] Predatory crimes are those based on theft, such as identify theft and maritime piracy. Market-based crimes are those based on counterfeiting and trafficking, including currency counterfeiting and trafficking in narcotics, small arms, people, and cigarettes. Lastly, commercial crimes are those based on tax evasion, regulatory violations, and criminal negligence. TCOs and other armed groups may also commonly engage in crimes including kidnapping, bribery, and subversion to further their goal of increasing their profits.

Indirect threats include societal costs from drug addiction, capital misallocated to corruption, and inefficiencies created by monopolies and market distortions. TCOs operating in states that cannot provide adequate services to their populations compound these problems by the diversion of funds through corruption, strained legal and health systems, as well as decreased productivity in legal systems, whether by diverting the workforce to illicit activities or removing the workforce due to drug addiction, human trafficking, or violence related incidents.[54] James Picard estimates that the worldwide direct costs of illegal drugs, human trafficking, excised goods, environmental crimes, and counterfeiting amount to $1.043 trillion, while indirect costs are estimated at $468 billion.[55]

Direct and indirect threats challenge a state's political legitimacy. TCOs seek profit, but in the pursuit of that profit—whether by controlling "turf," rigging elections, or denigrating the rule of law through corruption—TCOs may gain de facto political power or territorial control. This decreases the international community's incentive to pour aid and development funds into those societies most in need of strengthening foundational state institutions.[56]

Los Zetas, a Mexican TCO, was originally composed of deserters from Mexico's Special Forces Airmobile Group (GAFE), who acted as the Gulf cartel's private paramilitary force. They carried out assassinations, arms trafficking, human trafficking, and protected drug trafficking routes, eventually moving on to controlling large swaths of territory on behalf of the Gulf cartel. The group split from the Gulf cartel sometime between 2008–2010, after hiring themselves out to other cartels.[57] Today they are one of the largest, most violent cartels in Mexico and maintain cocaine-trafficking networks throughout Central America. They have hired former Guatemalan special forces soldiers (Los Kaibiles) as part of their effort to maintain a highly trained membership while increasing their control over Guatemalan trafficking. Los Zetas operate in Mexico, Guatemala, and the United States, as well as traffic drugs through several West African states bound for Europe. In April 2009, President Obama added Los Zetas to the list of traffickers and organizations subject to sanction under the Foreign Narcotics Kingpin Designation Act.[58]

Gangs

Gangs occupy an uncertain position in the armed group discussion.[59] By many accounts, gangs are smaller, more localized criminal organizations.[60] They are clandestine, organized, violent groups that seek economic profit, but like TCOs, they may have other motivations. One study noted that more than 50 percent of gang members surveyed joined for noneconomic reasons, including security, respect, or injustice.[61] Much like the TCOs discussed above, gangs may have been created to protect minority groups and evolved into predatory, crime-centered groups over time.[62] While some gangs may qualify as transnational actors that threaten the state and resemble TCO-terrorist hybrids, many do not. Gangs undoubtedly provide a law-enforcement challenge but have not, on a consistent basis, proven to be a threat equal to today's TCOs or TCO-terrorist hybrids.

MILITIAS

The variety of militia definitions may lead the analyst to view them as a "remainder set" of all of the armed groups left over that are not "obviously" insurgents, terrorists, or TCOs. Despite these initial misgivings, the literature addresses three different militia types exhibiting several common variables, making a comparative analysis possible. While the three militia archetypes run the gamut from insurgent-like groups to TCO- and terrorist-like groups, they all share several characteristics that differentiate them from the previous archetypes.[63]

Militias arise in weak and failed states as a response to the absence of central government power and legitimacy.[64] Militias are seen as both a cause and symptom of state decay. This failed state context is a key social driver for the creation, operation, and perpetuation of militias. Additionally, militias have a more predatory relationship with the population than other armed groups, although this will vary based on the militia type. What is more, many individuals join militias for protection, whether from the central government or other militias. Fourth, militia members tend to be young men and child soldiers, who also generally lack any specialized training. Last, militias have complementary political and economic objectives. Many militias strive for basic political autonomy in order to gain access to economic resources. Economic resources are mobilized and distributed to maintain internal discipline and group cohesion, as well as to enhance the leadership's political position. The sum of these factors show that militias are a result of a domestic environment nearly bereft of central authority, where training and resources are at a premium, and where the group challenges the state by their existence but is content to be left alone, rather than seeking to overthrow the state.

There are three militia types most frequently discussed in the literature. The first acts as a progovernment or pro-community-based armed force.[65] While it is private in nature, it is created for the purpose of protecting the community and is semiautonomous and semi-independent. It may be currently beholden to the community, and answer the call to defend the community in their time of need, but there is no guarantee that it will dissipate when the threat recedes, or that it will not take up its own, autonomous goals and act independently from the society that formed it. This progovernment militia may be regarded in some circles as a "paramilitary" group that operates as a paid government armed force, but does not exist as a legal or official branch of the state's armed forces. This might be because the group is charged with hunting down rebels, reducing crime, or carrying out a regime's "dirty projects," including ethnic cleansing or other human rights abuses. This use of unofficial military power further erodes the government's legitimacy by providing security that the central government cannot.[66] It may ultimately lead to community-based militias designed to defend against the central government itself.

The second militia type arises from the absence of central government power in a conflict or postconflict setting and acts as a more independent and autonomous armed force than the first model.[67] This militia type may have some connection to the local society and is frequently anchored in an identity community, whether clan, tribe, extended kinship network, or ethnic group. These groups rely on a "traditional" leader who most likely achieved his position by way of being the oldest, the most experienced, or the deftest in battle. The militia exists neither at the leader's behest nor for the discipleship of the leader, but the group exists for the group and they have a leader who is capable and drawn from the society the militia represents. This type of militia, as with the first group, is more concerned with group interests over those of the leader. This group may be somewhat predatory on the local population, as they may collect taxes or in some other way exploit the population in order to pay for their military activities. But this group may also provide basic economic and military services, as well as remain autonomous from the central state.[68] Once created, both the first and second groups may be difficult to control.[69] This may be especially true, as Kimberly Marten notes, because, much like organized crime, militias have an incentive to create the impression of instability. Otherwise, there would be no need for the militia's protection.[70] Instability and the lack of strong, central authority may lead to principal–agent problems, as the government and community are unable to control the militia.

The third type is the African militia or what many in the literature simply call "warlords."[71] In this situation, the warlord is the leader of a militia that operates independently and autonomously from the state—they exist simply for themselves.[72]

As Anthony Vinci has compellingly argued, these groups may create their own political community through initiation that is separate from the surrounding state, society, and local community.[73] These groups may even go so far as to prey on the ethnic group from which they draw many of their recruits, as the Lord's Resistance Army (LRA) does with the Acholi people in Uganda. Vinci has shown the creation of a new political community comprised solely of LRA members who have been initiated into the group leads to identifying non-LRA members as the "out-group." The LRA's predatory behavior toward the Acholi people is actually portrayed as preying on outsiders.[74]

This "warlord militia" is bound by common identity in the group and rarely seeks to protect a population or territory. This predatory group is concerned with looting, with exploiting natural resources, and with using these economic resources and profits to further a patronage system.[75] These groups may not be motivated by ideology in the same way that an insurgent or terrorist group may be. They may communicate a narrative centering on identity or ideology in an instrumental sense, but it is seldom the motivating factor. Economic profit may replace most other motivations. This can produce several advantages for a warlord militia, but it also comes at a potential cost.

The group is tied to a warlord who is central to the patronage system, which necessitates all economic relations flow through him. This ties the group's survivability to the warlord, as well as profits and continued "revenue flow" to the warlord's ability to secure new sources for looting and pillaging. An inability to deliver on profits can be reason to defect from the group. While coercion may be used to maintain group discipline, economic profit flowing from a patronage system is used on a constant basis to motivate fighters and maintain group cohesion. This may partially solve principal–agent, free-rider, coordination, and time-consistency problems. Nevertheless, these underfunded and underresourced militias create incentives for side deals and indiscriminate predation, leading to additional principal–agent and free-rider problems.[76]

The three militia models all exhibit the aforementioned common traits to varying degrees. Militias exist exclusively in weak and failed states, which provides constraints on and incentives to all militias. First, there is the basic desire to join a group that provides protection from others. Failed states cannot provide protection from other communities, nor from rogue government forces.[77] Joining a militia may represent a basic first step in securing survival.

Second is the degree to which these groups are beholden to the population. The first group—"procommunity" model—is really an extension of the community, closely akin to an insurgent group finding its recruitment and support from a particular community. Indeed, the community may have mobilized the militia and employ it as an unofficial, or unauthorized, armed force. This group still follows their own goals and may turn on the community, especially if taken over by a warlord-type leader. The second group—the "Chinese" model—falls in the middle. The militia may offer protection and seek recruits, as well as ensure that resource extraction and investment is carried out in an ordered and productive nature. There may also be some forms of economic predation, such as taxation and "forced giving" from the community.[78] Too much exploitation can lead the populace to turn on the group or seek them to defect to another protector. The third group—the "African" model—has severed ties to the local community and has become its own political community, predatory in nature, seeking to exploit whatever and whomever it can. This group has also severed ties to the state—save for the exploitation of infrastructure or other public goods—and is completely autonomous. While they do not represent a territory or the population living there, they may represent a group of people who have chosen to exist within the state, but outside of its norms, structure, and communities.

More broadly, most militia definitions assume membership is comprised of young males and children with no specialized training by the militia. Untrained militia troops may shrink from combat, prolonging a conflict. Deterrence strategies may work against militias, given the group's inability, or unwillingness, to engage a superior armed force. Militias may have an incentive to build up their capabilities to "demonstrate their lethality," leading to an arms race of sorts among militias. Since each group may be reluctant to engage in conflict, they may flee at the outbreak of conflict, or face an incentive to appear "irrational" and unwilling to back down from conflict.[79] Stories of West African militia men fighting naked, wearing life preservers into battle, or covering themselves in "holy oil" to "deflect" bullets may be both motivational tools for their own fighters and deterrents signaling to external groups.[80]

Militias seek to retain autonomy, but they are not necessarily looking to create a counterstate. Militias challenge the state's legitimacy, but that legitimacy is limited and already decimated, which leads to the militia's creation in the first place.[81] The militia's existence furthers the state's decline, but the militia cannot exist without basic state infrastructure.[82] Political power is a strategy to achieve greater economic profit, which in turn is redistributed in order to create greater political power.[83]

"COMMERCIAL" ARMED GROUPS

"Commercial" armed groups are employed to bolster a state's armed forces, provide local knowledge, or evade accountability.[84] PMSCs are the primary groups under consideration, but all armed-group archetypes may be hired as state proxies.[85] There is some disagreement as to whether PMSCs should be considered armed groups or whether they defy common armed-group definitions and characteristics. Complicating this is the political nature of these groups, as they are frequently based in "Western" countries and operating on behalf of "Western entities" in "non-Western" conflict zones.

"Commercial" armed groups bolster a state's military power by providing power projection capabilities, providing politically and economically inexpensive alternatives to a state's armed forces, and providing a force multiplier for existing state forces. This private use of military force for public interests obscures the public–private distinction, creating principal–agent problems for the state. Second, armed groups may provide local knowledge in the form of cultural, social, or ideological knowledge that is not available. This may occur when Western states intervene in non-Western states or more broadly when states undertake "extraregional" military operations. Third, employing armed groups allows states to evade accountability, both to their domestic populations and internationally. States intervening in neighboring states may fear military reprisal from the target state, domestic pushback from their own population, or international condemnation for intervening in the affairs of other states and find a solution in the use of armed-group proxies.

Chapter 2 discussed whether certain progovernment militias or PMSCs hired by the state should be considered as armed groups. Despite the argument that PMSCs lack autonomy and independence, the ability to differentiate an armed groups' loss of independence and autonomy due to whether they are employed by states or receive external support may be nearly impossible in practical analysis. PMSCs may be considered a separate type of armed group because they challenge the legitimacy of the state, they threaten or use violence, they are substate actors, they seek to remain somewhat clandestine, and they seek political and economic objectives. Moreover, unlike TCOs, they do not necessarily engage in illegal activities that carry long prison sentences. Politics, as well as the complexity and tensions of international versus domestic laws, create questions of legal liability in conflict zones. This is evident in many of the situations where states are likely to employ armed groups: extraregional interventions where there is a need for local knowledge and the desire to evade accountability. PMSCs may achieve a veneer of legality and legitimacy when under contract to the state in order to avoid legal retributions. This does not negate the fact that PMSCs are a principal–agent problem for the state and a challenge to state legitimacy and monopoly over the use of force.[86]

EVOLUTION, "HYBRIDIZATION," AND THE CRIME–TERROR NEXUS

Why are Armed Groups "Evolving"?

Armed groups adapt to environmental changes, foremost of which are government policies designed to counter armed groups, but also include great power competition, regional dynamics, development programs and humanitarian intervention, and access to safe havens. Competition with other groups in society, whether armed groups, NGOs, or foreign forces, may impel an armed group to create new capabilities or alter its strategic and operational calculus. Lastly, internal organizational needs and changes, such as changes in the leadership, organizational structure, or access to funding and resources, lead to group changes. This evolution may not be unidirectional or moving toward one particular endstate. Instead, groups must adapt to their environment or risk not achieving their goals or disintegration of their group.

Hybridization and the Crime–Terror Nexus

As part of the evolution process, armed groups may become hybrids, exhibiting characteristics of different armed-group archetypes. There are four broad categories to consider in this regard: opportunism, alliance, internalization, and hybridization.[87] Nearly all armed groups exhibit some of these characteristics, especially as they attempt to enter new operational areas. The constant adaptation required to achieve their goals means that there cannot be a "final stage" of armed-group evolution and hybridization.

Armed groups vacillating between the TCO and terrorist archetypes—the crime–terror nexus—have received the most attention in recent years due to a number of factors. These factors include changes in the post–Cold War environment, the need for funding, the ability to draw on resources beyond local populations, competition between actors, and the increased lethality of these armed groups. This crime–terror nexus demonstrates the four general "hybrid" categories.

The first step is opportunism. Nearly all armed groups will at some point seek funding, engage in operations, or espouse an ideology in a way that is not "true to form." They are not permanently forsaking their political objectives or ideological convictions. These are not long-term changes, as many groups fear that crime or terrorism may cheapen their message, make them appear illegitimate, or make them easier targets. They are simply bowing to environmental realities and constraints. Armed groups may use opportunistic economic or violent activities as force multipliers: to accumulate greater wealth, to conduct more lethal attacks, to ensure greater resiliency, and to expand recruiting. Additionally, they may secure basic organizational survival.

Second, groups may ally to acquire funding, access to materials, recruits, or other goods and services the group cannot attain alone. Groups may also seek to "balance" against the state, draining and dividing the state's efforts and legitimacy. TCOs may hire security to protect drug shipments or eliminate enemies, while terrorists may seek funding opportunities in an era of increased competition over scarce resources.

Third, armed groups may internalize various functions, developing greater in-house capabilities rather than create alliances. Politically motivated groups may routinely engage in illicit economic activities, while economically motivated groups seek political control and engage in terrorist tactics. For example, the US Drug Enforcement Agency (DEA) estimates that 60 percent of terrorist organizations are linked with the drug trade.[88] Internalizing the operations may initially be costly, as groups expand their membership and expertise. Over time, internalization reduces "transaction costs" associated with alliances, including economic middlemen taking their cut, delayed or unsuccessful military actions by "hired guns," and increased dependence on alliance partners.

Last, armed groups may ultimately become hybrid organizations. Hybrid groups simultaneously pursue economic and political objectives through a variety of means. These groups may resemble mercantilist states—they garner new resources in order to maximize profit, increase their size, and fund their conflicts. Conflict, in turn, is used to secure access to new profits, through natural-resource accumulation, control of territory and its population, or to secure the acquiescence of the governing body. Conflict is simultaneously an economic and politically motivated event.[89] Whether TCOs consciously pursue political objectives or seek only profit-maximizing strategies, the largest and most threatening TCOs blur the line between profit-seeking criminal organizations, terrorism, and insurgency.[90]

In the first two models—opportunism and alliance—armed groups do not radically transform or alter their activities, tactics, or strategies. Opportunism is an acknowledgement that armed groups do not perfectly adhere to any one archetype but may be prevented from or fear going too far outside of certain constraints. Alliances may be short or long term or may not last past one operation. These may lead to long-term changes through dependency, but they need not.

The second two models—internalization and hybridization—involve fundamental changes to the armed group in order to execute new tactics and strategies and accomplish new objectives. Politically minded groups may use illicit revenues to pay off members in the short run, seeking to overcome free-rider and time-consistency problems. Economically motivated groups may use increased violence to control turf, muscle out competition, and secure access to political power to protect their illicit activities and market control. As groups become less connected to the population, they may feel free to use terrorist tactics.[91] This has been the case with Mexican drug cartels, as they use car bombs, mass killings, and indiscriminate violence against the government, cartels, and civilians.[92] The level of violence has reached the point where several authors refer to them as "criminal insurgencies."[93]

The state faces several problems inherent in combating hybrid armed groups. First, these groups may be more lethal, successful, and expansive in their operations than previous groups. Second, hybrid groups may prolong a conflict based on their ever-changing means, tactics, and objectives. Third, the state faces difficulty in understanding the enemy and its motivations, intentions, and objectives in order to provide appropriate policies to combat the group. While counterterrorism or counternarcotic policies may be successful in one situation, they may not provide the necessary pressure on a hybrid armed group. Governments may be distracted by criminal activity and not pursue political challenges. States need to be cognizant of the full scope of an armed group's activities and pay careful attention to the change and evolution in an armed group's objectives.

Hybrid armed groups run the risk of losing members, creating ideological tensions, or creating splinter groups or factions within the armed group. Vanessa Neumann argues there may be more avenues and nodes within the crime–terror pipeline to attack that may bring groups down.[94] Engaging in criminal activity raises the risk of an armed group encountering principal–agent and coordination problems, but may help provide relief to the free-rider and time-consistency problem, with the constant influx of short-term economic benefits taking the place of future, but uncertain, commitments. Additionally, if economic benefits can be limited to group members then armed groups may be able to prevent free-riding by promising economic benefits unavailable to others. This aids in the time-consistency problem, as well.

Criminal activities and violence are the pursuits most common to all armed groups. This does not mean, however, that all groups will eventually evolve into TCOs or terrorists. It does mean that armed groups may be difficult to discern in practice. As groups adapt to external and internal circumstances, they are likely to alter their characteristics. This may lead groups to resemble terrorist groups when they lack a popular base and criminal groups when they lack external funding. These situations present the analyst with the complicated task of understanding whether the armed group's underlying ideology and motivations remain constant or hybridization has ushered in a fundamental group revision.

DISCUSSION QUESTIONS

1. Would criminal organizations be better off by ultimately seeking to control or depose governments? What costs and benefits do TCOs face in controlling territory as the political authority?
2. Manwaring argues that criminal organizations are a "new urban insurgency" that want to depose or control governments—which is it? Do they seek government control or not? Or do they just assume it by default?

RECOMMENDED READINGS

Isabelle Duyvesteyn, "How New Is the New Terrorism?," *Studies in Conflict and Terrorism* 27, no. 5 (2004): 439–54.

Vanda Felbab-Brown, *Shooting Up* (Washington, DC: Brookings Institution Press, 2009).

John MacKinlay, "Defining Warlords," *International Peacekeeping* 7, no. 1 (2000): 48–62.

Robert Mandel, *Dark Logic: Transnational Criminal Tactics and Global Security* (Stanford, CA: Stanford University Press, 2010).

Halvor Mehlum, Karl Ove Moene, and Ragnar Torvik, "Plunder and Protection Inc.," *Journal of Peace Research* 39, no. 4 (2002): 447–59.

Michael Miklaucic and Jacqueline Brewer, eds., *Convergence: Illicit Networks and National Security in the Age of Globalization* (Washington, DC: National Defense University Press, 2013).

Moises Naim, *Illicit: How Smugglers, Traffickers, and Copycats Are Hijacking the Global Economy* (New York: Anchor Books, 2006).

Robert I. Rotberg, ed., *Corruption, Global Security, and World Order* (Washington, DC: Brookings Institution Press, 2009).

Thomas M. Sanderson, "Transnational Terror and Organized Crime: Blurring the Lines," *SAIS Review* XXIV, no. 1 (2004), 49–61.

Stergios Skaperdas, "Warlord Competition." *Journal of Peace Research* 39, no. 4 (2002): 435–46.

NOTES

1. Michael V. Bhatia, "Fighting Words: Naming Terrorists, Bandits, Rebels and Other Violent Actors," *Third World Quarterly* 26, no. 1 (2005): 5–22.

2. Jennifer M. Hazen, "Gangs, Groups, and Guns: An Overview," in *Small Arms Survey 2010: Gangs, Groups, and Guns*, ed. Eric G. Berman, et al. (Cambridge: Cambridge University Press, 2010), 88. For "terrorism" as a more negative term ("evil") than "civil war" or even "genocide," see Roland Marchal, "Warlordism and Terrorism: How to Obscure an Already Confusing Crisis? The Case of Somalia," *International Affairs* 83, no. 6 (2007): 1100–01.

3. As Roland Marchal notes, George Kennan argued that understanding the different varieties of communism was useful in creating tensions within and between groups. See "Warlordism and Terrorism: How to Obscure an Already Confusing Crisis? The Case of Somalia," 1101.

4. James Khalil, "Know Your Enemy: On the Futility of Distinguishing between Terrorists and Insurgents," *Studies in Conflict and Terrorism* 36, no. 5 (2013): 428.

5. For example, see Anthony Vinci, "The 'Problems of Mobilization' and the Analysis of Armed Groups," *Parameters* 36, no. 1 (2006): 49–62; Ulrich Schneckener, *Spoilers or Governance Actors?: Engaging Armed Non-State Groups in Areas of Limited Statehood*, Sfb-Governance Working Paper Series No. 21 (Berlin, Germany: Freie Universität Berlin, 2009); and Hazen, "Force Multiplier: Pro-Government Armed Groups," figure 10.1.

6. For a similar approach that does not discuss fundamental problems all armed groups confront, see Richard H. Shultz, Douglas Farah, and Itamara V. Lochard, *Armed Groups: A Tier-One Security Priority*, INSS Occasional Paper 57 (Colorado Springs, CO: USAF Institute for National Security Studies, 2004).

7. For the role of ideas in foreign policy, see Judith Goldstein and Robert O. Keohane, eds., *Ideas and Foreign Policy* (Ithaca, NY: Cornell University Press, 1993). See also the concept of "securitization" in Barry Buzan, *People, States, and Fear: An Agenda for International Security Studies in the Post–Cold War Era*, 2nd ed. (Colchester, UK: European Consortium for Political Research Press, 2008).

8. Shultz, Farah, and Lochard, *Armed Groups: A Tier-One Security Priority*, 17–31.

9. Steven Metz, *Rethinking Insurgency* (Carlisle, PA: Strategic Studies Institute, US Army War College, 2007).

10. Ibid., 1.

11. James D. Fearon and David D. Laitin, "Ethnicity, Insurgency, and Civil War," *American Political Science Review* 97, no. 1 (2003): 80.

12. CIA, *Guide to the Analysis of Insurgency* (Washington, DC: US Government, 2012), https://www.hsdl.org/?view&did=713599.

13. Phil Williams, *Violent Non-State Actors and National and International Security* (Zurich, Switzerland: Swiss Federal Institute of Technology Zurich, International Relations and Security Network, 2008), 12.

14. Fearon and Laitin, "Ethnicity, Insurgency, and Civil War," 78.

15. Metz, *Rethinking Insurgency*, 13–14. See also William Reno, *Warlord Politics and African States* (Boulder, CO: Lynne Rienner, 1999).

16. Metz, *Rethinking Insurgency*, 9.

17. Fearon and Laitin, "Ethnicity, Insurgency, and Civil War."

18. Mao Tse-tung, "The Three Stages of the Protracted War," in *The Guerrilla Reader: A Historical Anthology*, ed. Walter Laqueur (Philadelphia, PA: Temple University Press, 1977).

19. Bard E. O'Neill, *Insurgency and Terrorism: From Revolution to Apocalypse* (Washington, DC: Potomac Books, 2005), 116.

20. Thomas H. Johnson, "Taliban Adaptations and Innovations," *Small Wars and Insurgencies* 24, no. 1 (2013): 7.

21. Kate Clark, "Continuing Conflict Is Not Victory: What the 2013 UNAMA Civilian Casualties Report Tells Us About the War," *Afghanistan Analysts Network*, published electronically February 11, 2014, http://www.afghanistan-analysts.org/continuing-conflict-isnt-victory-what-the-2013-unama-civilian-casualties-report-tells-us-about-the-war.

22. Ibid., 37.

23. Bruce Hoffman, *Inside Terrorism* (New York: Columbia University Press, 2006), 22–23.

24. Ibid., 24.

25. For a thorough discussion of terrorism definitions, see Alex P. Schmid and Albert J. Jongman, *Political Terrorism: A New Guide to Actors, Authors, Concepts, Data, Bases, Theories, and Literature* (New Brunswick, NJ: Transaction Publishers, 2005).

26. United States Code, Title 22, Chapter 38, § 2656f(d)(2). Legal Information Institute, Cornell University Law School, "22 USC § 2656f—Annual Country Reports on Terrorism," http://www.law.cornell.edu/uscode/text/22/2656f.

27. See Carol Rittner and John K. Roth, eds., *Rape: Weapon of War and Genocide* (St. Paul, MN: Paragon House, 2012) and Dara Kay Cohen, "Female Combatants and the Perpetration of Violence: Wartime Rape in the Sierra Leone Civil War," *World Politics* 65, no. 3 (2013). See also P. W. Singer, *Children at War* (Berkeley and Los Angeles: University of California Press, 2006).

28. For a discussion of al-Qaeda's setbacks predicated on their unwillingness to accommodate local "host communities," see Andrew Phillips, "How Al Qaeda Lost Iraq," *Australian Journal of International Affairs* 63, no. 1 (2009): 64–84.

29. It may be a misnomer to call terrorism the "weapon of the weak," as those who practice it are able to cause death and destruction, evade even the most vigilant state's surveillance and defensive measures, and effect policy change.

30. US Department of State, "Terrorist Designations of Boko Haram and Ansaru," media note, Washington, DC: US Department of State, November 13, 2013, http://www.state.gov/r/pa/prs/ps/2013/11/217509.htm#.

31. Mohammed Aly Sergie and Toni Johnson, "Boko Haram," Backgrounder: Council on Foreign Relations, February 26, 2014, http://www.cfr.org/nigeria/boko-haram/p25739.

32. For a debate, see Alejandra Bolanos, "Yes: The 'New Terrorism' or the 'Newness' of Context and Change," in *Contemporary Debates on Terrorism*, ed. Richard Jackson and Samuel Justin Sinclair (New York: Routledge, 2012) and Isabelle Duyvesteyn and Leena Malkki, "No: The Fallacy of the New Terrorism Thesis," ibid.

33. Russell D. Howard and Margaret J. Nencheck, "The New Terrorism," in *Terrorism and Counterterrorism: Understanding the New Security Environment*, ed. Russell D. Howard and Bruce Hoffman (New York: McGraw-Hill, 2012). Expressive violence is an additional factor for Mark Juergensmeyer, "Understanding the New Terrorism," *Current History* 99, no. 636 (2000): 158–63.

34. Martha Crenshaw, "The Debate over 'New' Vs. 'Old' Terrorism," in *Terrorism and Counterterorrism: Understanding the New Security Environment*, ed. Russell D. Howard and Bruce Hoffman (New York: McGraw-Hill, 2012).

35. Bolanos, "Yes: The 'New Terrorism' or the 'Newness' of Context and Change."

36. O'Neill sees terrorism as a form of warfare and subset of insurgency. See O'Neill, *Insurgency and Terrorism: From Revolution to Apocalypse*, 33.

37. Ibid., 34.

38. National Security Council, "Strategy to Combat Transnational Organized Crime: Definition," July 25, 2011, http://www.whitehouse.gov/administration/eop/nsc/transnational-crime/definition. The United Nations defines an "organized criminal group" as including three or more persons who gather over time to engage in serious crimes with the intent to make a profit. These groups are also transnational in nature. See United Nations Office on Drugs and Crime, *United Nations Convention against Transnational Organized Crime and the Protocols Thereto* (New York: United Nations, 2004).

39. National Security Council, "Strategy to Combat Transnational Organized Crime: Definition."

40. Ibid.

41. United Nations Office on Drugs and Crime, *The Globalization of Crime: A Transnational Organized Crime Threat Assessment* (Vienna, Austria: UNODC, 2010), 28.

42. West African criminal networks today may be small cells, composed of deal-making middlemen, possibly belonging to multiple criminal networks. They are adaptable, mobile, and project-based, rather than long-term enterprises. See Antonio L. Mazzitelli, "Transnational Organized Crime in West Africa: The Additional Challenge," *International Affairs* 83, no. 6 (2007): 1071–90.

43. Rachel Locke, *Organized Crime, Conflict, and Fragility: A New Approach* (New York: International Peace Institute, 2012). As the Chinese Triads and Italian mafia demonstrate, a complex, globalized environment with a multitude of actors may substitute for a weak state.

44. James Bergeron, "Transnational Organised Crime and International Security: A Primer," *The RUSI Journal* 158, no. 2 (2013).

45. Dipak K. Gupta, John Horgan, and Alex P. Schmid, "Terrorism and Organized Crime: A Theoretical Perspective," in *Faces of Terrorism: Multidisciplinary Perspectives*, ed. David Canter (Hoboken, NJ: Wiley, 2009), 125.

46. United Nations Office on Drugs and Crime, *The Globalization of Crime: A Transnational Organized Crime Threat Assessment*, 34.

47. Roy Godson and William J. Olson, "International Organized Crime," *Society* 32, no. 2 (1995): 20–21.

48. Gupta, Horgan, and Schmid, "Terrorism and Organized Crime: A Theoretical Perspective."

49. See World Shipping Council, "Top 50 World Container Ports," http://www.worldshipping.org/about-the-industry/global-trade/top-50-world-container-ports and Airports Council International, "Preliminary 2012 World Airport Traffic and Rankings," March

26, 2013, http://www.aci.aero/media/afc782a2-a258-4c49-a700-fea9047d15fb/News/Releases/2013/PR_260313_Prelim_2012_World_Traffic_Rankings-final_pdf.

50. Phil Williams, "Transnational Criminal Organisations and International Security," in *In Athena's Camp: Preparing for Conflict in the Information Age*, ed. John Arquilla and David Ronfeldt (Santa Monica, CA: RAND, 1997), 316–20 and United Nations Office on Drugs and Crime, *The Globalization of Crime: A Transnational Organized Crime Threat Assessment*, 29–31.

51. Robert J. Bunker, "Strategic Threat: Narcos and Narcotics Overview," *Small Wars and Insurgencies* 21, no. 1 (2010): 8–29.

52. Godson and Olson, "International Organized Crime," 21.

53. This draws from Justin Picard, "Can We Estimate the Global Scale and Impact of Illicit Trade?," in *Convergence: Illicit Networks and National Security in the Age of Globalization*, ed. Michael Miklaucic and Jacqueline Brewer (Washington, DC: National Defense University Press, 2013).

54. United Nations Office on Drugs and Crime, *The Globalization of Crime: A Transnational Organized Crime Threat Assessment*.

55. Picard, "Can We Estimate the Global Scale and Impact of Illicit Trade?," table 4, p. 57.

56. Locke, *Organized Crime, Conflict, and Fragility: A New Approach*, 7.

57. June S. Beittel, *Mexico's Drug Trafficking Organizations: Source and Scope of the Violence*, CRS Report R41576 (Washington, DC: US Congressional Research Service, April 15, 2013), 15.

58. The White House, Office of the Press Secretary, "Fact Sheet: Overview of the Foreign Narcotics Kingpin Designation," April 15, 2009, http://www.whitehouse.gov/the_press_office/Fact-Sheet-Overview-of-the-Foreign-Narcotics-Kingpin-Designation-Act.

59. For a thorough discussion, see Jennifer M. Hazen, "Understanding Gangs as Armed Groups," *International Review of the Red Cross* 92, no. 878 (2010): 495–520.

60. This notion is challenged by Max G. Manwaring, *Street Gangs: The New Urban Insurgency* (Carlisle, PA: Strategic Studies Institute, US Army War College, 2005).

61. Locke, *Organized Crime, Conflict, and Fragility: A New Approach*, 13.

62. On the evolution of street gangs, see Manwaring, *Street Gangs: The New Urban Insurgency*.

63. The most general definitions, encompassing all three models, can be found in Shultz, Farah, and Lochard, *Armed Groups: A Tier-One Security Priority*, 23 and CIA, *Guide to the Analysis of Insurgency*, 1.

64. Sabine C. Carey, Neil J. Mitchell, and Will Lowe, "States, the Security Sector, and the Monopoly of Violence: A New Database on Pro-Government Militias," *Journal of Peace Research* 50, no. 2 (2013): 250.

65. For example, see Keith Krause and Jennifer Milliken, "Introduction: The Challenge of Non-State Armed Groups," *Contemporary Security Policy* 30, no. 2 (2009): 204; Schneckener, *Spoilers or Governance Actors?: Engaging Armed Non-State Groups in Areas of Limited Statehood*, 9; Anthony Vinci, "'Like Worms in the Entrails of a Natural Man': A Conceptual Analysis of Warlords,*" Review of African Political Economy* 34, no. 112 (2007): 319. This category includes progovernment "paramilitary" groups that operate outside of official government channels. See Williams, *Violent Non-State Actors and National and International Security*, 11.

66. For example, warlords in Afghanistan provided security for trucking convoys, creating concerns over corruption and demonstrating the government's weakness. US House of Representatives, report of the Majority Staff, Rep. John F. Tierney (Chair), Subcommittee on National Security and Foreign Affairs, Committee on Oversight and Government Reform, *Warlord, Inc.: Extortion and Corruption Along the U.S. Supply Chain in Afghanistan*, June 2010, http://www.cbsnews.com/htdocs/pdf/HNT_Report.pdf.

67. This is similar to China in the 1910s–1920s, where the central government failed and local potentates rose up to defend their territory, while exploiting those around them for profit. For a general survey of some of the literature on Chinese warlords, see J. A. G. Roberts, "Warlordism in China," *Review of African Political Economy*, no. 45/46 (1989): 26–34.

68. This combination is at the heart of the roving versus stationary bandit discussion. See Mancur Olson, *Power and Prosperity* (New York: Basic Books, 2000).

69. Williams, *Violent Non-State Actors and National and International Security*, 12.

70. Kimberly Marten, *Warlords: Strong-Arm Brokers in Weak States* (Ithaca, NY: Cornell University Press, 2012), 8.

71. For a partial critique of warlord studies, see Marchal, "Warlordism and Terrorism: How to Obscure an Already Confusing Crisis? The Case of Somalia."

72. Krause and Milliken, "Introduction: The Challenge of Non-State Armed Groups," 204; Schneckener, *Spoilers or Governance Actors?: Engaging Armed Non-State Groups in Areas of Limited Statehood*, 11, 14; Williams, *Violent Non-State Actors and National and International Security*, 9; and Vinci, "'Like Worms in the Entrails of a Natural Man': A Conceptual Analysis of Warlords," 327–28. Williams, *Violent Non-State Actors and National and International Security*, 10 argues that militias may not have leaders, whereas a "warlord" is the leader of a militia. Because warlords require an armed group—the militia—to accomplish their objectives, they are subsumed here under the "militia" heading.

73. Vinci, "'Like Worms in the Entrails of a Natural Man': A Conceptual Analysis of Warlords," 319.

74. Ibid., 320.

75. Reno, *Warlord Politics and African States*.

76. See Jeremy M. Weinstein, *Inside Rebellion: The Politics of Insurgent Violence* (Cambridge: Cambridge University Press, 2007).

77. Schneckener, *Spoilers or Governance Actors?: Engaging Armed Non-State Groups in Areas of Limited Statehood* uses the label "sobel"—soldier by day, rebel by night.

78. Olson, *Power and Prosperity*.

79. This is similar to appearing irrational to "win" at the game of chicken. See Arthur A. Stein, *Why Nations Cooperate: Circumstance and Choice in International Relations* (Ithaca, NY: Cornell University Press, 1990).

80. As the name suggests, the "Butt Naked Brigade" led by Liberian warlord General Butt Naked would go into battle with nothing more than shoes and guns in order to strike fear into the enemy and as a sign of invulnerability. See Jonathan Stock, "The Penitant [*sic*] Warlord: Atoning for 20,000 War Crimes," Spiegel Online International, October 30, 2013, http://www.spiegel.de/international/world/general-butt-naked-warlord-blahyi-seeks-forgiveness-in-liberia-a-930688.html and Edna Fernandes, "Face to Face with General Butt Naked—'The Most Evil Man in the World,'" *Daily Mail*, November 27, 2010, http://www.dailymail.co.uk/news/article-1333465/Liberias-General-Butt-Naked-The-evil-man-world.html.

81. Marchal, "Warlordism and Terrorism: How to Obscure an Already Confusing Crisis? The Case of Somalia," 1095.

82. Vinci, "'Like Worms in the Entrails of a Natural Man': A Conceptual Analysis of Warlords."

83. See Reno, *Warlord Politics and African States* and Patrick Chabal and Jean-Pascal Daloz, *Africa Works: Disorder as Political Instrument* (Bloomington: Indiana University Press, 1999).

84. Carey, Mitchell, and Lowe, "States, the Security Sector, and the Monopoly of Violence: A New Database on Pro-Government Militias," 250.

85. Although the distinction is not absolute, private military companies may offer training, logistics, and service support, while private security companies offer security or combat services. For simplicity, the label "PMSC" will be used throughout this section. For an overview of private military companies, see P. W. Singer, *Corporate Warriors: The Rise of the Privatized Military Industry* (Ithaca, NY: Cornell University Press, 2007).

86. Ethan Corbin, "Principals and Agents: Syria and the Dilemma of Its Armed Groups Allies," *The Fletcher Forum of World Affairs* 35, no. 2 (2011): 25–46 and Janice E. Thomson, *Mercenaries, Pirates, and Sovereigns* (Princeton, NJ: Princeton University Press, 1994).

87. This section borrows from, but modifies, the crime-terror spectrum proposed by Tamara Makarenko, "The Crime-Terror Continuum: Tracing the Interplay Between Transnational Organised Crime and Terrorism," *Global Crime* 6, no. 1 (2004): 129–45.

88. Islam Qasem, Anna Michalkova, and Marjolein de Ridder, *Drugs, Crime and Terror: A Thriving Business*, WFF Issue Brief No. 09 (The Hague, Netherlands: World Foresight Forum, 2011).

89. See David Keen, "The Economic Functions of Violence in Civil Wars," *Adelphi Paper*, no. 320 (1998) and Reno, *Warlord Politics and African States*.

90. Manwaring, *Street Gangs: The New Urban Insurgency* and *A Contemporary Challenge to State Sovereignty: Gangs and Other Illicit Transnational Criminal Organizations in Central America, El Salvador, Mexico, Jamaica, and Brazil* (Carlisle, PA: Strategic Studies Institute, US Army War College, 2007).

91. Metz, *Rethinking Insurgency*.

92. Beittel, *Mexico's Drug Trafficking Organizations: Source and Scope of the Violence*.

93. Bob Killebrew and Jennifer Bernal, *Crime Wars: Gangs, Cartels and U.S. National Security* (Washington, DC: Center for a New American Security, 2010) and John P. Sullivan, "Counter-Supply and Counter-Violence Approaches to Narcotics Trafficking," *Small Wars and Insurgencies* 21, no. 1 (2010): 179–95.

94. Vanessa Neumann, "Grievance to Greed: The Global Convergence of the Crime-Terror Threat," *Orbis* 57, no. 2 (2013): 251–67.

Chapter Five

Internal Characteristics

Armed groups are shaped not only by the leader and his background, the membership's demographic and possible internal factions, or what ideology guides the armed group, but also by the context within which it operates. The context, as discussed in chapter 2, includes the current geopolitical environment; the role of different facets of globalization; the degree to which regional states, IOs, and NGOs play a role; the ever-present role of geography; and the history and cultural milieu from which the group emerges. These can have an impact on the norms, values, ideology, and strategic culture of the leaders and members of the group, as well as lead to shifts within groups over time and increase the distance, both physically and mentally, between leaders and followers. These factors may shape the narrative that the group creates, sometimes leading to different narratives within the same group. Armed groups, like states, are not monolithic organizations with a complete unity of effort, ideology, motivations, and interests from top to bottom. Instead, gaps and disagreements may emerge between the group's leadership and members, especially if these groups are from different cultures, time periods, or currently live in different regions. All of these contextual factors will affect armed group members differently.

In addition, these characteristics shape how groups engage their environment. This is not to say, however, that external influences play no role here. A group's leadership may be adversely affected by states' enacting decapitation strategies; a group's ideology may change, based on the perception or acceptance of that ideology in the international community, including among potential donor or sponsoring entities; and organization may be impacted by a state's relentless pursuit of a group's individual members.

The second factor that greatly impacts a group's characteristics is the government whose legitimacy they are challenging. Interaction between an armed group and the government (or governments, if external actors are involved) is a strategic one, whereby each group engages in independent, but interdependent, decision making.[1] Armed groups react to what the government is doing and what the armed group believes the government is likely to do. The armed group is still free to act consistent with its ideology, leader, or membership demands.

Armed groups may be greater than the sum of their parts, as evidenced by analysis of the interaction of the armed group's various components. It may not be enough to have an aggressive leader or radical ideology, but also a membership that can facilitate or is willing to accommodate indiscriminate or large-scale violence. The armed group's behavior emerges from the interaction of its individual parts.

Armed groups "produce" a number of "goods," whether services for their members, monetary benefits for the surrounding population, or security and violence. The provision of violence is seen as a key factor in understanding armed groups, yet most analyses consider it as a final product. Violence is both a good that armed groups produce, as well as an input into producing other armed-group goods such as internal cohesion, strategic communication, or ideological differentiation.

A fundamental point from this chapter is that many armed groups do not remain static, but change and evolve over time, especially as individuals are jailed, killed, or leave groups. In addition, armed groups are not unitary actors, meaning that there might be factions within the rank-and-file membership; leaders and followers may not agree on objectives, tactics, or strategies; and the strength with which various actors hold true to the motivating ideologies may ebb and flow.

These internal characteristics shed light on why groups are formed, their goals, and their justifications for the perpetration of violence; who belongs to groups and why; and how the group is organized. In many ways, these basic characteristics shape and are shaped by the group's ability to address the four fundamental problems presented in chapter 1: the free-rider, coordination, time-consistency, and principal–agent problems. Groups in their formation stage need to overcome the coordination and free-rider problems. How they do this will likely be shaped by their leadership and ideology, among other factors. These decisions subsequently establish organizational structure and membership that will constrain future group decisions as they grapple with principal–agent and time-consistency problems.

The principal–agent and time-consistency problems are evident where leaders maintain their positions through provision of tangible and intangible goods.[2] If members do not receive benefits now, but are promised them in the future, the group faces the time-consistency problem. Will the leader actually deliver on what he says, when he says? Moreover, this leads to oversight problems now, as short-term member rewards may not have a direct relation to the group's ultimate objective. Recruits may join for non-ideological reasons, such as following others in their social network. These members may need immediate social or economic rewards, which do not ultimately contribute toward directly achieving the objective. Members may have an incentive to seek short-term rewards at the expense of group cohesion or objectives, making it difficult for leaders to maintain discipline. This may mean that a group's strategy and use of force is geared toward purposive actions, but not the ultimate goal. An armed group's strategy may be geared toward maintaining group cohesion and loyalty.[3] Indeed, the longer the group exists the more focused on internal maintenance it becomes and the more its behavior may be explained by organizational prerogatives, rather than achieving final objectives or adhering to ideological principles.[4] This is another example where a group's characteristics and components parts are interdependent and integral to a thorough analysis.

LEADERSHIP

Leadership Roles in Armed Groups

Leadership in an armed group varies based on the size and objective of the group, the organization's functions, and the different group activities and interests. Leaders fulfill several key roles, such as motivating the group to fight, creating a common identity, coordinating basic organizational needs, outlining objectives, maintaining internal cohesion, and providing the public face for external relations. Leaders play both internally and externally oriented roles, based on a group's size, objectives, functions, and operational needs. They are also a product of both the environmental context and governmental pressure.

Different leaders excel at different roles. Nevertheless, one leader may seek to fulfill a multitude of roles in order to retain control or because of fears concerning security and the group's clandestine nature. This may mean that certain organizational needs and functions are unmet, hampering the group's efficiency and effectiveness.

Leaders are "rally points," helping overcome coordination problems. The leader can identify problems—or convince the population what their problem is—and then suggest an alternative narrative of who is to blame and what can be done about it. Individuals coalesce around the leader's ideology or identity, creating an armed group. Alternatively, leaders may arise as the group is formed, not as the initial catalyst but providing a stabilizing force in the incipient armed group.

Leaders are then key to perpetuating the group by providing guidance and direction on any number of issues, from matters of strategy and tactics to

providing the group objectives and acting as "statesman" to external supporters.

Leaders can be key to organizational issues, driving decisions related to
organizational structure, available resources, and strategy based on these
resources and the objectives the leader brings to the group and strategic
considerations regarding the group's narrative and objectives. Whatever
strengths or weaknesses the leader possesses may be passed along to the
group, constraining or enhancing its abilities in certain areas. The more en-
twined the leader and position, such that the position acquires authority from
the leader, the greater the likelihood that a challenge to the leader will be
seen as a challenge to the whole group. The leader's removal can create
dysfunction, reducing the group's legitimacy and effectiveness, renewing
coordination and other problems.

Leaders solve the principal–agent problem in small groups through the
use of soft power—espousing actions, ideology, or objectives others want to
emulate and achieve. Armed-group leaders may generate loyalty and dedication from the groups' members, such that the members want to carry out
operations and act in ways that directly benefit the leader and, by extension,
the armed group. Indoctrination is beneficial on this point as well, seeking to
ensure that when the leader gives a command, members follow to the utmost
of their abilities. This does not mean that a charismatic leader or radically
committed followers can overcome all problems that may lead to the principal–agent problem, simply because of utter devotion to the leader. But it
lessens the likelihood that members will actively seek to violate orders or
rules, and remain compliant with the leader's policies.

Groups may develop specialized leaders who devote time and expertise to
addressing specific functional issues within the armed group. This may further the principal–agent problem by creating overlapping areas of responsibility and factional divisions. Armed groups run by councils may be equally inefficient and unable to make decisions and direct members.

Dedication to a leader can also help solve the free-rider problem by motivating individuals to engage in behavior that benefits the group and the
leader because they want him personally to succeed and they have accepted
his narrative. Any organization faces the prospect of member defection, so
dynamic and skilled leaders are vital to maintain group cohesion and participation.

Lastly, persuasive or inspirational leaders are able to overcome the time-
consistency problem. If the leader generates an aura of trust, if he is believed
to be a religiously ordained figure, or if he possesses some other loyalty-
generating trait, groups that are founded or led by charismatic leaders are
more likely to overcome these issues. Leaders must be able to credibly commit to future actions. Demonstrating ideological zeal, lack of outside options,
and dedication to a cause allows the leader to commit to achieving future

objectives, while a group identity creates confidence the leader will not give benefits to nongroup members.

Three Aspects of Leadership

Assessing leaders involves considering three broad ideas.[5] The first is the context within which they rose to power.[6] This includes the leader's background and the environment within which a leader was raised or came of age. This also includes the leader's worldview, how he sees or interprets the actions and events around him on a global scale. Finally, why did the leader pursue this path toward armed-group leadership? Was he thrust into it suddenly, or has this been a carefully crafted path toward violence? The question of a leader's worldview may be key in understanding how he leads the group, as will understanding the context within which he first rose to prominence. But we should hesitate before creating a path-dependent argument. Once leaders assume their positions in armed groups, many other aspects may change. Members may be resistant or unwilling to accept a leader's philosophy in full; his background and upbringing may have no impact as he contorts his views to fit the current, local situation. And the reasons for assuming power—whether personal greed, "altruism," accession through the ranks, or an inner sense of "calling" to lead—may again need to be refined or subsumed given the needs of the group. The context within which a leader's persona and *Weltanschauung* were forged is important, but good leaders are flexible enough to adapt this to the present, and not be locked in by a rigid sense of where a group "should" go. Rigidity may lead quickly to disaster.

A second aspect of leadership is the leader's actions and ability to form and shape the armed group.[7] How did the leader first attain his role in the group and how does he maintain his grip on power? What sources of legitimacy or credibility does he draw on to lead? Furthermore, what factors does the leader exhibit as he attracts not only his leadership cohort, but also members and followers? The answers here may lie in the realm of intangible ideas such as charisma and the ability to inspire loyalty in others. They may be difficult to quantify, or to pinpoint. Nevertheless, intangible relationships between members and between members and leaders should not come as a surprise, given the networks or "cliques" of individuals who join armed groups in the first place. As discussed in the next section, those in armed groups may have relationships going back to their childhood years. Such bonds may be difficult to replicate or to understand at more than a superficial level. But they may have remained powerful over the years—and imbued members with a fierce loyalty to the group leader—that has greater force than relationships that emerge out of a legal relationship or a relationship built on fear of punishment.

Lastly, all leaders must, quite simply, exhibit the ability to lead.[8] What skills does the leader bring to the position? Does he excel at recruiting or attracting followers, while having no talent for strategic thinking? Does he make connections, or attract high caliber talent, while remaining in the background? Or is he a great communicator and motivator who provides an ideology and worldview that mobilizes the masses to follow him no matter the circumstances? These personal qualities increase or decrease the group's effectiveness in recruiting and maintaining members, undertaking successful operations, and achieving its goals. Again, the leader's ability to provide vision and objectives for a group, along with knowledge of how to coordinate the group's various activities, can be crucial in achieving its goals. But rigidity, and an inability to be flexible in the face of changing circumstances, or acknowledgement of a leader's own limitations, may doom a group to obsolescence and eventual dispersal. This is especially clear in insular groups facing issues of groupthink. As discussed in the organization section, armed groups are by their very nature clandestine. Many groups run the risk of turning inward to such an extreme degree that they quickly generate the most negative aspects of groupthink. This applies to the leader of a group, as well as its members.

Leadership Archetypes

Max Weber laid out three leadership types to legitimate domination.[9] These are charismatic, traditional, and legal. The charismatic leader inspires his followers and generates a personal loyalty and possesses a special quality that makes others want to take up arms and follow him. The traditional style of leadership is formed based on a tradition or custom of ruling. A dominant leader—whether the eldest, most physically powerful, clan leader or head of household, or simply the next in dynastic succession—controls a group based on a perceived right or tradition of leading. Lastly, the leader in a rational-legal system holds power through the position and authority granted by the legal office he occupies. This position is given its power through laws, a constitution, elections, or other set of formalized rules.

While Weber classified leadership into three types, most armed groups are led by either charismatic or traditional leaders. The third leadership type, rational-legal, may be found in larger, more established groups, but they are unlikely for several reasons. First, armed groups are not well-established bureaucracies with formal rules and laws. Older, hierarchical groups may resemble traditional bureaucracies, but this does not mean leadership selection is based on a "free and fair election" within a set of rules and laws. Transfer of power is frequently contentious and may involve the use of force, intimidation, and other means of coercion.

A leader's status as a "rally point" requires the ability to connect with and lead group members, as well as inspire others to join, raise funds, and communicate with external audiences. The coordination and free-rider problems punish leaders who do not provide a rally point by creating incentives to leave the group or follow new objectives and strategies.

Armed-group members are unlikely to feel bound by traditional rules and norms in many other aspects of their behavior and thus are not likely to "play by the rules." Armed-group members may feel little moral or ethical regard against using violence to advance themselves, may feel they are using violence in greater service to a cause, or simply out of self-interest in securing greater monetary, social, or psychic rewards from leading the organization.

Those challenging for a leadership position may employ support from senior leadership in another armed group (important in groups looking to ally with al-Qaeda, for example), connections to external state support and funding, or other social, economic, or political networks that provide the challenger with the capabilities to assume leadership. Few challenging for a leadership position will be concerned with questions of outside "corrupting" forces.

These four basic reasons motivate against armed groups possessing a purely rational-legal leadership model and thus push toward either a charismatic or traditional leadership model, both of which are more helpful in overcoming the coordination problem, the principal–agent problem, the free-rider problem, and even possibly the time-consistency problem.

Charismatic Leaders

Charismatic leaders have a rare gift that sets them apart from their followers. Charisma is traditionally viewed as a personal quality that imbues an individual influence over others. This influence is not derived through fear of punishment, but through desire to emulate or accept the leader's actions or vision.

The leader may not actually possess any special abilities or talents. The leader's actual capabilities, skills, and power may be irrelevant, as what is important is that the leader convinces a group of people that he has them. Those who are held in high esteem or elevated as religious figures may lead social movements. And yet many more thousands or millions may not find those leaders or their beliefs credible.

Charismatic leaders excel at identifying a group of people and explaining their problems. Many people have grievances, whether due to social, economic, or political discrimination or inequalities. A key factor is presenting a simple version of the grievance that resonates with a population and includes a target for their collective anger or disappointment. Many people know they are poor or lack education or employment. Charismatic leaders pinpoint why this is the case and who is to blame, whether another ethnic group, a particular social class, religious authorities, or even "foreign powers," such as corporations, NGOs, international agencies or institutions, or past colonial powers.

Moreover, charismatic leaders provide solutions to people's problems. Individuals recognize they have been passed up for promotion, prevented from worshipping or using their native language, or driven from their homeland by a particular group. These aggrieved individuals, however, may lack a plausible, appealing strategy for righting the perceived wrong. The charismatic leader provides focus and direction for an armed group by making the people believe he is responsive to their plight and is "one of them."

The charismatic leader must continually prove himself, since he may not have other leadership characteristics on which to fall back. Failure to provide the answers and strategies may result in loss of faith in the leader. The leader may prove himself in battle, as Ahmad Shah Massoud demonstrated in Afghanistan, by repulsing multiple Soviet advances up the Panjshir Valley between 1980 and 1985.[10] This might be accomplished by gaining international recognition for the group, as Yasser Arafat was able to do for the PLO.

Charismatic leaders can play the role of "political entrepreneur" or "ethnic activist" in order to rally individuals and mobilize armed groups.[11] Ethnic activists identify with an ethnic group, building cohesion within the group and separation from outside groups. Political entrepreneurs mobilize identity groups to use as the basis for their quest for political power. Charismatic leaders are ideally suited to galvanize those with grievances and push them to the next level of organization and armed-group creation.

Charismatic leaders may also bring several disadvantages to armed groups. The leader, due to his larger-than-life personality or aura surrounding him, may draw unwanted to attention to an armed group. Charismatic leaders risk making the fight personal and ignoring the needs or interests of the group. If a leader becomes larger than the group, seeks additional power outside of the group's objectives, or subverts the group's ideology or beliefs in order to catapult himself to greater levels of power, the group risks disintegrating. Charismatic leaders may succumb to the trappings of power, or believe themselves to be more important than their current situation and worthy of greater accolades.

Charismatic leaders may also be inflexible. The consistent worldview and strategy that propelled the group to unrealized heights, may be rigid and unable to successfully adapt to a changing environment. Additionally, ideological or strategic changes may risk the leader's credibility.

Lastly, charismatic leaders may be the ultimate embodiment of a group. A single strike removing the leader may destroy the group if the group is too reliant on the leader for motivation, ideology, organization, and strategic guidance. Alternatively, factional splits may arise in groups, as others seek legitimacy or challenge the charismatic leader over differences in ideology, strategy, or tactics. This is not unique to charismatic leaders—traditional leaders who maintain their positions through force or claim to a divine right to rule may face challengers to rule. However, in a charismatically led group, so much of the leadership and direction of the group may be centered in an individual who appears to possess a unique talent or vision that his removal irrevocably hinders the group's operations. An anointed successor may not possess the needed skills to lead a group, falling back on a more traditional, less inspirational, leadership style.

Traditional Leaders

Clan chiefs, tribal leaders, and politicians in political systems lacking a strong rule of law have long operated along the lines of traditional leaders. In this scenario, leaders place themselves at the center of political and economic networks in order to become the conduit through which economic benefits and political power flow. Traditional leaders direct this economic largesse to political allies while attempting to cut allies and rivals alike off from alternative sources of funding. Access to sources of funding aside from the traditional leader, such as from MNCs, states, or diasporas, decrease the traditional leader's legitimacy and increase the power of his rivals. As long as the traditional leader can maintain his position as the central node in the economic and political relationship with the armed-group members, he retains legitimacy and the means to allocate the spoils of war, maintaining cohesion and increasing recruitment.

Charismatic leaders maintain legitimacy through their hold over members through a "force of will," and they may also resort to dispensing social recognition or "honor" for service to the armed group, along with material rewards.[12] Traditional leaders rely to a greater degree on economic incentives, as well as the fear of punishment, to motivate and energize group members, as the fear of "exit and defection" are ever-present realities.[13] Overlapping forms of legitimation will help any leader overcome coordination and principal–agent problems associated with maintaining group cohesion and working toward a single objective.

Charismatic leaders possess several advantages in helping armed groups overcome fundamental problems of formation and perpetuation. Finding these leaders may be more difficult. Traditional leaders may overcome some of the disadvantages associated with charismatic leaders but may have a harder time overcoming fundamental problems. An armed group's organizational structure may create incentives for a particular leadership type, while adjusting to the leader's narratives and policy making.

ORGANIZATION

"Organizations are systems of coordinated action among individuals and groups whose preferences, information, interests, or knowledge differ."[14] Organizations serve three main functions: core, instrumental, and expressive. Additionally, two broad organizational types are discussed here: hierarchical organization and network organizations. Armed groups exist along a spectrum of organizational structure, with many groups a combination of hierarchical organization—signified by some type of vertical power relationships capped by a leader—with networked lower levels dispersed into cells that are frequently geographically organized and relatively autonomous from each other.

Why Do Groups Choose the Organization They Choose?

Organizations may be structured by multiple complementary constraints and incentives. First, a group's organization may arise from the group's ideology.[15] A group's organization allows it to accomplish certain goals and is a function of what the group believes and is striving to attain. Armed groups requiring outreach to a population may organize to provide greater member involvement, engage in increased strategic communications, and build an alternative governing structure to the state. McCormick argues, "A hierarchical organization, even for a revolutionary purpose, was antithetical to the movement's libertarian principles."[16] Monarchists, some religious fundamentalists, and other groups organized around a central authority figure may prefer hierarchical group organization. This enables a religious leader to more closely monitor his members' adherence to religious tenants.

A group seeking economic profit may want to keep all functions "in house," much like an MNC. MNCs are designed first to reduce transaction costs. For an armed group, this may mean reducing the likelihood of exposing operations to law enforcement or the military through weak alliances between armed groups. MNCs are also structured to operate in a bureaucratic, legal environment. Armed groups do not meet legal regulations, norms, or treaty requirements and may be less hierarchical and more accepting of the principal–agent problem. Armed groups are more concerned with exposing their operations to the state.

Underfunded groups may suffer from greater principal–agent problems or free-rider problems as members seek alternative sources of revenue. This may create a more loosely based organizational structure that is unable to monitor its members. A group seeking external support may create some hierarchical structures dedicated to fundraising, as rank-and-file members may not be savvy in addressing potential external supporters, sensitive to the ebb and flow of international politics, or possess the ability to make personal connections to further their fundraising or external support needs. Image may be important to outside supporters, who may not be willing to donate money or aid or take up a diplomatic mission on behalf of unpolished members.

The complexity of the groups' operations and objectives affect its organization. The more complex its operations or the longer the time horizon for achieving its objectives, the more likely a group will need a more rigid, hierarchical structure in order to coordinate large numbers of people and resources across multiple regions, while maintaining actions directed toward achieving a future objective. Complexity introduces the need for more specialized skill sets, with groups within the organization focused on specific skills including intelligence, crime, and mission execution.

A leader may have incentives to favor one structure over another. A leader may feel the need to closely monitor his group, whether through a hierarchical structure or a network with a central node through which all objectives, strategies, and funding flow. This may also coincide with the quality of membership composition or ideology.

The presence of a mass base brings with it the need to manage and train people, extract resources, pursue strategies on multiple fronts, and carry out a variety of operations. In addition, larger, more complex organization is needed to monitor the membership in order to overcome coordination, time-consistency, free-rider problems, and most commonly, principal–agent problems.

Finally, the external environment, notably geographical factors as well as government actions against the armed group, are key to organizational structure. Government crackdowns can force a group to quickly decentralize to avoid detection and for general survival. Alternatively, weak and failed states with a political leadership seeking outside funding and networks for support may coopt armed groups, creating more hierarchical groups that are directly involved in political decision making, such as occurs in "criminalized states" such as Guinea-Bissau. [17] A group's geographical dispersion may necessitate a networked approach with logistics, operational planning, and communications handled by local cells.

In short, a group's organization can be an expression of every other characteristic, just as the organizational structure may impact all other aspects of the group. A small insurgent group, needing a dedicated group and mass base to achieve its goals, may find it necessary to pour money, time, and effort into strategic communications and other factors that will secure greater external support. The organization may concentrate on influencing media outlets and communicating the governing regime's inadequacies and the inequalities inherent in the state's political and economic system. For a small, aggressively pursued terrorist group unconcerned about generating a mass base, but focused on communicating its message through violence, reducing the government's legitimacy, and avoiding law enforcement or the military, a networked organizational structure that provides ideological justification and narratives, while facilitating funding and operations, may be most appropriate. A large TCO, facing constant law-enforcement scrutiny, a need to keep track of production and profits, as well as ensure communication, transportation, and coordination among its members, will likely have a more formally structured hierarchical organization with clear disciplinary rules and a means of coordinating a wide array of operations and logistics. A group's organization thus responds to supply-and-demand incentives, from the need to secure resources to the need to provide members with the ability to express their messages and accomplish their goals.

Organizational structure can determine a group's resiliency, the ability to recover from a devastating attack. It also can determine whether a group is able to generate sufficient internal resources to maintain operations, as well as what type of control an armed group has over its membership. More loosely structured organizations may find that while they are more difficult to combat and more able to evade detection, their members may be less responsive to leadership's desires or less effective in their attacks. More loosely organized groups may also find that, with less control over the group, the group is likely to carry out actions contrary to the central, motivating ideology or objectives of the leadership.

By contrast, more hierarchically organized groups with succession plans may be less susceptible to state-decapitation strategies and more resilient in the face of repeated attacks. Furthermore, a hierarchically organized group may have less trouble keeping members focused on the ultimate objective. Hierarchical organizations may be unable to adapt to changes in the environment, changes in state policies, changes in external funding, and changes in the international environment. Their increased bureaucracy may naturally increase their inefficiency, overhead costs, and a host of other factors that may remove the advantages that an agile, networked fighting force may possess.

Group's Functions

A group's organization provides several functions for the group and its members. Core functions include coordinating actions among various members and leaders, maintaining unity, and making resources available to accomplish basic tasks. Instrumental functions are operations designed to accomplish a group's main objectives, including training members, establishing logistical networks, undertaking combat operations, and communicating with the external environment. Expressive functions primarily serve to establish and maintain identities. The most basic is to coordinate the members and their actions. Organization—whether based on ideology, objectives, or a leader's charismatic persona—can help solve the most basic of coordination problems. Organizations coordinate the members' disparate activities and provide unity to a group of people who may have differing preferences, incentives, information, and objectives, but who possess some common thread that ties them together. Organizations may also provide basic services to its members and passive supporters, whether training and education, logistical support, or communication among like-minded individuals. Lastly, organizations provide an outlet for their members to express their identities, whether rooted in the desire to conduct violence or to show their support for and championing of a cause greater than themselves.

Factors affecting whether the organization is able to effectively translate will and interests into action include the scope and complexity of the organization, the presence of factions and the degree of uniformity among the members and compatibility between the members and leaders, and the degree to which the group's actions are coordinated.

Armed groups may be drawn from the same ethnic or kinship group, they may come from a particular region, or may simply be adherents to the same cross-cutting ideology. The greater the degree of differentiation among the membership, however, the more trouble the armed group will have in agreeing on strategy and tactics, creating a coherent narrative, and accomplishing its goals. If there is great disagreement such that factions form with distinct leadership, splinter groups may form and defect from the armed group.

An armed group's organizational cohesion affects a variety of group functions. It may create conflicting policies between different organizational branches or factions within the branches; it can hinder operations through the misallocation of resources; it may lead to principal–agent problems, decreasing the leadership's informational awareness; or it can undermine external support and make it easier for authorities to disrupt whole networks if infighting and disunity spillover into the public arena. Dysfunction and a reputation for inefficiency may also deter possible recruits seeking a successful, viable organization, increasing the coordination problem and creating free riders.

Al-Shabaab in Somali faced internal fighting in 2013, leading to the ouster of the more locally focused leader. The new faction, under Ahmed Abdi Godane, is likely to be more predatory toward the local population, seek more global objectives, and brings with it foreign fighters.[18] This split and reorientation may be the driver behind Al-Shabaab's attack on the Westgate Mall in Nairobi, Kenya in September 2013.

A group's objectives may impact its organizational structure and cohesion. An insurgent group seeking to overthrow and replace a government may form a shadow government. Alternatively, the group may infiltrate the government and seek political office and power through subversion.[19] The group may also provide services to its members and supporters. All of these factors entail resources, manpower, and organizational competence and increase complexity.

Armed groups are clandestine for purposes of survival, as they fear government repression. An armed group's clandestine nature comes at a price for organization and decision making.[20] Its size and structure remain unknown quantities. Individuals, believing the group is small and not large enough to achieve its objectives, may not join the group. This creates a coordination problem, as the group will not appear to have a critical mass necessary for self-sustainability. A group's secrecy may lead to free-riding if members believe that the group is unable to monitor them. In addition, the group's clandestine nature closes down decision making and can lead to groupthink.[21] There is also an "action bias," which may encourage risk taking, especially if the group is walled off from society and reality.[22] In short, if the member's perceptions are altered due to the group itself trying to remain hidden, the member may be more tempted to engage in free-riding, lack the ability to coordinate with others in the group, and find it more difficult to exchange information or carry out operations in a classic principal–agent scenario.

Social networks based on friendship, kinship, or discipleship help terrorist groups overcome the free-rider and coordination problems. They do this by providing a shared collective identity and emotional feelings for in-group members. They also create a sense of "virtue" between those who have not left the organization. They discourage a member's departure through the loyalty and "emotional intimacy" created between members. It is this "in-group love" that is much more likely to motivate group members, instead of negative reactions to the world around them. People are willing to kill to protect friends and family, but less willing to do so out of hate.[23]

Hierarchies vs. Networks

The difference between hierarchical and networked organizations highlights armed groups' ability to overcome the four fundamental problems addressed in this book. Hierarchic organizations reduce the cost of the coordination, free-rider, principal–agent, and time-consistency problems. This comes at a cost of a loss of freedom of movement to evade government repression, inability to rapidly adapt to change, susceptibility to decapitation strikes, and inefficiency in operational planning and execution. The group is likely to speak with a single voice, reducing the costs of acquiring external funding, while a succession plan may reduce the risk of removing the leader. Lastly, the time-consistency problem may increase if individuals believe factional competition reduces the leadership's ability to credibly commit.

Hierarchic organizations reduce the cost of the principal–agent problem by establishing clear avenues of authority and oversight, along with the free-rider problem and coordination problem due to the structure's strength in exerting control over the members. The time-consistency problem may be overcome if the member believes the group is large or successful enough to achieve its goals and deliver on its promises. But the group may be too large, or there may be competing interests in the group, such that an individual may not believe the group can deliver on its promises. Decapitation strategies may not be effective if there are well-established lines of succession and authority. [24]

Network organizations are more difficult for authorities to disrupt and have lower overhead and logistical resource costs while improving operational efficiency and success, as local cells are able to supply specific, targeted, local intelligence and bring local expertise to bear on operations and recruitment. The armed group's embeddedness in the local environment allows cells to adapt more quickly and avoid possible operational failures. [25] Networks allow greater and freer flow of information and open local decision making to dominate a fluid environment. [26]

All organizations suffer from principal–agent problems. O'Neill argues that the organization must develop into a more complex organization as it escalates the level of violence or prepares to carry out a protracted war strategy. [27] While this does not necessarily imply that organizations must become more hierarchical, it does imply that the organization needs to have greater control over its members, since "the effective use of people will depend on the skill of insurgent leaders in identifying, integrating, and coordinating the different tasks and roles essential for success in combat operations, training, logistics, communications, transportation, and the medical, financial, informational, diplomatic, and supervisory areas." [28] By contrast, network organizations solve the principal–agent problem by devolving decision making and information accumulation to local cells, flattening the decision-making process and increasing adaptation and decision-making speed. [29]

Local cells in a network organization may lack training, resources, ideological fervor, clear sense of narrative, and have differing objectives, all forms of the principal–agent problem. Additionally, these organizations may be vulnerable at the hubs that connect various nodes, as targeted limbs may disrupt communications and leave individual nodes or cells isolated. [30] Mokhtar Belmokhtar's relationship with AQIM, as highlighted in chapter 1, is a case in point. Belmokhtar's group was affiliated with AQIM, as well as having a relationship with the central al-Qaeda leadership independent of AQIM. Belmokhtar's illicit economic activity did not sit well with the AQIM leadership, nor did his habit of not answering emails, not attending meetings, and not taking care of the record and book keeping. Despite multiple attempts to rein in Belmokhtar, AQIM was unable to do so. The decentralized nature of the organization increased the principal–agent problem and Belmokhtar eventually split from AQIM, arguing that he would carry out his operations in his own way, while working in parallel with al-Qaeda central's strategic plans.

Organizational structure ultimately depends on a multitude of factors, including resource constraints, coordinating ideology and internal discipline, leadership type and strength, and operational and organizational needs. Networks provide advantages in adapting to environmental changes or government repression, while hierarchies provide structure and coordination across wide-ranging operational needs. Armed groups strike a balance between these organizational structures best suited to achieving their specific needs.

Leaderless Organization

It is questionable whether truly leaderless organizations are possible, as groups may need to coalesce around a charismatic or traditional leader, especially in order to mobilize the masses. A leaderless group may arise after a group loses their leader, yet maintains a high level of indoctrination or strong identity sufficient to move people toward achieving their goal with no external influence or motivational force. Alternatively, the group may arise out of an egalitarian or anarchic ideology that rejects leadership. Small groups may also not see the need or desire for leadership, as they lack complex or multifaceted organizational functions to be addressed. Even without formal leadership, there may be subtle or informal forms of leadership within groups.[31] This is not to say that true leaderless organizations cannot arise or exist. It will be difficult, however, to maintain a coherent, unified organization, especially as it grows, with no vertical relationships that ultimately establish leadership positions.

Leaderless groups may be difficult to find, track, and combat due to their diffuse, disconnected organization. There is little need for communication between cells within the organization, there is no concern with decapitation strategies, and factions are not likely to cause significant damage to the group.

The disadvantages to a leaderless group are that they suffer from all of the fundamental problems: coordination, free-riding, principal–agent, and time-consistency. Without the unifying presence of a leader, leaderless groups may quickly degenerate into rival factions with no coherent ideology. It will be difficult for such a group to maintain a coherent, unified organization that is able to recruit new members, execute complicated strategies, or provide even the most necessary resources to achieve their goals.

Internal Regulation

One important consideration, along with how a group is structured and organized, is how the group is internally regulated. Internal regulations help leaders maintain oversight of group members and address the principal–agent problem. Given constraints on armed-group leaders and their organizational structure, leaders seek to ensure that all members are working toward a common goal. One author has suggested a general typology of various forms of internal regulations, including oaths, codes of conduct, standing orders, standard operating procedures, operation orders, military manuals, internal organization documents, and penal or disciplinary codes.[32] A key additional component of many internal regulations will be a group's ideology. Internal regulations are likely to reinforce, and be reinforced by, adherence to particular ideological precepts.

MEMBERSHIP

The most fundamental questions surrounding an armed group's membership are how does the armed group identify, recruit, train, motivate, and retain their members?[33] Armed groups must overcome the coordination problem early on so that the group appears to be large enough to succeed. The coordination game creates power among groups, which is self-reinforcing. The more people join a group, the more likely the group is able to recruit new members and impose sanctions on those who do not join.

Armed groups face pressures to coordinate and seek to solve these problems through a common objective, charismatic leader, or ideology. Actors face costs from the state, their social networks, and their greater community by joining and staying in an armed group. These costs may be economic, social, or political, and may vary in size. Understanding them allows the analyst to consider who is vulnerable to mobilization into a group, who may be dissuaded, and what role the state may inadvertently play in driving individuals into an armed group.

Identify Possible Members

The armed group, whether by the leader, a membership committee, or individual members, must survey people in order to find new group members to replenish those captured, killed, or who have left. This is made more difficult by the fact that the armed group wants to remain clandestine and does not wish to advertise, the group does not come into contact with potential non-members on a regular basis, the group does not know *a priori* who it can trust, and potential recruits may not know that the armed group is looking for new members. These problems are all part of the coordination problem, where the group may want people to join, potential members are looking for opportunities to join, but the two sides may not have the ability to coordinate their search. Armed groups may identify potential members from select populations in order to mitigate this coordination problem.

Armed groups may identify members among the poor, as these disadvantaged members of society are in need of money, food, stability, shelter, and employment. Identifying members among orphans and children is another way of resolving the coordination problem, as these individuals are also likely to be unemployed, seeking to satisfy their basic needs, seeking family-type social structures, and looking to cement their identities. Armed groups may also seek members among their own ethnic or religious group, whom the armed group may feel, *a priori*, it can trust. This helps the armed group overcome its isolation from the general public and the principal–agent problem.

Recruit Members

Once the group has identified possible members, the armed group must recruit individuals. This can take one of several broad approaches. Members can voluntarily join, with few hurdles to membership; the armed group may be highly selective, admitting members only after a series of tests or initiations; or the members may be coerced into joining. Members who voluntarily join do so for a host of reasons, from matters of shared kinship or grievances, to promises of power—monetary and material, spiritual, or in future governing roles.[34] Leaders may make economic promises or ideological appeals, or appeals rooted in the leader's legitimacy. This legitimacy may stem from a charismatic appeal, a traditional leadership appeal as the group elder, or as a legitimate leader based on previous experience and activity as a political party leader, legal defender, or member of the government. The narrative the group and its leader provide is extremely important and must not only "speak" to the potential member but also motivate them to accept the risks and costs that come with joining an armed group. This points to the difficulties recruitment has in overcoming two basic problems.

One problem is that regardless of the narrative the leader or group presents, unless the member joins voluntarily without the promise of incentives, the group faces a time-consistency problem. While a group has a long-term goal, members will likely need short-term benefits or incentives to keep them engaged. Furthermore, the potential member does not know whether promises the group makes will be kept. This may be compounded during the recruitment phase as leaders make promises to highly sought-after potential members. Even if the group offers no incentives, a new member may have his own expectations as to what he might receive from group membership.[35]

Moreover, the group faces a free-rider problem. Joining an armed group entails a number of real, potentially life-ending costs for a member. The group must thus convince the member that joining the group provides enough benefits that it offsets the potential costs in doing so. Because the group is likely unable to credibly commit to providing those benefits immediately to the new recruit, the armed group can overcome the free-rider problem and its associated time-consistency problem in two ways. The group can promise the new recruit immediate incentives upon joining, whether training, a salary, housing, food, or the satisfaction of some other immediate need. Eventually, the group may once again face the time-consistency problem, as the recruit may expect a salary, food, or housing every day, week, or month. Alternatively, the armed group may move to a more selective means of recruitment, involving standards or initiations to joining a group and the associated benefits group membership provides.

The second broad method by which groups may recruit members is through a highly selective process or by enacting initiation rituals as the final step in joining the group. Once the member has passed these potentially arduous hurdles, the group will have greatly reduced several problems. The group can make greater claims that any future benefits will go directly to the initiated, "elite," or "selected" group member and not the population as a whole. This assures the member that joining the group does bring benefits and reduces the free-rider problem. Additionally, the group reduces the time-consistency problem by credibly demonstrating to the member that it is willing to invest in the recruit's future because it has spent the time and effort to invest in his recruitment, and that the group is able to funnel benefits to the member and away from the general population, ensuring that it can provide short-term gains on the long road to achieving the group's objectives. The group can also ensure that the recruit is trustworthy through an extensive and rigorous recruitment process. A series of trials, tasks, or an initiation narrows down the members to those who desire to remain with the group, while affording the group an opportunity to check the recruit's background and verify his "credentials."

The third recruitment method is through coercion. This may occur by threatening harm to the individual if he does not join, threatening the individual's family with harm, or by placing the recruit into some other untenable situation that coerces them into joining. The LRA has been accused of forcing children to kill fellow abductees, parents, or siblings and then bringing those children into its ranks as members. The children have nowhere else to go due to the legal and psychological fear of returning to society.[36] Armed groups that recruit through coercion may face the greatest free-rider, coordination, and time-consistency problems. The member is an unwilling member and may strive to leave at any time, fail to carry out a leader's orders, or report false or misleading information to a leader. A coerced member may make greater short-term demands on the group in exchange for not defecting. The coerced member requires greater oversight, increasing the cost of maintaining a group composed of coerced members. In this situation, the group has to pay off the members, employ ever-greater amounts of force or indoctrination to maintain discipline and organizational coherence, or spend greater amounts on surveillance of the group.

Forced coercion might only be considered where the group had access to a large, initial resource base; generous external support; or it might lead the group to allow the members to loot and pillage in order to satisfy group demands and maintain members.[37] The first two seem unlikely, as an armed group with an initially large resource endowment, or the ability to call upon significant external sources of funding, would be able to use incentives instead of coercion to attract new recruits. It seems likely that armed groups are forced to use coercion due to an unappealing narrative, lack of legitimacy among the people, or a lack of resources to offer as incentives to joining. This creates a cycle whereby the use of violence against the local population is likely to lead to increased alienation and the need for coercion to recruit members, including children.[38]

Government brutality may push people into armed groups. Che Guevara's "Foco" theory of insurgency argued the government's harsh response to insurgent attacks would motivate people to join the armed group, once they saw how evil the government was.[39] Others examine more broadly whether increased government repression or the government's indiscriminate use of force leads to an increase in group membership or attacks.[40] This highlights the fact that there is a "push-pull" effect in members joining an armed group, whereby they are recruited or pulled into the group through social networks, armed group coercion, or the lure of economic or other incentives, while government oppression may push the population into an armed group in search of protection or freedom from grievances.

Training Members

Training, which may include indoctrination, can be used to not only increase the lethality, efficiency, and success of the group, but may also create group cohesion and decrease instances of defection. The lack of a training program may be overcome by bringing in already trained members, as Los Zetas drug cartel does with Mexican and now Guatemalan special forces.[41] Some armed groups, notably militias, do not provide any training, nor do they necessarily seek those who already have training, as is the case with the LRA's use of child soldiers. Those who recruit trained members or provide their own training, whether in small unit tactics, bomb making, or other aspects, can ensure a known, consistent quality.

Training may be difficult, however, given the level of resources and sanctuary—both in a physical and mental sense—available to the group. Members must have the necessary expertise to train them, as well as the physical and mental space in which to absorb this training. Training camps require physical space and relative stability, made more difficult as the government or external powers hunt down the armed group. [42]

Motivating Members to Fight

Anthony Vinci succinctly argues members may be motivated through loyalty, cooperation for survival, economic incentives, and coercion. [43] Sageman argues that the al-Qaeda members he studied did not fight against an outside enemy, rather they fought for each other out of a sense of cohesion and loyalty. [44] Survival, whether of the armed group or a clan, ethnic or nationalist group, or sectarian group, can be a powerful motivator. While mercenaries and private military contractors fight for economic profit, others may fight to correct what they see as economic inequalities or a sense of relative deprivation between groups. Individuals may fight given the promise of economic benefits for family members should the armed-group member die in combat. This can be seen in the extreme case of some suicide bombers, whose families are cared for after they kill themselves. [45] Members may be coerced into fighting by threat of injury or death administered by the group if they do not fight. In addition, leaders can use "hostage taking," whether physically holding families and loved ones or threatening to release damaging information, to coerce the individual to fight.

Retaining Members

Retaining members may overlap with how individuals are motivated to fight. There may be ideological or economic motivations for staying, as well as group dynamics that encourage and build group cohesion and trust. All of these create benefits that help the group overcome the time-consistency problem. An armed group may make promises now about benefits it will convey to the member once the group has achieved their goals in the future. The member may have little reason to believe that the group will keep its promise in the long run and may seek short-term ideological and economic incentives and benefits to remain a member.

A member may be ideologically committed to the cause and need little outside encouragement to remain a member of the group. He may believe that his or his family's spiritual wellbeing, or future role in a new political order, can only be achieved through group membership. Leaving the group would be a betrayal of the ideology, other members, and the leader, and throwing away the potential to achieve the desired goals. At the same time, if the group diverges from its stated ideology, or acts contrary to the group's ideology, the member may have an incentive to leave.

A member may alternatively receive economic benefits. This may also apply to the member's family. Groups might provide a base salary, along with periodic monetary bonuses. Groups might provide social welfare services or training. Too much group dependence on external support, however, could incentivize the members into defecting to the better-endowed external supporter. At the same time, large monetary benefits in the short term may incentivize members to either do little toward achieving the group's ultimate goals or even work at odds with achieving the group's goals. This creates two, intertwined problems. Short-term monetary benefits may lead to the creation of a moral hazard problem, whereby the monetary benefits leave the member free to pursue activities that the group believes are inappropriate. Additionally, the moral hazard problem may be exacerbated by the principal–agent problem, because the group leadership has difficulty monitoring the member's activities.

Groups seek to build a sense of cohesion and trust among the members and leaders through ideology, indoctrination, or internal regulations. Nearly all clandestine groups face trouble establishing trust and credible commitments between group members. As Joseph Pistone, aka Donnie Brasco, an undercover FBI agent stated about the mafia: "Everybody's . . . trying to keep as much as they can, pass along as little as they can get away with, regardless of what the rules say. They always fudge. They figure, they're out doing the job, who wants to give up half of what they get to somebody that's not even there? So you never told anybody the whole story with money . . . That was the standard."[46] This can prevent members and leaders from trusting each other and tear the group apart.

There are three broad ways to overcome the principal–agent problem and create greater trust and cohesion: third-party oversight and enforcement, removing options, and hostage taking.[47] Third-party oversight and enforcement by a reliable, external party to the armed group is rarely available. Removing options to leaving or defecting may entail costs such as identifying members of the group. Hostage-taking, such as through shared kinship and violence or social networks, is plentiful in many armed groups and can be used to create credible commitments and ensure cooperation.

Kinship and social networks are traditional sources for recruits, which provide family members a stake in future outcomes and profits of the criminal organization, and make it easier for the group to seek retribution in the event of a family member's defection. Shared violent acts implicate each actor, such that each knows that the other has committed violence and none will be able to defect and implicate the other without implicating himself. Campana and Varese find that even in mafia clans based on shared kinship, shared violence had a stronger effect on cooperation. Overlapping kinship, social networks, and violence lead to cooperation in nonviolent actions and play a role in strengthening group loyalty and retaining members.[48]

Social networks may provide volunteers for armed groups and were key to providing members for al-Qaeda, but they also bring local customs and norms, social bonds that may transcend a group's ideology, and a possible attachment to more localized ideas than is presented in a global ideology.[49] Moderate factions may eventually leave a group or seek negotiations with the governing regime, while factions holding to a more extreme position may be cast out of a group.[50]

IDEOLOGY

Mary Kaldor and others in the "new war" discourse believe that contemporary conflicts are no longer Cold War ideological clashes, arguing instead that today's conflicts are motivated by identity.[51] This belies two points. The first is that identity, by itself, may not be enough to motivate somebody to fight, as identity may be more of a permissive than proximate cause. Leaders may motivate individuals by using ideology, wrapped around a group identity, to explain and justify that group's actions. Identity may not be helpful in justifying why a group should commit suicide bombings, seek particular objectives, or not target specific individuals. Second, ideology may be used to create a new identity specific to a group. Ideology subsumes the notion of identity while providing a broader prism through which to examine an assortment of armed groups.[52]

Definition of Ideology

Ideology is, at its most basic, a shared set of ideas, beliefs, myths, and values that not only promotes a lens through which to understand the world, but also links the members of the group through communicated symbols and identity. This does not mean that all group members adhere to identical versions of an ideology, and the degree of "buy-in" from the leadership may far outstrip the rank-and-file membership. A group's ideology provides a motive and framework for armed action, and discusses the allocation of power as well as to what ends power should be used. "Ideology" is a neutral concept, although it has garnered negative connotations depending on the audience and form in which it is presented. Ideology serves different roles across multiples audiences, whether in-group members, potential supporters, the government, or international audiences. Ideology must be communicated in order to be effective, which may require group member indoctrination, strategic communication to spread the group's ideology, and acting in concert with the tenants of the group's ideology. Lastly, successful utilization of ideology is frequently characterized by flexibility and adaptability in the face of contextual changes. Groups unable to adapt will find their message unable to sustain their membership or their cause.

Common ideologies include nationalism, religious traditions, and variants of socialism, liberalism, and more abstract concepts of egalitarianism. While ideologies are collections of norms, values, beliefs, myths, practices, and culture links, armed-group leaders may need more specific directives in order to provide group objectives or motivate individual actors. More abstract ideologies need a practical grounding in order for them to provide the objectives, organization, or strategy and tactics that members rely on. Likewise, while abstract or general platitudes may help attract a broad set of members, this can backfire by bringing in members too diverse to maintain group cohesion, or will provide no compelling idea or motivation for those seeking meaning beyond themselves. Too specific, and the group risks alienating potential supporters. Too broad, and supporters may see little of value to joining the group.

Ideology's Role

In its broadest consideration, ideology may aid a group in three general ways. Ideology can provide a definition of the problem the group faces. This can be religious or ethnic persecution, loss of sacred homeland, or inability to share in economic profit. Charismatic leaders are frequently able to motivate a group based on their ability to identify "the other," enemy, or scapegoat for the group. This is often done by relying on an ideological framework that can be used to undergird the group.

Ideology may also propose a solution to the problem the group faces. This is translated as the group's objectives. When linked with the definition of the problem, ideology provides a linked and coherent story or narrative about who and what is to blame and how to fix the problem.

Ideology may not only provide motivation to group members but also specify and legitimize the means to solve the problem. A group's ideology may detail or constrain the strategic and tactical steps needed to achieve the group's objectives, specify a particular type of organizational structure, or even justify previously taboo actions to achieve the group's goals.

Ideology, then, explains how power is allocated, how power should be allocated, and how the group should strive to correct this imbalance of power. It should come as no surprise that a charismatic leader might promote a specific ideology in order to gain influence over a group of people. Charismatic leaders not only identify people in distress, but also identify the cause of their distress, as well as provided a readymade solution to the people's distress. Ideology, which can be packaged and "sold" to a desperate, disadvantaged, or willing audience, is a powerful tool that leaders wield in a multitude of ways.

Ideology is also a malleable product, not simply handed down from the leadership to the members for them to accept. The interplay between leaders, group members and their family politics, the local context, and external actors may shape and create new identities and ideological narratives.[53]

Ideology, then, is not only framed by elites to be passed onto unknowing followers, but is modified based on the needs and circumstances of the followers.[54] These actors may have different uses for ideology, with elites using ideology to address larger, structural problems in society, and followers using ideology to address immediate grievances. Different audiences not only experience and adapt an ideology to meet their needs, but this discourse creates a new, unique identity and ideology that differentiates the group from others.

We can further break down some of the internal roles that ideology plays in an armed group. As first discussed, ideology can define a group's problem and solution, which clarifies the armed group's goals. Furthermore, ideology may promote a particular organizational structure, whether promoting a leader to an unrivaled position, creating a more egalitarian structure, or decentralizing power to the point that there is no central leadership.[55] These organizational structures may correspond to a religious ideology or cult of personality, a socialist or egalitarian ideology advocating for greater equality among its members, or a political ideology of a "leaderless revolution." Ideology may also be used to create internal cohesion and greater discipline among members. This can increase the gains made from a group's strategy and tactics, retain members, and focus the group's efforts on the stated objectives. Moreover, ideology can legitimize the group's strategy and tactics within the group. Members will likely be asked to not only carry out violent acts, but violent acts members may be resistant to entertain. Killing women and children and other noncombatants, undertaking suicide bombing, and engaging in other actions that may be expressly forbidden in a culture or religious tradition are commonly employed tactics among not just terrorist groups but insurgents, TCOs, and militias. Overcoming the psychological, cultural, and social norms against such actions is a key role for ideology. An ideology may justify such unpalatable or previously viewed taboo actions through religious, moral, or economic arguments, or by pointing to the extremes to which the government or enemy is willing to go.

Ideology, when communicated to outside actors, can be used principally to justify and legitimize an armed group's actions to both a domestic and international audience. While group members must be convinced to carry out unpalatable violent acts, the cultural context within which they are committed may also render those actions taboo. Gaining influence over this population will thus require the same types of justifications of the actions as occurred within the group. This can also occur at the international level, as ideology can be used as a link to populations or states espousing similar views. Armed groups seek sympathy and support in international organizations and forums, as well as political, military, and monetary support from international audiences. Armed groups may exaggerate or "play up" one tenant of their ideology in the hopes of drawing in this broader audience, while minimizing other aspects that lack a broad level of acceptance. Juan E. Ugarriza noted that both Laurent Kabila's insurgents in the Democratic Republic of the Congo and the FARC in Colombia were faced with global skepticism of socialist causes after the fall of the Soviet Union. These groups turned to nationalism and anti-imperialism in order to appeal to wider audiences. They did not forgo their socialist messages, but instead highlighted other aspects of their ideology in order to attract both domestic and international support.[56]

Ideology may also be used in differing roles, depending on the armed-group type. Given the manner and nature of terrorist tactics, which involve attacks against noncombatants, terrorist group ideologies frequently must emphasize ideological arguments that erode constraints on the use of violence. Terrorist ideologies are well developed in terms of legitimizing the use of force. Insurgents, given their need to build a mass base and construct alternate governance structures, may use ideology to build unity, strengthen their legitimacy, and undermine the legitimacy of the target state. Both of these groups employ ideology in the struggle to define the problem, but terrorist ideologies, whether because of their emphasis on legitimizing violence against noncombatants or the extremity of other claims, have a more difficult time mobilizing popular support, whereas insurgent ideologies are frequently predicated on the notion of presenting a viable alternative governance structure.

TCOs and militias may not necessarily have formal ideologies but do have worldviews and unwritten, limited political objectives. TCOs, given their focus on profit and monetary gain, appear to be outside the realm of political, religious, or nationalist ideologies, nor rely on identity as it relates to ethnicity or religion. TCOs, however, may be said to have an ideology surrounding greed. Militias are often held together by ethnic identity or shared kinship, but these more narrow aspects of ideology may be created as part of the process of group formation and through committing violent acts. Many militias do desire territorial sovereignty and maintain political objectives that are accompanied by more traditional political ideologies. Much like TCOs, militias may possess hybrid ideologies that blend political and religious ideologies with commercial motivations. Broad definitions of ideology, such as "overarching cultural systems that nevertheless may be influenced or shaped by power and economic relations," leave the door open as to whether TCOs represent a different type of ideology than traditionally envisioned.[57] The culture and identities created by shared kinship and violence in criminal networks, shaped by the struggle to gain economic, if not political, power, may create a mixture of political and "commercialist" ideologies.

In a more theoretical sense, ideology can provide solutions to the principal–agent, time-consistency, coordination, and free-rider problems for all of the armed groups under consideration. Ideology's creation of internal cohesion, definition of objectives, constraining tactics, centering the group on common myths, and aiding in the advancing and creation of common identities creates linkages that draw disparate individuals together to engage in collective action. The coordination problem is more easily solved among those who hold similar views on the inequalities and injustices in society. Principal–agent problems can be reduced when members of a group see the leader speaking on behalf of an ideological community. Time-consistency problems, where individuals may not believe that gains promised in the future will be delivered due to changing leadership preferences, can be mitigated because the member is a part of a like-minded community, holding to common beliefs. An armed group adhering to a religious ideology may believe that true believers and those carrying out actions on behalf of the group are granted access to enlightenment or a place in the afterlife. This motivation, not only to follow the precepts of the leadership but also in believing that future promises will be fulfilled, may not rely on the leadership itself but on the perpetuation and espousing of a strong ideological foundation.

In the end, armed groups need to show coherence and balance between the group's ideology, objectives, and policies. If there is a disconnect between a group's strategy and tactics and its ideology, especially as it might concern indiscriminate violence or religious hypocrisy, the group may have trouble attracting new members and current members may defect from the group. Failure to reconcile an armed group's ideology and objectives may rob an armed group of the legitimizing force needed to use violence in achieving that objective.

The leader and members who shape and are subsequently constrained by the group's organizational structure, ideology, and external factors discussed in the next chapter seek to achieve certain economic or political objectives. Failure to do so may increase the costs of maintaining membership and a loss of group legitimacy.

OBJECTIVES

Armed groups work toward objectives or goals, as any other group. This fundamental point stands in contrast to the idea that many armed groups today only seek survival or exist simply to commit violence. Individual members of a group may have as their individual motivation violence for the sake of violence, but groups have a larger, collective objective. In many cases, this objective may be set by the leader, but at the same time may be an articulation of the group will. As discussed with charismatic leaders, one of the traits that propelled them to their position of leadership is the ability to bring voice to a group's grievances and bring with them a set of goals, values, and ideology. This ideology may not only justify the group's actions, but also delineate objectives. Whether imposed by a leader or as an expression of the will of the people, all groups have an ultimate objective. Those groups that achieve their objective or find their objective is no longer attainable either adapt to the new environment or quickly wither. This is especially true for insurgent groups that may be better in opposition than in governing. The skill sets required to fight the government may not necessarily be complementary with governing.

At the most fundamental level, this book delineates objectives into two categories, political and economic objectives. Political objectives as a category subsumes a host of other objectives that may be popularly sought by groups but which, on closer inspection, boil down to a fundamental challenge against the state or even state-system as it exists today. If politics is, in Harold Lasswell's famous quote, "who gets what, when, and how," then nearly all armed groups are fighting for political objectives.[58] Even groups with economic objectives, discussed next, may seek de facto political objectives. Insurgent and terrorist groups challenging a state do so because they seek to change the political system. Religiously oriented terrorist groups are also seeking a political change—they want the government to either espouse a religious viewpoint, to be run or directed according to religious dictates, or, in the case of al-Qaeda's objectives, for the state system to be abolished and a new type of political organization, the caliphate, to be substituted in its place.[59] The political objective may vary—institution of a right-wing or left-wing government, a greater redistribution of goods to certain minority groups, or the imposition of religious laws—but in the end, these all entail a political change and present a political challenge to the existing government.

Groups with economic goals—namely TCOs and militias, but at times, potentially all groups seek economic objectives—do not set out to challenge the state politically. The group seeks greater profit, albeit by subverting the laws of the state. But the TCO does not necessarily want the state to change its laws. By changing its laws, the state may make an illicit product legal, which reduces profits to the armed group and transfers them to the state. If the state legalizes the production and consumption of alcohol, the profits from alcohol sales accrue to the state and the price of this now legally traded commodity is likely to drop. While there may be other societal costs and issues associated with alcohol consumption, these are not issues with which the armed group is necessarily concerned. Instead, the armed group may prefer for alcohol—or drugs, small arms, or prostitution—to remain illegal. This artificially inflates the price, allowing the armed group to be not only the sole provider, or at least not face competition from the state, but also to set prices due to a limited market with limited information.

As TCOs mature or expand in scale and scope, they may increasingly challenge the political legitimacy of the state through the violation of laws, de facto control of territory, and corruption and subversion in the name of furthering their economic objectives. These are not the group's primary objective and the groups frequently do not want to replace state services with their own. Nevertheless, this evolution into a political and not just economic challenge to the state may bring additional attention and focus from state security services, as the Mexican "war" with the drug cartels demonstrates. As TCOs with economic objectives control more territory, move into providing services to the population, and replace the government in many regions, whether through corruption or subversion, they demonstrate that armed groups are difficult to label, flexible and adaptive to their surroundings and situations, and ultimately a challenge in multiple ways to the state's ability to govern.

There are nine types of insurgencies, according to O'Neill. The first five, he argues, are "revolutionary," as "they seek to change an existing political system completely."[60] These types are: anarchist, egalitarian, traditionalists, apocalyptic-utopians, and pluralists.[61] Additionally, secessionist groups transcend revolutionary objectives, as they want to create a new state; reformists are nonrevolutionary; preservationists are status quo groups that frequently fight other nonstate actors; and commercialist groups seek political power in order to accumulate wealth.[62] All serve political objectives, where the ultimate aim is some type of political change with an eye toward political legitimacy. The last goal, a commercialist insurgency, is described as "nothing more than the acquisition of material resource through seizure and control of political power."[63] He further notes that "such groups are essentially self-aggrandizing nihilists, although predators would also be an appropriate term."[64]

Kydd and Walter identify five general terrorist-group objectives. These can be generalized to accommodate most of the armed-group types under consideration here. These objectives are regime change, territorial change, policy change, social control, and status quo maintenance.[65]

A different take points out that terrorists generally cluster around similar objectives during different periods, creating distinct objectives waves. Rapoport argues that modern terrorism has gone through four waves, with none of the motivations ever disappearing, but certain ones becoming more salient in different periods. The Anarchist wave began with Russian terrorism in the 1880s, the anticolonial wave began in the 1920s and lasted for forty years, the New Left wave came after that, followed by the current religious wave in 1979. Nationalist groups existed during all of these periods, influenced by the major features of each wave. Today, Rapoport argues that the "most significant, deadly, and profoundly international attacks" originated with Islamic groups.[66]

Likewise, the literature on "new war," "new terrorism," and "new civil wars" have all postulated similar ideas, namely, that "old" objectives of political change, revolutionary overthrow of governments, or nationalist goals of autonomy and independence, are being replaced by conflicts over identity that eschew traditional categorization.[67] Armed groups may seek this at a local level, creating intractable identity conflicts that end in genocide, "ethnic cleansing," or reach indecisive conclusions that flare up every few years. At the international level, groups may seek the revolutionary over-throw of the international political system revolving around state sovereignty and the implementation of new forms of political organizations that reflect identity claims based on "civilizations" or other broad identity categories.[68]

All of these discussions of armed-group objectives bring a common trait to the fore, namely that objectives may be influenced by environmental factors and the international context. Rapoport's four waves highlight that while nationalist or other objectives are always present, they may take on characteristics to reflect popular sentiments sweeping through many populations. Armed groups, seeking external support, are likely to alter their objectives to reflect popularly held views. As the end of the Cold War demonstrated, many groups altered their objectives to reflect the unpopularity and lack of resonance communist or Marxist causes had in the international search for donors.

There are numerous problems with identifying an armed group's goals. The goals themselves may change, or a group may have conflicting goals. This may be due to schisms among the group's membership, factional leaders staking out territory as they attempt to solidify control over the group, or internally inconsistent dialogue. The group may also have misleading rhetoric, possibly due to internal factionalism. There may be ambiguous goals and confusion between ultimate and intermediate goals.[69] Finally, outside observers may not be able to differentiate between a group's ultimate externally oriented objective such as regime change and objectives that seek to accomplish other, sometimes internal purposes, such as to create group cohesion.[70]

Goals and objectives may be long term, as exemplified by al-Qaeda's grand strategy stretching out two hundred years in the future.[71] Many armed groups may have goals that are long term in nature, much as many states have long-term goals. This creates problems for both the armed group and the state combating them. The difficulties that armed groups face are encapsulated in the time-consistency problem. While the ultimate objective is only going to be achieved in the future, armed groups must keep their members motivated in the short-term. Otherwise, these members will leave and seek short-term gains elsewhere. States have the advantage of supplying goods and services to their citizens, whether infrastructure in order to carry out economic exchange, emergency services in the event of a disaster, or, perhaps most importantly, security services to protect the citizens and state from internal or external aggression. Although a state may seek long-term territorial expansion, defeat of an enemy, or spread of a particular norm or value, the citizens recognize short-term benefits to being members of the state and are satisfied enough to stay and maintain the state's resource base.

Armed groups, by contrast, may not be able to provide services to their members and may be unable to provide regular, short-term benefits to membership in the group. Long-term objectives are thus more difficult to satisfy, as members may leave to seek gains elsewhere. Armed groups have an incentive to either hide the true objectives from the group's membership, or to create shorter-term goals, which lead to an ultimate, future objective. A group's ability to maintain the organization and recruit new members will be hampered if the group's objectives are only likely to be achieved too far in the future. The role of ideology and internal regulations are increasingly important the more distant the attainment of the group's objectives appear.

Armed-group goals may, by necessity, be more long term in nature, given the need to engage in protracted warfare. Carving out an autonomous area, achieving a monopoly on an illegitimate market in a region, forming a new country, or overthrowing the governing regime in an existing country are unlikely to be achieved quickly. This is due to the nature of the objectives themselves, as well as the strategies used to achieve them. The objectives themselves are complex and may involve convincing tens of thousands of people that their current government in some way lacks the necessary legitimacy to govern. They may also involve a radical change to that government, which would mean a new way of life for the population. These types of changes will not come easily, even with a willing population. Additionally, the strategies frequently employed to achieve these goals may rely on a protracted struggle. Armed groups lack the capabilities to rise up overnight and achieve their goals through decisive confrontations with government armed forces. Therefore, the complex, revolutionary changes that many armed groups seek are unlikely to be quickly fulfilled through protracted strategies. Clearly, armed groups have several problems when attempting to achieve their goals.

Group members may have joined a group with different objectives from their own. While a group may seek autonomy or greater profit, members may have joined because of friendship and camaraderie. This creates a possible principal–agent problem, where group members, motivated to achieve differing objectives than the group, do not follow orders that would benefit the group over their own relations. This creates a free-rider problem, where the member may seek his own aggrandizement at the expense of the group, since he may not fully embrace the group's ideology and objectives. Moreover, because the group is likely to make promises based on future achievement of its goals, the member may disbelieve them and look for payouts in the short term. This time-consistency problem is likely to increase the more distant the achievement of the group's objectives. It should come as no surprise that groups with long-term objectives may set intermediate goals, alter their goals in the face of membership desires, provide additional benefits, or employ coercive measures to maintain group membership and discipline. The stronger the adherence to a central ideological vision, the more likely group members are to remain focused on the ideologically established goals.

TCOs focus on economic goals, which creates several differences from those focused on political goals. Recruiting members may be easier for TCOs, as crime is a more potent draw and less likely to expose the individual to injury or death than politically motivated violence carried out against the government. These organizations may not face the same degree of the time-inconsistency problem that other groups face. Although a TCO's long-term objective may be to attain a monopoly over drug trafficking in a particular market, or to control all criminal activity in a region, the long-term goals are simply an enlargement of the group's short-term goals. Whether engaging in petty crime such as pickpocketing or small-scale arms smuggling, all criminal activity for a TCO entails profit. As the group expands in power and their operations expand in scale and scope, the group continues to make profit, albeit on a greater scale. Long-term gains do not come at the expense of short-term gains. Group members receive constant payouts from the criminal organization, overcoming their desire to leave and seek short-term gains elsewhere.

Armed groups with economic goals may also find their basic organizational and strategic needs are less complex than groups with political goals, as they are focused less on overthrowing the government than in evading government forces. Insurgent groups must not only fight government troops, but also prepare an alternative governing structure and maintain an alluring ideology that will motivate people to join and fight for the group. TCOs, by contrast, do not need to develop compelling ideologies or prepare to both fight and govern. They instead possess an ideology—if greed or the attainment of ever-greater wealth can be said to be the basest of ideologies—that has widespread appeal. And because they do not want to rule a country or region—although they may de facto control territory—they do not require the dual governing structures and extra effort that is required to communicate these wishes to the masses. Instead, they must deal with other TCOs and gangs, while evading government scrutiny. This does not necessarily make it easy for TCOs to operate, but it may reduce the costs to members of engaging in such a group, thus decreasing the complications from not only the coordination problem, but also the free-rider problem.

TCOs may face greater principal–agent problems due to constant short-term gains and members' ability to conduct side deals and maintain illegal activities outside the purview of the TCO leadership. Whether individual members are transporting drugs, buying weapons to sell in alternative markets, or creating counterfeit money, they all have an incentive to pocket some of the illicit goods or profits and not report the transactions to the TCO leadership. Likewise, the TCO leadership may possess information about the size of an illicit transaction such as money laundering, trade-based money laundering, or other difficult to observe illegal transactions that they do not share with members, allowing the leadership to withhold profits to which the members are "entitled."

The internal elements discussed in this chapter—leadership, membership, organization, ideology, and objectives—are fundamental in understanding the basic composition and internal constraints on an armed group's operations, whether violent or nonviolent. Each influences the other, such that leadership is constrained by group membership, as members are influenced and constrained by the group's ideological underpinnings. These interdependent factors set the stage for the elements discussed in the next chapter, while subsequently being shaped by them. To understand how a group interacts with its external environment—whether through violent confrontations with police or armed forces, or by nonviolent communications seeking influence over a potentially sympathetic population—the next chapter outlines not only how a group's internal construction and factors interact with its external environment, but how the external environment shapes and constrains a group's internal decisions.

DISCUSSION QUESTIONS

1. What are the costs/benefits to an armed group that adopts a leadership council or becomes leaderless?
2. What are the costs/benefits to having an armed group led by coercion instead of charisma?
3. What disadvantages does the armed group's clandestine nature place on these internal characteristics?
4. What problems is the group likely to encounter if it recruits members from outside the "target" demographic?
5. Is ideology used to exploit the social situation? Or does the social situation drive ideology?
6. Can an armed group maintain ideologies for both internal and external consumption?
7. How might an armed group keep members motivated and focused on long-term goals?
8. Why might leaders and followers have different ideologies?

RECOMMENDED READINGS

John Arquilla and David Ronfeldt, *Networks and Netwars: The Future of Terror, Crime, and Militancy* (Santa Monica, CA: RAND Corporation, 2001).

Bernd Beber and Christopher Blattman, "The Logic of Child Soldiering and Coercion," *International Organization* 67, no. 1 (2013): 65–104.

Ori Brafman and Rod A. Beckstrom, *The Starfish and the Spider: The Unstoppable Power of Leaderless Organizations* (New York: Portfolio, 2007).

Peter W. Singer, *Children at War* (New York: Pantheon Books, 2005).

Abdulkader H. Sinno, *Organizations at War in Afghanistan and Beyond* (Ithaca, NY: Cornell University Press, 2010).

Jeremy M. Weinstein, *Inside Rebellion: The Politics of Insurgent Violence* (Cambridge: Cambridge University Press, 2007).

Michael Wessells, *Child Soldiers: From Violence to Protection* (Cambridge, MA: Harvard University Press, 2009).

NOTES

1. For strategic interaction more broadly in international relations, see David A. Lake and Robert Powell, eds., *Strategic Choice and International Relations*(Princeton, NJ: Princeton University Press, 1999).

2. Martha Crenshaw, "Theories of Terrorism: Instrumental and Organizational Approaches," in *Inside Terrorist Organizations*, ed. David C. Rapoport (New York: Columbia University Press, 1988), 19.

3. Ibid., 20, 21.

4. Ibid., 21.

5. This section draws heavily on Dieter Rucht, "Leadership in Social and Political Movements: A Comparative Exploration," in *Comparative Political Leadership*, ed. Ludger Helms (New York: Palgrave Macmillan, 2012).

6. Ibid., 102.

7. Ibid., 106–07.

8. Ibid., 109–12.

9. This section draws from Max Weber, "Politics as a Vocation," in *From Max Weber: Essays in Sociology*, ed. H. H. Gerth and C. Wright Mills (New York: Oxford University Press, 1958).

10. J. Bruce Amstutz, *Afghanistan: The First Five Years of Soviet Occupation* (Washington, DC: National Defense University Press, 1986).

11. Stefan Wolff, *Ethnic Conflict: A Global Perspective* (Oxford: Oxford University Press, 2006), 82–83.

12. Weber, "Politics as a Vocation," 80–82.

13. Rucht, "Leadership in Social and Political Movements: A Comparative Exploration," 106.

14. James G. March and Herbert A. Simon, *Organizations* (Cambridge, MA: Blackwell, 1993), 2.

15. Juan E. Ugarriza, "Ideologies and Conflict in the Post-Cold War," *International Journal of Conflict Management* 20, no. 1 (2009).

16. McCormick, "Terrorist Decision Making."

17. On criminalized states, see Douglas Farah, "Terrorist-Criminal Pipelines and Criminalized States: Emerging Alliances," *PRISM* 2, no. 3 (2011). On Guinea-Bissau, see Alexander Smoltczyk, "Africa's Cocaine Hub: Guinea-Bissau a 'Drug Trafficker's Dream,'" Spiegel Online International, March 8, 2013, http://www.spiegel.de/international/world/violence-plagues-african-hub-of-cocaine-trafficking-a-887306.html.

18. Farouk Chothia, "Will Somali Islamist Purge Strengthen Al-Shabab?," *BBC News*, http://www.bbc.co.uk/news/world-africa-23146744.

19. On shadow governments and organizational complexity, see O'Neill, *Insurgency and Terrorism: From Revolution to Apocalypse*.

20. This draws from McCormick, "Terrorist Decision Making," 486–90.

21. On groupthink, see Irving L. Janis, *Groupthink*, 2nd ed. (Boston: Houghton Mifflin, 1982).

22. McCormick, "Terrorist Decision Making," 488.

23. Marc Sageman, *Understanding Terror Networks* (Philadelphia: University of Pennsylvania Press, 2004), 154–56.

24. Without a leader or a clear succession plan, groups may struggle to fulfill their obligations. See ibid., 140.

25. Ibid., 146.

26. John Arquilla and David Ronfeldt, "The Advent of Netwar (Revisited)," in *Networks and Netwar: The Future of Terror, Crime, and Militancy*, ed. John Arquilla and David Ronfeldt (Santa Monica, CA: RAND, 2001).

27. O'Neill, *Insurgency and Terrorism: From Revolution to Apocalypse*, 116, 21.

28. Ibid., 116.

29. Arquilla and Ronfeldt, "The Advent of Netwar (Revisited)."

30. Sageman, *Understanding Terror Networks*, 140–41.

31. Rucht, "Leadership in Social and Political Movements: A Comparative Exploration," 113.

32. Olivier Bangerter, "Regulating Armed Groups from Within: A Typology," *Small Arms Survey Research Notes*, no. 13 (2012): 1–3.

33. Shultz, Farah, and Lochard, *Armed Groups: A Tier-One Security Priority*. and Vinci, "The 'Problems of Mobilization' and the Analysis of Armed Groups."

34. Sageman argues al-Qaeda did not engage in top-down recruitment and that members joined based on social and kinship networks. See Sageman, *Understanding Terror Networks*, 107–14.

35. Those joining a group due to "relative deprivation" or "rising expectations" seek short-term benefits even without the group's promises. See the classic statement on relative deprivation in Ted Robert Gurr, *Why Men Rebel* (Princeton, NJ: Princeton University Press, 1970).

36. Anthony Vinci, "The Strategic Use of Fear by the Lord's Resistance Army," *Small Wars and Insurgencies* 16, no. 3 (2005): 371.

37. See Jeremy M. Weinstein, *Inside Rebellion: The Politics of Insurgent Violence* (Cambridge: Cambridge University Press, 2007).

38. See Vinci, "The Strategic Use of Fear by the Lord's Resistance Army," 365. and Kevin C. Dunn, "The Lord's Resistance Army and African International Relations," *African Security* 3, no. 1 (2010): 46–63. The LRA has sought to "cleanse" the Acholi people in northern Uganda, for whom they originally fought against the government, leading to alienation and making coercion and abduction of children a necessity for increasing its membership. On the LRA's child recruitment, also see Christopher Blattman and Jeannie Annan, "On the Nature and Causes of LRA Abduction: What the Abductees Say," in *Lord's Resistance Army: Myth and Reality*, ed. Tim Allen and Koen Vlassenroot (London: Zed Books, 2010).

39. J. Thomas Moriarty, "The Vanguard's Dilemma: Understanding and Exploiting Insurgent Strategies," *Small Wars and Insurgencies* 21, no. 3 (2010): 476–97.

40. Jason Lyall, "Does Indiscriminate Violence Incite Insurgent Attacks? Evidence from Chechnya," *Journal of Conflict Resolution* 53, no. 3 (2009): 331–62.

41. June S. Beittel, *Mexico's Drug Trafficking Organizations: Source and Scope of the Violence*, CRS Report R41576 (Washington, DC: US Congressional Research Service, April 15, 2013) and Tim Padgett, "Guatemala's Kaibiles: A Notorious Commando Unit Wrapped Up in Central America's Drug War," *Time World*, July 14, 2011, world.time.com/2011/07/14/guatemalas-kaibil-terror-from-dictators-to-drug-cartels.

42. For the effects of drone strikes and other government actions on degrading armed group's abilities, see chapter 7.

43. Vinci, "The 'Problems of Mobilization' and the Analysis of Armed Groups," 52–54.

44. Sageman, *Understanding Terror Networks*.

45. "Palestinians Get Saddam Funds," *BBC News*, March 13, 2003, http://news.bbc.co.uk/2/hi/middle_east/2846365.stm.

46. As quoted in Paolo Campana and Federico Varese, "Cooperation in Criminal Organizations: Kinship and Violence as Credible Commitments," *Rationality and Society* 25, no. 3 (2013): 265.

47. Ibid., 267.

48. Ibid.

49. Al-Qaeda is riven with factions, based on social and regional networks, that want to focus their attention on local ("near") enemies, while others argue that the controlling "far enemy" must be eliminated before any changes can take place. See Sageman, *Understanding Terror Networks*. Infighting among factions over this issue has also occurred in al-Shabaab in Somalia. See Farouk Chothia, "Will Somali Islamist Purge Strengthen Al-Shabab?" *BBC News: Africa*, published electronically July 3, 2013, http://www.bbc.co.uk/news/world-africa-23146744.

50. Osama bin Laden distanced himself from the Armed Islamic Group in Algeria because of their high level of violence. See Lauren Vriens, *Backgrounder: Armed Islamic Group*, Council on Foreign Relations, May 27, 2009, http://www.cfr.org/algeria/armed-islamic-group-algeria-islamists/p9154.

51. Mary Kaldor, "In Defence of New Wars," *Stability: International Journal of Security and Development* 2, no. 1 (2013) 1–16.

52. Ugarriza, "Ideologies and Conflict in the Post-Cold War," 84.

53. Juan E. Ugarriza and Matthew J. Craig, "The Relevance of Ideology to Contemporary Armed Conflicts: A Quantitative Analysis of Former Combatants in Colombia," *Journal of Conflict Resolution* 57, no. 3 (2012): 445–77.

54. Thomas A. Marks, "Ideology of Insurgency: New Ethic Focus or Old Cold War Distortions?," *Small Wars and Insurgencies* 15, no. 1 (2004): 107–28.

55. Ugarriza, "Ideologies and Conflict in the Post-Cold War."

56. Ibid. On Colombia, see Ugarriza and Craig, "The Relevance of Ideology to Contemporary Armed Conflicts: A Quantitative Analysis of Former Combatants in Colombia."

57. Ugarriza, "Ideologies and Conflict in the Post-Cold War," 84. Bard O'Neill borrows "commercialist" insurgency from Steven Metz. See O'Neill, *Insurgency and Terrorism: From Revolution to Apocalypse*, 28–29.

58. Harold D. Lasswell, *Politics: Who Gets What, When, How* (New York: Peter Smith Publishing, 1936).

59. Mark E. Stout et al., eds., *The Terrorist Perspectives Project: Strategic and Operational Views of Al Qaida and Associated Movements* (Annapolis, MD: Naval Institute Press, 2008).

60. O'Neill, *Insurgency and Terrorism: From Revolution to Apocalypse*, 20.

61. Ibid., 20–24.

62. Ibid., 24–29. These main goals are echoed by the CIA, which lists revolutionary, reformist, separatist, resistance, and commercialist goals. See CIA, *Guide to the Analysis of Insurgency* (Washington, DC: US Government, 2012), https://http://www.hsdl.org/?view&did=713599.

63. O'Neill, *Insurgency and Terrorism: From Revolution to Apocalypse*, 28.

64. Ibid.

65. Andrew Kydd and Barbara Walter, "The Strategies of Terrorism," *International Security* 31, no. 1 (2006): 52–56.

66. David C. Rapoport, "The Four Waves of Modern Terrorism, " in *Attacking Terrorism: Elements of a Grand Strategy*, ed. Audrey Cronin and James Ludes (Washington, DC: Georgetown University Press, 2004), 47, 61.

67. As a general example, see Mary Kaldor, *New and Old Wars: Organized Violence in a Global Era* (Stanford, CA: Stanford University Press, 2007).

68. Samuel Huntington, *The Clash of Civilizations and the Remaking of World Order* (New York: Touchstone, 1997).

69. O'Neill, *Insurgency and Terrorism: From Revolution to Apocalypse*, 29–31.

70. Crenshaw, "Theories of Terrorism: Instrumental and Organizational Approaches," 20.

71. Stout et al., *The Terrorist Perspectives Project: Strategic and Operational Views of Al Qaida and Associated Movements*, 139.

Chapter Six

External Characteristics

External characteristics are interdependent with each other, as well as constrain and are intertwined with internal characteristics. An armed group may find that its brutal tactics contradict its strategic communication and hamper its ability to secure external support. A group's ideology may be key to not only designing strategy and limiting tactics, but also provide a set of possible like-minded external supporters. The interplay between these two sets of characteristics is fundamental to understanding an armed group's operation.

STRATEGY

An armed group's strategy, like any other strategy, is a process for matching available means to desired ends. Strategies tell us how the armed group is going to use its available resources (means) to achieve its goals or objectives. Tactics link together to achieve the strategy and ultimately achieve the group's goals. While strategy originally referred to the use or threat of military force to achieve political objectives, the term is more broadly construed today to include nonmilitary actions as well, including the use of strategic communications, provision of economic or general welfare services, or psychological operations.

Strategy is frequently conceived of as constituting "ends-ways-means." Both the armed group and state have ends, their ultimate objectives or goals. While these are usually political in nature, TCOs and militias may have economic ends. Groups may have multiple goals, but these usually fit together in a hierarchy, where the achievement of small goals leads to the ability to seek an ultimate goal. Unsuccessfully achieving one goal does not mean that a group's ultimate goal cannot be achieved, but achieving a group's ultimate goal may increase in difficulty or time required.

A group has a collection of means or resources, such as members, weapons, or external support to use in achieving its objective. A group may be able to use all of these means to accomplish their goals, or they may find that different strategies or tactics are needed to make full use of their means. Furthermore, the means may be directly under a group's control, or the group may need to mobilize these means in pursuit of its broader objectives.

A group's "ways" is the strategy a group uses to connect its means to its ends. It is not just a plan of action. It signifies how a group will use the resources at its command to influence a population, such that the population will pressure the government to change its policy to the armed group's desired goal. A strategy may be aimed directly at the government or external actors, as well as the population. This acknowledges at least three potential audiences, and a comprehensive strategy will examine how to influence each one. While an armed group may have three different strategies leading to the achievement of one ultimate goal, it will be incumbent on the armed group to rectify those strategies with each other in its attempts to achieve its goals.

There is a range of theorizing and coherence to armed-group strategies, with some groups going to great lengths to create an overarching strategy that is routinely revisited and strictly adhered to, while others apply a more haphazard approach.[1] It is also difficult for the government to discern a group's true strategy, as well as its objectives, since these may be closely guarded secrets. State-armed group interaction places a great emphasis on information, both in terms of the government gathering information concerning the group, its members, its objectives, and its strategy, as well as in terms of the armed group gathering information concerning the state's regime type, domestic politics, and constraints. Certain strategies may be more applicable against particular regime types or domestic political situations and tracking these may greatly aid the armed group in achieving its goals.

Strategies can come from the leader, a group within the leadership, or copied from an existing model, such as writings by Mao, Mariguela, or Guevara. Additionally, both internal and external factors will influence the strategy that the group is able to design or implement. Because strategy connects means to ends, the group's means provide constraints on the options available. While the group may be able to secure access to additional means from eternal sources or through their own criminal operations, armed groups may encounter great difficulty in securing even the most basic resources.

Due to their limited military capabilities, armed groups are likely to shy away from frontal or direct attacks on government forces. When they do attack government forces, it is likely to be as hit-and-run raids. These tactics are part of a strategy of "protracted war," where the armed group hopes to "prolong the conflict long enough for the government to judge that it is better to negotiate a settlement."[2] This prolonged conflict strategy hopes to wear down the government's will to continue, or may lead to a "death by a thousand cuts," where any one military blow is not a decisive victory, but the accumulation of the cuts leads to the slow disintegration of the government's military power and legitimacy among the people. This is not universal, as the Communist Party of India-Maoist (CPI-Maoist) group had between 6,500–9,500 members in its armed wing in the mid- to late-2000s and thousands more active and passive supporters.[3] Likewise, the Mexican drug cartels have tens of thousands of armed soldiers to face off against the Mexican military and law enforcement.

Additionally, a group's ideology or organization may alter its strategy. If the group is too decentralized in structure, the leadership may be unable to motivate cells to carry out operations that would further achieve strategic goals. If a group is too centralized, operations that revealed group membership might be removed in order to maintain secrecy and security for the group. Ideology may influence a group's tactics and strategy, particularly in the realm of what targets are legitimate.[4] While law enforcement and armed forces members may be "legitimate" targets, according to the armed group's ideology, killing noncombatants may be viewed as unethical, immoral, or in some other way a violation of the group's ideology. These ideological constraints will hamper a group's strategic thinking, either limiting the group's options or opening up different options than traditionally considered. Government will be able to respond best when it fully understands these and other external and internal constraints a group faces as it constructs and carries out its strategy.

Three actors lie outside the armed group's control, but which the armed group nevertheless seeks to exploit in creating its strategy.[5] These highlight the interactive nature of strategic planning. The first actor is the state. An armed-group strategy may be predicated on the notion that a regime type or domestic political situation will produce a given government reaction, leading the group to follow a particular strategy. The domestic population is another key actor. Gaining influence over this group will be the lynchpin for any armed group and failure to secure the support of the people, or at least their neutrality, against the government, will likely lead to failure. International actors—states, other armed groups, or international organizations—also play a role. Their reactions, support, or intervention on behalf of the government may lead to success or failure for the group. While the armed group cannot control these three audiences, they need to create strategy that manipulates them in order to achieve its goals.

This highlights perhaps one of the greatest problems with creating an armed-group strategy: the armed group faces a coordination and free-rider problem in mobilizing the population. The armed group must target the will of the government and domestic and international audiences and be able to sustain their level of effort over the long run. The group must target intangible factors—"influence" over the people or sapping the government's "will"—while generally possessing fewer, less sophisticated weaponry than the state, lacking basic supplies and logistical support, and with a strategy that hinges on motivating people to risk their lives for an abstract, ideological cause.

Strategies must not only seek to achieve a group's objectives, but build a group's capabilities and membership, while degrading the government's legitimacy. The state, on the other hand, starts with advantages in manpower and military might, infrastructure and some level of legitimacy, along with the advantages of controlling the political, economic, and possibly social environment. They may also control the will of the people, especially in situations where the government is elected or relies for support on a majority of the population.

There are a wide variety of armed-group strategies that can be modified and used to achieve a nearly endless number of goals. At the heart of these strategies is a desire to legitimize the armed group, delegitimize the state, and draw the population to the side of the armed group.

Terrorist, Insurgent, and Militia Strategies

Terrorists, insurgents, and militias share common bonds of political objectives and frequently employ violence against competitors. Each group may differ in their formulation of a given strategy according to their objective, organization, ideology, leadership, and relationship with the population. Each of the three archetypes is briefly discussed before moving to a broad consideration of violent and nonviolent strategies.

Terrorists rely on strategies that primarily target violence against civilians. The logic is one of indirect compellence—the terrorist targets the civilian, as a weak and easily scared entity, with the aim of pressuring the civilian to enact political change. Strategies aimed at achieving political objectives frequently use violence as a form of communication and seek to capture the attention of the widest audience possible. Attacking the government is frequently beyond their capabilities, whether because of a lack of military capability, political support, economic funding, or organizational robustness. Terrorist groups may use nonviolent strategies, but these are secondary to the use of violence to sow uncertainty and fear. Furthermore, there is a debate as to the effectiveness of terrorism in the long run. While terrorist groups may achieve goals in the short run, some question whether this is a successful, long-term strategy.[6] Engaging in strategic discussions and outlining and creating a group's strategy does not mean that a group will be successful. It means that armed groups consider their objectives and the means at their disposal to accomplish those goals and does not imply complete information, perfect execution, or certainty of the target's response.

Insurgents and militias show some of the most varied use of strategies, employing both violent and nonviolent strategies. Insurgent groups, due to their desire to win over populations, their greater command of resources, and more complex organization, use violence against the government, while less frequently targeting noncombatants. Both insurgents and militias may provide services to the population to further erode the government's legitimacy, while drawing on other nonviolent strategies to complement their use of violence.

All groups employ some combination of strategies of compellence and strategies of leverage.[7] Building from this, group strategies may include one of four broad categories: coercion, provocation, spoiling, and outbidding.[8] All of these strategies are protracted in nature, as armed groups lack the military capabilities to directly confront the state's armed forces and secure the state's capitulation. Because of this, the armed group usually relies on unconventional tactics, whether against the state, other armed groups, international forces, or the population.

In addition, armed groups may use several nonviolent strategies to gain leverage over the government. Terrorists are unlikely to use these nonviolent strategies, as they are frequently underfunded, organizationally unable to mobilize the resources, and unconcerned with winning over the population. Insurgents and militias, on the other hand, may make greater use of these strategies, with militias likely more limited in their options due to their failed state operating environment. The use of nonviolent strategies may be limited for all armed groups due to their initial small size, ideologies, and objectives.

All armed groups pose a threat to the state's legitimacy. While some strategies rely on controlling territory and the population therein, others seek popular support without concern for territory, while others seek neither popular support nor territory. In the case of TCOs, the population is not only something to be "won" or "lost," but also potential "consumers" or a "market" to be "captured," bringing an added dimension to armed-group strategies.

Coercion

This category encompasses a combination of strategies that impose costs on the government or population in order to achieve the group's goals. The use of force also implies the potential for the future use of force and it is this uncertainty that provides the armed group with greater leverage than their low-level military capabilities might otherwise suggest.[9] The armed group seeks attrition through many small attacks, with the ultimate goal of wearing down the government's will to continue or by draining the government's resources as they combat the insurgent or terrorist group.

Once an attack is carried out, a group has no more leverage. It must threaten another attack in order to seek additional policy concessions from the state. Attacks may be used to create credibility, by demonstrating that a group has the ability and will to carry out an attack while diminishing the state's credibility to provide security.[10] While dictatorships can be targeted by all types of groups, terrorist attacks that aim to coerce the public to pressure their government for a change in policy are more likely to come against democracies, given the obvious increased role of domestic politics in democracies versus dictatorships. This is not to say that terrorists cannot or will not attempt to coerce political or social elites connected to dictatorial regimes, but that it is far more common in democracies.[11]

Insurgents may believe they will defeat the government on the battlefield, whether with a conventional force, as elaborated in Mao Zedong's third phase of insurgency, or possibly through the use of weapons of mass destruction (WMD).[12] Mao built up his conventional force by first indoctrinating the population in order to overcome the free-rider problem; second, he advocated a campaign of ever-increasing guerrilla warfare attacks against the government, culminating in conventional conflicts against government forces. This was to be a protracted conflict involving coercion against the state, as well as the population in cases where communist indoctrination was not enough to motivate them to fight against the government. Much of Mao's protracted, coercive strategy was predicated on using ideology to motivate the people, demonstrating that ideology is a key factor in many different aspects of an armed group.[13]

Provocation

An armed group may attack the government in the hope of provoking a disproportionately large counterstrike.[14] The government's harsh counterstrike is seen as "revealing" the government's true intentions or policy and has the effect of driving the domestic population to support the armed group and to take up arms against the government, decreasing the state's legitimacy, or trigger an international intervention.[15] Che Guavera first advocated this strategy with a rural-based "vanguard" launching attacks on the government and ultimately sparking government repression and popular sympathy.[16] Carlos Marighella adopted this strategy to an urban setting. Writing about transforming Brazil in the late 1960s, he advocated relentless attacks on the government. The outcome, he said, was that "the government has no alternative except to intensify its repression. The police networks, house searches, the arrest of suspects and innocent persons, and the closing off of streets make life in the city unbearable. The military dictatorship embarks on massive political persecution. Political assassinations and police terror become routine."[17] "The general sentiment" among the population concerning these harsh government crack downs "is that this government is unjust, incapable of solving problems, and that it resorts simply to the physical liquidation of its opponents."[18]

Provoking the government into overreacting may also lead to an international intervention in the name of preventing a humanitarian disaster, genocide, or some other feared atrocity.[19] International intervention in Libya in 2011 was predicated on the perceived likelihood of the Libyan regime committing atrocities against the insurgents, militias, and civilians in Benghazi.[20]

Spoiling

Armed groups may try to stop or sabotage peace agreements. Through the use of violence, the armed group casts doubt as to whether the moderates who negotiated the treaty can keep their commitment and implement the peace accord.[21] Hamas attempted to play the role of spoiler against the Oslo Accords and various actors seek to undermine peace and stability in Afghanistan. Instability allows militias and TCOs to economically exploit domestic instability and uncertainty, furthering their economic objective.[22]

Outbidding

An armed group may use violence in competition with another armed group as both seek to garner the support of a population, demonstrate their prowess, signal their policy positions, and stake a claim as the "legitimate" representative of a group by outbidding another group in the use of violence.[23] According to Hoffman, Hamas began the modern practice of suicide bombing in order to compete with and distinguish themselves from rival groups. The fear of fading power relative to Hamas motivated Fatah in November 2001 to set up a suicide unit, the al-Aqsa Martyrs Brigade.[24]

Outbidding may also occur as a group undergoes a period of internal discord. In an environment where exit from a group is possible, members may seek groups that match their preferences. Groups have an incentive to demonstrate their prowess, capabilities, or signal their resolve and objectives by committing violence to differentiate themselves and attract new recruits.[25]

Transnational Criminal Organizations' Strategies

TCOs seek to maximize profit by committing serious crimes while using force, or the threat of force, to intimidate rivals and the government or protect and expand their markets and turf.[26] While TCOs may act in ways similar to other armed groups, in many cases their violence is not perpetrated for the purpose of communicating broader messages to the populace. Since TCOs do not seek political objectives, they are not necessarily looking to influence the population in the same way that politically motivated groups are. TCOs do not need to delegitimize the state or increase their own legitimacy, insofar as they are looking to replace the state. TCOs mainly need to convince possible recruits that they are unlikely to get caught or that the profits are great enough to offset the threat of arrest. While terrorists or insurgents may invite harsh government retaliation in order to generate support, TCOs refrain from provoking state repression. TCOs are likely to employ basic levels of coercion against rivals and law enforcement, with the possibility of some version of outbidding to demonstrate their status vis-à-vis rival organizations. However, a greater level of TCO violence is likely to invite increased government scrutiny and law-enforcement challenges.

All armed groups may also use several nonviolent strategies, including corruption, infiltration, and competition. These are especially prevalent among TCOs that want to avoid government repression. Corruption involves bribing government officials or local security forces to create a context within which TCOs are free to operate. Corruption is frequently a part of weak and postconflict states, as the population may suffer from the time-consistency problem. These populations may not believe the government can provide promised goods in the future, whether economic advancement, education, or health care. When long-term economic rewards appear unlikely, civilians turn to more immediately beneficial, but ultimately market-distorting and harmful, practices such as corruption.

TCOs may infiltrate the government. This "political–criminal nexus" is corruption fully realized, as the TCO controls certain aspects of the state's leadership.[27] The state leadership may also seek out linkages with TCOs in order to line their pockets from illicit transactions. In either scenario, state leaders use the resources of the state to directly benefit TCOs. This creates the ultimate rentier or "criminalized state," as exemplified by political–criminal connections in West Africa states.[28]

Moreover, TCOs may be direct competitors with the state. The TCO may provide services that the state would normally provide, which further delegitimizes the state. TCOs may also place additional burdens on the state's legal or health facilities, tying up already overburdened infrastructure and service provision. These may be by design, as through tactics of "lawfare." Lawfare is "designed to destroy the enemy by using, misusing, and abusing the legal system and the media in order to raise a public outcry against that enemy."[29]

Policy–Strategy Mismatch

A group's means, including threats and violence, are applied so as to achieve a political or economic objective, whether to overthrow the state, spark a mass uprising, or gain monopoly control over trafficking networks. The difficulty comes in matching the strategy with the objectives sought. Force is never perfectly applied and the outcomes are not always those anticipated. A group's strategy must constantly be reexamined and altered, given the current context and the reaction from the governing regime, the population, and international audiences.

Expressive vs. Instrumental Violence

There are two main ways in which armed groups may use violence: for expressive or instrumental purposes.[30] Expressive violence uses violence as a symbolic gesture. Violence can be its own goal, where individuals commit violence for the sake of violence. Individual motivations may run from violence as "art" to lashing out in madness. The expressive use of violence implies that violence is the goal and strategy. If individuals commit violence for no other reason than to commit the violent act, there is no strategy involved. Tactics, strategy, and ends may blur together, as killing others, and possibly oneself if it is a suicide attack, is the expression of a desire to kill others in a "stylish" manner, to express the attacker's innermost feelings, or to undertake "symbolic" violence against a target. The attack serves no purpose, other than to express oneself.

The instrumental use of violence envisions force as a tool or instrument to accomplish a political or economic goal, such as detonating a bomb to terrorize a population into pressuring the regime or assassinating the leader of a country in order to bring about political change. Violence is used to wield influence or control over others. Violence is not the final product; it is a means to carry out a strategy to achieve an objective.

Any one individual's true motives are difficult to discern. There may be multiple explanations for why an individual carried out an attack. Armed groups, as organizations, are more likely to use violence in an instrumental way, communicating the reasons for an attack. The very presence of al-Qaeda "policy documents," for example, demonstrates that armed groups are not just engaging in expressive violence.[31] Armed groups may also harness an individual's desire for expressive violence to further the group's strategy and achieve its objectives.

Instrumental violence may be both simultaneously tactical and strategic. Bombing a gathering of elected officials removes these individuals from power, which is a tactical action. The broader message this attack sends—deterring future politicians by creating the fear and uncertainty of future attacks—is a strategic action. People opposed to the insurgent group will be afraid to run for office, the state will lose legitimacy, and the insurgent group will achieve its goal of delegitimizing the state. The deterrent value of armed group violence—"the expectation of *more* violence that gets the wanted behavior"—is one of the key advantages that armed groups possess in asymmetric warfare.[32]

TACTICS

Tactics are the use of a group's instruments of power while engaged with the enemy. Strategy, as we have seen, directs the use of all of those instruments to achieve a group's objectives. The use of IEDs in Iraq or Afghanistan is a tactic to inflict casualties as part of insurgents' strategy to incrementally increase costs and degrade the international community's will, ultimately creating political pressure on foreign powers to withdraw from those countries. Tactics are frequently discussed in terms of short-term or small-scale actions utilized by small units. Additionally, tactics may create "strategic effects." For example, the use of suicide bombings or a WMD attack may have a much greater impact than shooting two local officials. The line between tactics and strategy may blur as large-scale attacks lead directly to political change. Nevertheless, all tactics have a place in the strategic context, "meaning its place in the group's overall conception of ends and means as well as its role in government-challenger interactions in a given environment."[33]

An armed group's tactics reveal they generally lack the ability to be a larger, conventional force. This does not mean that armed-group tactics are different from small units in a conventional military. Many of the tactics will rely not only on less technologically advanced weaponry or equipment, but also may involve more basic ambushes, bombings, or other actions that do not require advanced communications or material to execute. Armed groups are better served with tactics that do not play to a state' technological or operational superiority. Many of these tactics may also entail low risk for the armed groups. The scarcity of resources and manpower and the lack of resiliency force some groups to use more conservative, low-risk tactics. These may prolong the conflict, as each attack is only a small step toward completing a group's objectives. They may also place a group's success in jeopardy, as low-risk tactics are likely also low-reward tactics.

Conflicts involving armed groups, whether "new wars," "civil wars," or "intrastate wars," create hazy distinctions between combatants and noncombatants, areas of conflict and areas of peace, tactical and strategic level effects, and soldiers and law enforcement.[34] Because these tactics target populations, cities and towns become the zones of conflict, where there are no established frontlines, and law enforcement may become the primary security actors. Armed-group violence is frequently assumed directly by the population, which has a greater impact due to the soft, less resilient nature of the population at large when compared to the government. The next section briefly focuses on several widely used armed-group tactics, including bombings, kidnappings, human trafficking, suicide attacks, and unconventional attacks using WMD.

Bombings

The most prevalent terrorist tactic from 1970–2007 was bombings, which accounted for nearly double the next most frequently used terrorist tactics.[35] The wide availability of materials—from household chemicals and commercially available fertilizers, to surplus war munitions ubiquitous in many post-conflict theaters—combined with their relative ease of design, creation, and lethality, makes these ideal weapons. Additionally, they may be created and left for forces to discover later, allowing the creator time to flee the scene and create more bombs.

Kidnapping

Kidnappings account for only 3 percent of terrorist tactics between 1970–2007, but they have become a well-known tactic in Africa, ranging from AQIM to Somali pirates.[36] James J. F. Forest argues that AQIM is using the "'rhetoric of Islamism' to justify criminal activity."[37] He also notes kidnappings are vastly underreported worldwide, with upwards of 80 percent of kidnappings for ransom never reported to the authorities.[38] Kidnappings of high-profile foreigners make the news, but most victims are local. One study estimates that $1.5 billion was paid to kidnappers in 2010, but because only a small percentage of kidnappers demanded money, it is far more likely that kidnapping is used to seek political concessions.[39] The incident rate of kidnappings as a percentage of overall terrorist tactics has remained relatively steady, as kidnappings as a terrorist tactic have increased at the same time as the overall number of terrorist attacks has increased. There has been a geographic shift over the last few decades of the focal point for kidnapping, from South America to the Middle East and finally to South Asia. The Abu Sayyaf Group (ASG), whose stated goal is to turn the Philippines into an Islamist state, has engaged extensively in kidnapping, likely as a result of Libya's Muammar Qaddafi paying the group $25 million for the ransom of several Western hostages. Fellow Islamic extremists have since accused ASG of "selling out" and becoming little more than a TCO.[40] This highlights the danger for groups too focused on crime to face the potential danger of decreasing their legitimacy.

Human Trafficking

Human trafficking, involving forced labor, recruitment of child soldiers, sex trafficking, slavery, and other forms of indentured servitude, involves the threat or use of force or coercion to exploit people, frequently women and children.[41] Human trafficking can occur within a state's borders and across them, with a multitude of state laws complicating the issue. While human trafficking is a crime with a victim, human smuggling is an illegal activity in which people willingly engage. National authorities and the situation on the ground frequently blur the distinction between trafficking and smuggling. Those who have willingly paid to be smuggled across a border may be coerced into paying more money at the destination or held in isolation or under other unlawful conditions that would constitute a threat of force or coercion.[42] The nebulous division between trafficking and smuggling, combined with their transnational scope, make these difficult problems to combat. Estimates vary widely as to the number affected, with surveys showing that sex trafficking is investigated and brought to trial more often than labor trafficking, which may be more plentiful than reported. The International Labor Organization estimates the number of those in forced labor at 20.9 million as of June 2012, with the US Federal Bureau of Investigation estimating in 2006 that human trafficking generated nearly $10 billion annually for organized crime.[43]

Suicide Attacks

Suicide attacks have received substantial attention in the years since the 9/11 attacks, despite their modern inception in the 1980s.[44] All armed groups may employ suicide attacks, with varying degrees of popular support and motivations, against both combatant and noncombatant targets.[45] While academic discussions of suicide attacks are not unified in a multitude of ways, we can make several broad points and provide a platform on which to build our discussion of analyzing this particular armed-group tactic.

Suicide attacks are not the most common terrorist tactic, nor are they necessarily the most successful. Martha Crenshaw estimates that since 1980s, out of more than twenty thousand terrorist incidents (which does not include domestic incidents prior to 1998), there have been fewer than 1,500 suicide attacks.[46] Furthermore, Assaf Moghadam estimates that only 24 percent of suicide attacks have led to major policy changes.[47] They do, however, receive a substantial amount of media coverage, in that they are generally more lethal than conventional terrorist attacks and are designed to communicate a message far beyond their local, intended target.[48] Killing oneself in order to kill others for a cause may seem anathema to most people. The strident message that this tactic sends to the target and others viewing the attack and its aftermath help to justify the terrorists' view that the benefits of these attacks greatly outweigh any costs.

These tactics also benefit from being relatively inexpensive, easy to perpetrate, believed to have a greater likelihood of success, and are easier to execute than conventional terrorist attacks.[49] This is largely due to the human delivery vehicle, who is able to negotiate his or her way past obstacles, overcome problems, and make an informed, last-minute decision as to the ideal time and place to strike. All of this leads to the fundamental question of why these attacks are not used more often. If they are easy, cheap, and successful, why have more groups not carried them out to a greater degree?

Terrorists, insurgents, and militias may all use suicide attacks. The phrase "suicide attacks" highlights the notion that "suicide terrorism" refers specifically to those groups—terrorists, by most definitions—that carry out suicide attacks against noncombatants, while insurgents do so against government or military targets.[50] When carried out against the military, suicide attacks are not "terrorist" attacks. This is not to say that terrorist groups may never carry out attacks against the government or military, but if the purpose of terrorism is to create fear among civilians in order to pressure the government to make policy changes, then terrorist groups, by definition, should only be seeking to kill noncombatants as part of their broader strategy.

Insurgents, seeking the support of the people, may be unwilling to use suicide tactics that are designed to kill and injure those whose support they seek. Insurgent groups are more likely to target military forces. Militias, who may occupy a middle ground between insurgent and terrorist, are more likely to be predatory toward the population they control. Nevertheless, because these groups are primarily active in failing or failed states where the central government has crumbled, suicide attacks against government forces may not be part of their greater strategy. For many militia groups, they are the local or regional authority and, while preying on the population economically, may not find much use for suicide tactics. TCOs are similarly constrained as insurgents, in that their goals require a population to act as consumers for their product or as supporters and workers in their criminal networks. Eliminating the population through suicide attacks—or any large-scale attacks—decreases their consumer base and may turn the population to seek support from the government, especially as the TCO may not provide alternative sources to government services.

While any group may use suicide attacks, Islamic terrorist groups have been responsible for a majority of suicide attacks since 9/11.[51] This raises questions about the role of religion in justifying or motivating suicide attacks. Religious ideology may help an armed group overcome various internal problems related to the coordination problem and the free-rider problem. Individuals must overcome strong norms against suicide, as well as a basic self-preservation instinct. A combination of religious justifications and grievances may help armed groups overcome the taboos inherent in this tactic.[52] No matter the individual motivation to undertake a suicide attack, the organization is drawn to them for instrumental reasons—to credibly communicate messages about the likelihood of future attacks, a group's dedication to a cause, or a group's policy positions, such as its unwillingness to negotiate. Suicide attacks send a message that is designed to reach far beyond their intended target.

WMD Attacks

Terrorist groups have expressly stated their desire to obtain WMD. Other groups may have little incentive to acquire these weapons. They are too indiscriminate for the insurgent and would adversely affect the very population with whom they want to generate legitimacy. WMD would do little for a militia, save for invite massive retaliation from the state and also adversely affect a population. Even if the militia were antagonistic and predatory against the local population, WMD use might adversely affect the territory they control. TCOs do not desire to overthrow governments, nor bring unwanted attention on themselves. WMD would bring unwanted state repression, as well as the risk of killing off their customer base.

The question of how armed groups would gain access to WMD, specifically nuclear weapons, has been frequently discussed, but with little solid evidence to support various claims. Examining the technical and empirical difficulties in acquiring the needed resources and building a nuclear weapon, John Mueller argues terrorists are unlikely to be able to construct a nuclear device.[53] Keir A. Liber and Daryl G. Press note states would not transfer nuclear weapons to armed groups, as neither the supporting state nor the terrorist group could remain anonymous.[54] Taking a different approach, Tim Sweijs and Jaakko Kooroshy state chemical and biological weapons may be easier to obtain. Additionally, these weapons may be more tailored through biochemical engineering, and it is not the catastrophic nuclear attack that is the most likely threat today. Many states have sought to use advanced riot control chemical weapons that incapacitate, rather than kill.[55] This could open new avenues for armed groups, but it is unclear whether mass incapacitation sends the same message as mass killing and whether these weapons are of use to armed groups.

Tactics–Strategy Mismatch

Armed group's tactics may not successfully fulfill the group's strategy and help in achieving the group's objectives. Tactics that work against the achievement of a group's strategy also work against the successful achievement of a group's objectives. Armed groups should constantly evaluate their tactics in light of their effect and the reaction they generate.

Issues to consider when examining the possibility of a tactics–strategy mismatch include whether the tactics are more costly for the enemy than for the group; whether the tactics are sustainable, in terms of manpower, materiel, and in generating the desired results from the target; and whether the armed group is able to successfully integrate the tactics into their overall ideology and strategy. There is also the question of whether tactics can stand alone, or whether they need additional factors to generate a strategic effect.

Certain tactics may only work if accompanied by a verbal or written explanation, or if carried out in a particular time period or in a particular location. This context specific nature of some tactics may be misperceived and need further elaboration on social media or through some other strategic communication.

As with a group's strategy, it is possible that one attack or operation may lead to an unexpected success or failure that the group must either capitalize on or quickly seek to rectify. While one attack may not destroy a group, it may lead to such a reaction from the government that it brings much more government attention than was intended. These outlier tactical successes or failures may be difficult to predict, but a sustained campaign of indiscriminate violence, or an attack carried out on an unprecedented level or in a unique and possibly norm-violating manner—such as the 9/11 attacks or a WMD strike—may bring with it unknown, but potentially negative consequences. Large-scale attacks or actions that strike at the very heart of a society's norms may provoke the government into a reaction far beyond what the armed group envisioned.

STRATEGIC COMMUNICATIONS

Armed groups use strategic communications to control the flow of information to a target audience—whether the host government, domestic population, or international audience—with the strategic goal of developing a narrative. This narrative is a means of framing a conflict in a context that is ideologically advantageous to the armed group. All armed groups, no matter their objective, want to create a narrative, a story for public consumption that can attract domestic and international supporters and generally build the group's legitimacy. The group's ideology provides the content that is distributed through communication and information operations. The goal of communicating with outsiders is to relate ideas to deeds and seek greater acceptance of the group's ideas. As many of today's conflicts are "wars amongst the people," according to Rupert Smith, access to the media in order to directly control the group's message is a key component in the contemporary security environment.[56]

Violence may not be sufficient to convey an armed group's message, or may be misinterpreted by those viewing it. Alternatively, state-run media outlets may purposely try to misrepresent an armed group's actions, or present an attack in the worst light possible for an armed group. Independent media may also misinterpret an attack or other deed, necessitating that the armed group provide their own explanation of why they undertook an attack and the reasoning behind it.

Strategic communication can be instrumental in the early stages of an armed group, when the group is attempting to establish itself and seeks greater membership. Strategic communication can be hampered by state repression, as individuals and groups with similar ideologies may find it difficult to coordinate and join together due to constant monitoring, harassing, and jailing potential or presumed members. While using nonviolent means of communicating their ideology and goals to the outside may be all that many groups are able to perform in the early stages of their existence, violence quickly becomes the means by which armed groups communicate their ideology and objectives.

Nonviolent strategic communication can take many different forms, from letter writing, to the publication and dispersal of anonymous pamphlets, to the Mexican drug cartels' use of sheets hung from freeway overpasses advertising employment or providing warnings to other cartels, the authorities, or civilians.[57] While pre-Internet communications also relied on radio and television, these were generally indirect means of communication. The armed group, having committed an act of violence, would then hope to capture the attention of a wide audience through television or radio news coverage. Armed groups, however, generally did not have their own strategic communication infrastructure.[58] Groups such as Hezbollah and al-Qaeda today may own, operate, and control their own media outlets, including television and radio stations. Hezbollah operates *Al Manar* ("The Beacon"), a satellite television station broadcasting from Beirut, Lebanon. The channel has music videos, news reports, sports programs, dramas, and family programming, many with anti-Israel and anti-United States messages. Their website contains links to Hezbollah Secretary General Hassan Nasrallah speeches and other Hezbollah propaganda.[59] A second Hezbollah media outlet, *Al Moqawama* ("The Resistance"), is geared more toward supporters and potential supporters and broadcasts martial music, Nasrallah speeches, and other propaganda to further the Hezbollah narrative.[60] These media outlets allow groups to directly control the message they are trying to communicate.

The advent of the Internet has allowed armed groups to control their own low-cost communication infrastructure and reach a wider audience. Today, terrorists and many other groups see the Internet more as a tool than a target.[61] Cyberterrorism, where groups may target corporate or government websites, or seek to take down opposition websites, is not necessarily the greatest online threat from most armed groups. Instead, it is the armed group's use of the Internet as a "force amplifier" that is key to understanding how and why groups use any and all online resources available, often without government interference or even awareness that such sites or activity exists.[62]

The Internet has proven to be an ideal tool for nonstate armed groups. It has been key in targeting multiple audiences at the same time, as groups provide different websites for those with a passing interest, and password-protected or more anonymous forums for members. Websites, Facebook pages, blogs, chat rooms, and Twitter accounts allow for the anonymity that groups desire without exposing them to increased state surveillance. While any public or external activity runs the risk of bringing increased scrutiny to the armed group, the greater levels of anonymity available by logging into chat rooms from cybercafés, for example, provides a method by which armed groups can balance both the need to provide an unfiltered message and public presence with security to protect the group and its members. Furthermore, with the explosion of smart phones throughout many areas that lack traditional telephone lines, Internet access, and radio and television stations, Internet access has opened up vast new audiences that armed groups previously lacked the ability to contact.[63]

One difficulty of a strategy of relying solely on the Internet is the ability to fully radicalize an individual may only come about through face-to-face contacts.[64] If a precursor to joining an armed group is membership in a social network, it may be more difficult to convince an individual not in a social network to join, or for him to be accepted by other members, without face-to-face interaction.

There are three main audiences that all communications target. The first is the domestic population, to include current and potential supporters. Communications to this group may include information on how to join the group, what the group's ideology and objectives are (or at least watered down or "contextually acceptable" objectives and goals), and information that attempts to further shape the context within which the armed group is operating. As with every audience, the information and narrative attempts to increase the armed group's legitimacy, while diminishing the government's legitimacy. Presenting the armed group as successful, with reasonable objectives that are prohibited by the government, is all part of creating a narrative.

Another frequent target is the government and their domestic supporters. Communications may seek to delegitimize the government's ideology, to highlight supposed crimes or atrocities the government has committed, or to inform government employees and civilians of the futility of their actions. Casting doubt on or disparaging government actions, noting government's inconsistencies or discriminatory policies, or influencing those charged with creating government policy are targeted at both potential supporters and enemies. While it may be more difficult to sway those in the military or law enforcement who are dedicated to combating the armed group, sowing the seeds of doubt and chipping away at the government's legitimacy is part of the long-term political struggle accompanying any group's violent acts.

Finally, armed groups may target the international community. This can range from international organizations such as the United Nations to neighboring or regional states to influential—frequently wealthy or politically connected—individuals. Armed groups may be seeking international recognition, monetary aid, humanitarian relief, or military aid in their fight against the government. The importance of external support is discussed in more detail below, but the ability to attract an international audience and supporters may mean the difference between an armed group's success and failure. While more sophisticated communications may target all actors at once—and the overlap in messages is unavoidable—the plethora of media outlets means that groups can narrowly target key audiences with specifically tailored messages.[65]

Al-Shabaab live-tweeted their attack on the Westgate shopping mall in Nairobi, Kenya, in September 2013. While their Twitter account has been taken down several times, they have had upwards of twenty thousand followers and post in both Arabic and English. The group defended and clarified the reasoning behind the attack, warned Kenyans there would be future attacks in retaliation for Kenya's forays into Somalia, and provided a narrative of the conflict in Somalia.[66]

While the variety of audiences may mean a variety of messages, certain themes are likely to emerge from any armed-group communication.[67] One theme is the justification of the use of violence. Frequently, armed groups will argue that due to their weakness and government repression, the group is unable to make their voice heard. Violence is the group's only means of access to the political process. Moreover, communiqués attempt to delegitimize the government and cast it in the worst possible light. Strong, unequivocal language arguing of the "evil nature," "illegitimacy," or "crimes" the government is alleged to have committed are targeted at both armed group and regime supporters. This plays into the armed group's narrative whereby the government and its possible external allies are victimizing and unfairly discriminating against those in society whom the armed group represents.[68] These messages strike at the government's legitimacy and seek to both tear down the government and simultaneously build up the armed group's legitimacy. Correspondingly, while armed groups justify their use of violence, they also want to appear nonviolent and attempting peaceful solutions. This builds support with potential domestic supporters, who may find this as more evidence of the government's illegitimacy or discrimination, as well as attracting support from the international community and potential supporters who do not necessarily want to be seen supporting violence. While the appearance of nonviolence and apparent willingness to negotiate does not mean it is actually occurring, it may generate necessary political capital among many different parties, both foreign and domestic.

Armed groups also use violence as a means of strategic communication, as Marighella notes, "Each individual urban guerrilla operation is in itself a form of armed propaganda."[69] Given the nature of armed groups—clandestine, loosely organized, and oftentimes lacking popular support—it is difficult for armed groups to credibly communicate their intentions, goals, and capabilities. The need to make credible threats, so that their demands and calls for policy change will be taken seriously, forces them to use violence to back their threats. Violence signals the group's resolve and capabilities to the government, while it also communicates the group's goals and even ideology to the population at large.

The success or failure of armed-group attacks is also a form of communication, as great success may be used as a recruiting tool and a demonstration of a group's "legitimacy" and "efficacy," which strengthens external support and internal cohesion.[70] Failure may demonstrate that a group lacks the capabilities, knowledge, or ability to successfully plan and execute an attack, which can demoralize those in the group, while creating an impression of illegitimacy among the population writ large. Even if the attack's success or failure is a coincidence of factors, the armed group can trumpet any fortuitous outcome as a recruiting and propaganda tool, while the state can use a group's failed attack to further marginalize, demoralize, and denigrate the group.

Armed groups' use of violence as a form of strategic communication presents them with two problems. The first is how to contend with attacks that fail. Potential sponsors or members may react poorly to a failed attack. Groups may deny responsibility for a failed attack, place the blame on others, or declare "success" by claiming the event brought important issues to light. The second problem is the degree to which violence—and its outcomes— work against a group's message. The Taliban attempted to explain their failed and headline-grabbing attack on fifteen-year-old Malala Yousafzai in 2012. After an outpouring of support and outrage at the attack, a senior Taliban leader claimed she was attacked because she "smeared" the Taliban, not because the Taliban disapproved of girls' education.[71] Likewise, the Armed Islamic Group's (GIA) indiscriminate use of violence in Algeria in the 1990s alienated many potential supporters, both domestically and internationally.

Armed groups signal their interests, intentions, and objectives through the use of violent and nonviolent measures. Violence demonstrates a group's commitment to a cause and increases pressure on the population and government to enact policy change in ways other methods may not be able to replicate. Nevertheless, violence is frequently a blunt instrument that may not deliver the message an armed group desires. Nonviolent communications are frequently needed to better connect with the desired population.

EXTERNAL SUPPORT

The most important aspect to whether a group survives and succeeds is external support.[72] External support is frequently characterized as a set of *linkages* in a larger network rather than as a strict bilateral relationship. This means that rather than rely on one big sponsor state as was common during the Cold War, armed groups may rely on multiple, smaller contributions from regional states, other armed groups, refugees, and diaspora populations.[73] This network and linkage between diverse actors means that the armed group receiving the aid has demands placed on it from multiple sources, all wanting their own payback for support—the armed group may be in a difficult position to actually deliver what the supporter wants.

There are three broad motivations for why outside groups support armed groups. Governments may seek to satisfy pressure from domestic constituencies who maintain ideological, ethnic, or religious ties with an armed group. A second motivation concerns the supplier-armed group alignment on ultimate objectives and the supplier's inability or unwillingness to act. The supplier may lack the capacity to act, they may lack the domestic support to act and need to do so surreptitiously through an armed group, it may be cheaper to act through an armed group, or the supplier may simply wish to free-ride on the armed group's actions. Alternatively, the supplier seeks to use this support to pressure the targeted state, with the armed group's needs or interests tangential to the supporting state's interests.[74]

External armed-group support exists across several dimensions. The external support may be open or clandestine, as well as direct or indirect (or "active" versus "passive" support, in Daniel Byman's language). Moreover, this support may be willingly or unwillingly provided. All of these dimensions come with varying degrees of costs and benefits. Given the differing reactions these dimension are likely to generate, state may have an incentive to not only provide clandestine support, but also disavow knowledge of it. Open, active support may be used to signal and seek leverage over the state hosting an armed group.

At the same time it must be noted that armed groups—and their external supporters—are playing a multiple-level game. Armed groups are playing a game with the actor(s) supporting them, the government(s) opposing them, and, in some cases, their domestic constituency if they are not responding to the domestic base of support. These issues apply not only to the armed group, but in the case of the various governments involved as well. These multiple constituencies all have their own costs and benefits, which makes understanding when external actors will support armed groups—and what is required from armed groups to secure external funding—a challenging proposition.

For both the supplier and target (armed group), there is a principal–agent problem—one group cannot control the other group or dictate a particular policy. The armed group cannot force the multitude of states, diaspora and refugee groups, NGOs, and others to give it supplies, or to not supply a rival—there are too many suppliers, leaving the armed group with little power or sway, and the suppliers may have other armed groups they could support. The states, armed groups, diaspora and refugee groups, NGOs, and others cannot force the armed group to attack or act as it wishes because each supporting group is providing a smaller amount of aid than one of the superpowers in the past—each group has less overall influence with each armed group it supplies. In addition, the state, group, or NGOs will be hurt if there is a human rights violation and may not want to be associated with an armed group.

External support is a product of supply and demand. From the supply-side perspective, one of the most immediate points concerns the effects of the end of the Cold War. The break up of the Soviet Union and Warsaw Pact flooded the markets with small arms at the same time official backing and funding of communist insurgents evaporated. The United States no longer supplied anti-Communist insurgents in the Global South and the remaining major powers were reluctant to get involved in conflicts tangential to their national security. Democratic countries may also be mindful of armed-group proxies who violate international norms or laws, reducing their incentives to risk state support of autonomous, independent actors. States must be concerned with the oversight problems inherent in the principal–agent problem in a globalized world. The implication is that as more countries transition toward democracies, there may be fewer state-sponsors of armed groups.

The decrease in defense spending across the major power reduces available funds for armed groups and smaller states. This decrease in funding to smaller states has led to the need for alternatives to conventional forces. In order to project power and pursue regional foreign-policy goals, smaller states are forced to rely on less expensive alternatives such as armed groups. Relatedly, the oft-noted desire by Western politicians to avoid casualties, not risk expensive military equipment in a time of austerity, and appease domestic constituencies is yet another factor.[75]

Additional supply-side factors involve the degree of ideological agreement between the supporter and armed group, as well as the conviction with which the supporter not only holds the ideology, but also desires its furtherance or dissemination.

State sponsors may be particularly loath to commit resources to armed groups if it means potential retaliation from the target state.[76] This may be the fear of direct military retaliation, or the violation of economic, political, or social relations between the supporter state and the target state. US citizens' support of the Irish Republican Army created difficulties between the US and UK governments, based on their wide-ranging "special relationship."

The demand-side of the external support equation involves examining key aspects of the armed group. A group's leadership and ideology are key to whether they receive aid. Armed groups must understand their audience and how to connect with potential supporters. This can be accomplished through a charismatic leader or the presentation of an appealing ideology that resonates with those the group is trying to persuade.[77] Groups craft well-honed "strategic narratives" in which they demonstrate their legitimacy, expose government brutality, and present their case in a cogent, compelling story. Excessive violence, inept strategic planning, or inarticulate spokesmen reduce the likelihood of securing external support.

In addition, armed groups have some degree of local resourcing and self-reliance the group can maintain. Groups from areas with more "lootable" resources, such as diamonds or timber, may be more successful and find it easier to secure political recognition or legitimacy from outside groups. Poorly resourced groups may have such a high need for support that external groups believe they are not viable actors. Groups with few resources, weak leadership, few members, and a dearth of operational success may find external support difficult to attract.

Open/Clandestine

States may openly acknowledge their support for an armed group for several reasons. The first is to send a message to a rival state in order to demonstrate power capabilities and create a deterrent effect. Second, open support of an armed group signals the target government and the international community. External support and recognition may confer legitimacy on the armed group and weaken the legitimacy of the target government. Third, it signals the domestic population in the home state that the state is supporting a similar ethnic or religious group. This may create domestic unity through the rally round the flag effect.

Clandestine support may be due to negative political ramifications of being linked to a group accused of human rights violations, or that is seen as an enemy of the state. States may want to support insurgents overthrowing a government, but cannot gather enough intelligence to discern the group's true objectives or preferences.

Active vs. Passive Support

State and nonstate actors actively aid an armed group when they act on its behalf. States provide passive support by not prosecuting individuals who provide aid or travel abroad to fight with an armed group or by turning a blind eye when an armed group uses a state's territory for sanctuary. States provide passive support because there is domestic political support for an armed group, the armed group poses little threat to the host government, there is a low cost to inaction by the host government, and the state may lack the capacity to deny support to the armed group.[78] Passive support also provides the state diplomatic cover, as it can deny that it actively supported the armed group. Active and passive support may be provided at the same time, such as providing training, materiel, and safe haven to an armed groups.

Willing/Unwilling

Willing support for an armed group is a directed policy by the state as part of furthering its own policies with the goal of achieving a particular objective. Unwilling support for an armed group comes when a state is unable to control its borders, lacks the capacity to stop illicit activity, or in some other way is unable to stop an armed group from exploiting the state and its resources. This is also a problem for NGOs or charities that may not be able to differentiate between insurgent members and noncombatants when providing humanitarian aid or services. Armed groups may also steal supplies or interdict aid deliveries. In addition, diasporas may find it difficult to differentiate between legitimate and illegitimate charity organizations when making donations.

Political Ramifications

The political ramifications of these three dimensions—for both the state or nonstate supplier and the armed group seeking support—are key factors when considering whether and how to support a group. Some states may fear the political backlash from their domestic populations if they do not aid fellow ethnic or religious groups. States may face domestic or international condemnation for supporting groups accused of human rights violations, or are at odds with large minority groups within the country.

States may also fear retaliation by the target government. External support for an armed group against a legally constituted government is considered intervention and a violation of sovereignty under international law and norms.[79] Supporting an armed group inside of a rival country is likely to lead to conflict between the two states. Additionally, while supporting armed groups may potentially lead to the overthrow of a rival, or at least tying up military capabilities and draining resources, it may have further, regional effects. The 2013 civil war in Syria pits armed groups backed by Iran, the United States, and Saudi Arabia in opposition, while also drawing in Russia, Turkey, Israel, and Jordan. Russia's offer to sell air-defense missiles to Syria was met with US urging to not inflame the region and upset the balance of power, especially in regard to Syrian–Israeli relations.[80]

The armed group may seek open, direct support from a state or international organization in order to garner legitimacy. Nevertheless, armed groups, as discussed in chapter 2, are clandestine organizations by nature, and any exposure may create problems. Armed groups may desire passive or clandestine support, in order to not be associated with a state that they view as ideologically hostile and working at odds with their ultimate objectives. Additionally, they may fear that open acknowledgement of support provides outside actors a new avenue to attack.

The last, and potentially most negative, aspect of external support from the perspective of the armed group is the degree to which the supporting actor will demand changes to the group's policies, operations, or objectives. The armed group may be giving up some amount of freedom in return for external support. The principal–agent problem that states face—the question of whether the state can provide adequate oversight of the armed group in order to ensure the satisfactory accomplishment of their goals—impacts the armed group as well. The armed group is the target of the state's oversight, and as such, the state may find that it wants to limit or proscribe the group's actions. At best, the state may make suggestions about tactics, targets, or routine procedures. At worst, from the armed group's perspective, states may dictate objectives, strategies, or ideological constraints.

What Does Support Look Like?

This section briefly outlines some of the types of support armed groups receive.[81] Because of the varied nature of armed groups—their differing objectives, ideologies, and leadership—the form support takes will vary widely, and the importance of any one type of support will vary by group and the environment. Two commodities—money and safe haven—provide the greatest boost to an armed group, no matter the group and circumstance. The remaining issues have all been key to a variety of armed groups. It should also be noted that while we frequently think of support in a physical sense, many of these factors, as exemplified by both money and safe havens, can be thought of as having a "mental" or "virtual" form that means the support occurs through online resources or provides intellectual freedom or like-minded individuals who share the group's ideology, narrative, or objectives. As such, support may be offered in overlapping and complementary forms.

Money, according to Robert J. Art, is the "most liquid asset of all" and has the "highest fungibility" among all forms of statecraft.[82] It can be used to buy "good press, top-flight international negotiators, smart lawyers, cutting-edge technology, bargaining power in international organizations," along with being able to generate military power.[83] While all of these apply to armed groups, many groups have more basic needs, such as purchasing weapons and ammunition, paying salaries and social services for the group's members, or bribing officials. As the most "fungible" form of power, money can also be used to buy political or legal representation or support for a group, and provide online safe havens and means of recruiting for an armed group. Many groups have difficulty generating money internally and must engage in illicit activities or attract external supporters. Armed groups today resort to crime, in many cases, as external support has decreased with the end of the Cold War.

Safe haven is the second key form of support for most armed groups. Sanctuary is frequently presented as a physical refuge, often across state borders, an isolated geographic space, or ungoverned territory. These may also include ideologically like-minded communities in a physical or virtual safe haven. Mental retreats may be as important as physical space. A group's inability to rest, train, and regroup may decrease the group's overall success.

In addition to money and safe havens, there are additional two broad categories of support. Intangible support includes political support and propaganda, intelligence, training, organizational aid, and inspiration. Tangible forms of support include direct military support and the provision of weapons and materiel. Armed-group competition for influence over a given population may lead them to favor certain forms of intangible support. Tangible support, given its greater visibility, may entail greater political risks from external sources and occur less frequently than intangible aid. Intangible forms of support can translate into the successful completion of kinetic operations or political subversion, while tangible support may be parlayed into propaganda, aid in gathering intelligence, or increase recruitment.

Political support and propaganda can be accomplished by planting stories in newspapers, publishing pro-armed-group tracks, favorably mentioning armed groups in official government documents, or not including groups on the US State Department's Foreign Terrorist Organization list.[84] Additional actions can be taken through press conferences or pushing for international recognition through voting in the United Nations or other international organization. A state may oppose international assistance to the host government opposing the armed group.

The United States may meet with armed-group leaders in the White House or allow Congressional members to meet with armed-group leaders. President Reagan was photographed with a "Stop Communism Central America" t-shirt, which he used to bring further attention to his fight with Congress over $100 million in funding for the Contras in Nicaragua.[85] On another occasion, he drew parallels between the Contras and America's Founding Fathers:

> Yet despite all the repression and Soviet intervention, the people of Nicaragua still cling to their dream of freedom. In the best tradition of our Founding Fathers, they formed a democratic resistance against tyranny, one of the larg-

est peasant armies in the world, with more than 17,000 freedom fighters called contras. And as the contras have grown stronger, the Communist regime has grown shakier.[86]

President Reagan also publicly championed the Afghan resistance against the Soviet invasion:

> Coincidentally, the day after Afghanistan Day, this country plans to launch the third Columbia space shuttle. Just as the Columbia, we think, represents man's finest aspirations in the field of science and technology, so too does the struggle of the Afghan people represent man's highest aspirations for freedom. The fact that freedom is the strongest force in the world is daily demonstrated by the people of Afghan. Accordingly, I am dedicating on behalf of the American people the March 22d [*sic*] launch of the Columbia to the people of Afghanistan.[87]

In both of these cases, President Reagan supported the armed groups by legitimizing their objectives and goals and tying them directly to major US accomplishments and the founding ideals of the country. This public, political support sent clear signals to the Soviet Union, the public, Congress, and the armed groups concerning US support and objectives.

Training may come from states that directly run training camps for armed groups, as Libya did in the 1980s.[88] Individual armed-group leaders or members who are former military officers may have received military training in the United States, UK, France, China, the Soviet Union, and now Russia as part of their military service prior to joining an armed group. Leaders or members may also have been educated at overseas universities prior to returning to their countries to lead armed groups.

Outside states face difficulty in supply intelligence and organizational aid and both are seldom decisive to a group's success. Local forces are likely to have better intelligence than outside forces and understand the local environment in ways the external forces may not. In much the same way, organizational aid may be of limited value, as the armed group will be better suited to organize in a manner that best suits the local environment, culture, and personalities within the group.

The last intangible form of support, inspiration, may help an armed group with the coordination problem in its initial formation but is unlikely to sustain the group for long. Outside inspiration may evoke powerful emotions for the creation of a group or create a rallying point or demonstrate that the armed group is part of a larger, more international movement, but if continued outside inspiration is required to maintain the group, members are likely to lose confidence in the group's leaders. Inspiration provided from outside sources, bereft of local input, may not fully address, or may even be at odds with, local practices and customs.

States and nonstate actors may also provide tangible support to an armed group, such as direct military support in the form of providing irregular troops or others to fight alongside armed groups, airstrikes in support of armed groups, military airlift or other such military aid, or full-scale conventional military operations carried out in addition to or in lieu of armed-group troops. While rare, this provides not only tangible aid but also intangible propaganda support. The Pakistani Taliban announced in July 2013 that they had sent troops to fight alongside al-Nusra Front, an al-Qaeda affiliate in Syria. This not only increased pressure on the Assad regime, but also exacerbated tensions between the Free Syrian Army and the al-Qaeda affiliated insurgents, who had just assassinated a top Free Syrian Army commander.[89]

A related issue is the provision of weapons and materiel to the armed group. These can take the form of small arms, vehicles, or food and supplies, or potentially "game-changing" weapons such as man-portable surface-to-air missiles. These weapons and supplies may be directly provided from the government's stores, or more indirectly supplied through illicit market purchases or third parties.

What Does Support Do?

External funding is integral to many other areas considered here: it may determine resource availability and impact an armed group's means, strategy, tactics, and organization. One of the most fundamental aspects of outside support is the degree to which it can make an armed group a viable threat to the government. Outside support may be key in the beginning of the armed group's life, as the group has to overcome problems including a potential lack of organization, lack of members, lack of resources, and very basic logistical issues including a lack of weapons, meeting places, and means of communication. Armed groups must initially overcome the free-rider problem, whereby the group must convince enough members to join the group and risk injury, death, or material destitution and government persecution, while any concessions they win from the government will be distributed to the entire population or the subset of the population the group seeks to represent. External support makes it easier for the group to not only organization itself, but convince potential members it is a viable group with some likelihood of achieving success.

Support for an armed group can bring increased domestic and international visibility. States may directly advocate for a group on the international stage, which benefits armed groups in several ways. This potentially increases a group's legitimacy and credibility by demonstrating outsiders' commitment to the group; it can bring in other supporters who may not have known a group existed; it can highlight the group's successes, creating a bandwagoning effect; or it may bring pressure on the government to end the conflict. The internationalization of a conflict is frequently accompanied by increased scrutiny.

Support can also increase the lethality and scale of armed-group operations. This is due to the added money, material, or manpower at a group's disposal. The United States provided the Afghanistan mujahedeen with surface-to-air missiles, which allowed the various groups to attack Soviet helicopters. Libyan support of Tuareg insurgents—both actively through Libyan use of Tuareg mercenaries and passively through Libya's inability to control their armories after the state's collapse—enabled the Tuaregs to return to Mali and seize control of the northern half of the country.[90] French entrance into the American Revolution internationalized the conflict, as Britain feared French challenges not only in Europe, but also in the Caribbean. This lent credibility to the American colonists and constrained British actions.[91]

External support may provide the armed group political support and propaganda effects, in addition to military success on the ground, by "internationalizing" the conflict. This signals that the armed group is part of a larger movement and may help overcome coordination and free-riding problems by demonstrating that the armed group is successful. In addition, tangible support's visibility credibly commits the state to supporting the armed group. Alternatively, visible external support may be seen as demonstrating that the armed group is unable to attract members on its own, lacks the capabilities to carry out their own military operations, or is unable to provide a credible alternative to the government. Additionally, the influx of "foreign fighters" may erode the credibility and legitimacy of the armed group and create tension between "locals" and "foreign fighters." External support is key to an armed group's success, but may be a double-edged sword for fledgling armed groups. Visibility and timing are important factors in determining whether armed groups can effectively channel support to achieve their objectives.

DISCUSSION QUESTIONS

1. At what point does an armed group become beholden to an external supporter?
2. If suicide attacks are cheap, easy, and successful, why do we not see more groups perpetuating more of these attacks?
3. Who decides what the strategies and tactics are: leaders, followers, or some other actor?
4. What penalties, if any, does an armed group face if it is caught lying in its strategic communications?
5. Some argue that broadcasting interviews with terrorists or providing excessive coverage of a group, its goals, and its operations confers

legitimacy and "global actor" status on them. Does this lead to the conclusion that media should be forbidden from talking to these groups and airing interviews or stories?

6. How might a group's choice of strategy and tactics be difficult to reconcile with its strategic communication?

RECOMMENDED READINGS

Daniel Byman, *Deadly Connections: States that Sponsor Terrorism* (Cambridge: Cambridge University Press, 2007).

Brigitte L. Nacos, *Mass-Mediated Terrorism: The Central Role of the Media in Terrorism and Counterterrorism* (Lanham, MD: Rowman and Littlefield Publishers, 2007).

Robert I. Rotberg, *Corruption, Global Security, and World Order* (Washington, DC: Brookings Institution Press, 2009).

United Nations Global Initiative to Fight Human Trafficking (UN GIFT) and UN Office on Drugs and Crime (UNODC), "An Introduction to Human Trafficking: Vulnerability, Impact and Action," Background Paper, 2008.

United Nations Office on Drugs and Crime (UNODC), *Global Report on Trafficking in Persons, 2012* (New York: United Nations, 2012).

United States Department of State, *Trafficking in Persons Report 2013*, June 2013, http://www.state.gov/j/tip/rls/tiprpt/2013/index.htm.

NOTES

1. See Brynjar Lia and Thomas Hegghammer, "Jihadi Strategic Studies: The Alleged Al Qaida Policy Study Preceding the Madrid Bombing," *Studies in Conflict and Terrorism* 27, no. 5 (2004): 355–75. As the authors note, a "jihadi strategic studies genre" does not imply perfect cohesion. See also Dima Adamsky, "Jihadi Operational Art: The Comig Wave of Jihadi Strategic Studies," *Studies in Conflict and Terrorism* 33, no. 1 (2009): 1–19.

2. CIA, *Guide to the Analysis of Insurgency*, (Washington, DC: US Government, 2012), https://www.hsdl.org/?view&did=713599. 10.

3. Uppsala Conflict Data Program, UCDP Conflict Encyclopedia: India, CPI-Maoist, Uppsala University, July 26, 2013, http://www.ucdp.uu.se/gpdatabase/gpcountry.php?id=74&regionSelect=6-Central_and_Southern_Asia#.

4. See Kai M. Thaler, "Ideology and Violence in Civil Wars: Theory and Evidence from Mozambique and Angola," *Civil Wars* 14, no. 4 (2012): 546–67.

5. This corresponds with Audrey Kurth Cronin, "Ending Terrorism: Lessons for Defeating Al-Qaeda," *Adelphi Paper* 47, no. 394 (2007): chap. 1.

6. See Bard E. O'Neill, *Insurgency and Terrorism: From Revolution to Apocalypse* (Washington, DC: Potomac Books, 2005), fn. 34, p. 69., who argues that it is only effective when combined with other forms of warfare. See also Max Abrahms, "Why Terrorism Does Not Work," *International Security* 31, no. 2 (2006): 42–78.

7. Cronin, "Ending Terrorism: Lessons for Defeating Al-Qaeda," 11–22.

8. Jeffry A. Frieden, David A. Lake, and Kenneth A. Schultz, *World Politics: Interests, Interactions, Institutions* (New York: Norton, 2010), 392–97. They adapted their structure from Andrew Kydd and Barbara Walter, "The Strategies of Terrorism," *International Security* 31, no. 1 (2006): 49–80. While the original formulation focused on terrorist groups, these strategies are applicable to all of the armed groups considered here. Cronin includes punishment and attrition under compellence, with provocation, polarization, and mobilization under leverage. She argues that spoiling and outbidding are tactics, but it is unclear how these differ from mobilization. See Cronin, "Ending Terrorism: Lessons for Defeating Al-Qaeda," 11–22.

9. Frieden, Lake, and Schultz, *World Politics: Interests, Interactions, Institutions*, 392.

10. Ibid., 393.

11. Ibid., 394.

12. CIA, *Guide to the Analysis of Insurgency*, 10.

13. Thomas X. Hammes, *The Sling and the Stone* (St. Paul, MN: Zenith Press, 2006), 44–55. See also J. Thomas Moriarty, "The Vanguard's Dilemma: Understanding and Exploiting Insurgent Strategies," *Small Wars and Insurgencies* 21, no. 3 (2010): 476–97.

14. Phil Williams, *Violent Non-State Actors and National and International Security* (Zurich: Swiss Federal Institute of Technology Zurich, International Relations and Security Network, 2008), 15.

15. Kydd and Walter, "The Strategies of Terrorism," 69–72. See also Gordon H. McCormick, "Terrorist Decision Making," *Annual Review of Political Science* 6 (2003): 484.

16. Moriarty, "The Vanguard's Dilemma: Understanding and Exploiting Insurgent Strategies."

17. Carlos Marighella, *Manual of the Urban Guerrilla*, trans. Gene Hanrahan (Chapel Hill, NC: Documentary Publications, 1985), 93–95.

18. Ibid.

19. CIA, *Guide to the Analysis of Insurgency*. 10.

20. See "The Crisis in Libya," International Coalition for the Responsibility to Protect, http://www.responsibilitytoprotect.org/index.php/crises/crisis-in-libya.

21. Kydd and Walter, "The Strategies of Terrorism," 72–76.

22. On Afghanistan, see Cyrus Hodes and Mark Sedra, "The Search for Security in Post-Taliban Afghanistan," *Adelphi Paper* 47, no. 391 (2007): 17–33.

23. Kydd and Walter, "The Strategies of Terrorism," 76–78. This resembles Cronin's "mobilization." See Cronin, "Ending Terrorism: Lessons for Defeating Al-Qaeda," 19–20.

24. Bruce Hoffman, *Inside Terrorism* (New York: Columbia University Press, 2006), 147, 63–64.

25. Martha Crenshaw, "Theories of Terrorism: Instrumental and Organizational Approaches," in *Inside Terrorist Organizations*, ed. David C. Rapoport (New York: Columbia University Press, 1988), 23–24.

26. This discussion borrows from Rachel Locke, *Organized Crime, Conflict, and Fragility: A New Approach* (New York: International Peace Institute, 2012), 4–6.

27. Roy Godson, ed. *Menace to Society: Political-Criminal Collaboration around the World* (Piscataway, NJ: Transaction Publishers, 2003).

28. Douglas Farah, "Terrorist-Criminal Pipelines and Criminalized States: Emerging Alliances," *PRISM* 2, no. 3 (2011): 15–32. See also Antoni L. Mazzitelli, "Transnational Organized Crime in West Africa: The Additional Challenge," *International Affairs* 83, no. 6 (2007): 1071–90. This more broadly resembles Reno's conception of patronage politics in many African countries. See William Reno, *Warlord Politics and African States* (Boulder, CO: Lynne Rienner, 1999).

29. Susan W. Tiefenbrun, "Semiotic Definition of 'Lawfare,'" *Case Western Reserve Journal of International Law* 43, nos. 1 and 2 (2011): 29–60.

30. See the discussion in Stathis N. Kalyvas, *The Logic of Violence in Civil Wars* (Cambridge: Cambridge University Press, 2006), 23–28.

31. Lia and Hegghammer, "Jihadi Strategic Studies: The Alleged Al Qaida Policy Study Preceding the Madrid Bombing," 356.

32. Thomas C. Schelling, *Arms and Influence* (New Haven, CT: Yale University Press, 1966), 3. Italics in the original.

33. Martha Crenshaw, "Explaining Suicide Terrorism: A Review Essay," *Security Studies* 16, no. 1 (2007): 161.

34. For example, see Martin van Creveld, *The Transformation of War* (New York: Free Press, 1991).; Rupert Smith, *The Utility of Force: The Art of War in the Modern World* (New York: Vintage Books, 2008); and Mary Kaldor, *New and Old Wars: Organized Violence in a Global Era* (Stanford, CA: Stanford University Press, 2007).

35. Gary LaFree, Laura Dugan, and R. Kim Cragin, "Trends in Global Terrorism, 1970–2007," in *Peace and Conflict 2010*, ed. J. Joseph Hewitt, Jonathan Wilkenfeld, and Ted Robert Gurr (Boulder, CO: Paradigm, 2010), 56.

36. Ibid. For example, see Oarhe Osumah and Iro Aghedo, "Who Wants to Be a Millionaire? Nigerian Youths and the Commodification of Kidnapping," *Review of African Political Economy* 38, no. 128 (2011): 277–87.

37. James J. F. Forest, "Global Trends in Kidnapping by Terrorist Groups," *Global Change, Peace and Security* 24, no. 3 (2012): 324. Kidnappings and drug trafficking have become AQIM's main sources of funding. See Islam Qasem, Anna Michalkova, and Marjolein de Ridder, *Drugs, Crime and Terror: A Thriving Business*, WFF Issue Brief No. 09 (The Hague, Netherlands: World Foresight Forum, 2011).

38. Forest, "Global Trends in Kidnapping by Terrorist Groups," 312.

39. Ibid., 322, 24.

40. IISS Armed Conflict Database, "Background: Philippines (ASG)," https://acd.iiss.org/en/conflicts/philippines--asg-f55d?as=E12DFD99A21F45CEBF1903733FDB7D3E.

41. United Nations Office on Drugs and Crime, *United Nations Convention against Transnational Organized Crime and the Protocols Thereto* (New York: United Nations, 2004).

42. Alison Siskin and Liana Sun Wyler, *Trafficking in Persons: U.S. Policy and Issues for Congress*, CRS Report Rl34317 (Washington, DC: US Congressional Research Service, August 28, 2008), 34–35.

43. Ibid., 7–9.

44. As many assert, suicide attacks—whether by the Assassins, Russian anarchists, Japanese kamikazes, and others—are nothing new, but the tactic is currently *en vogue* among certain armed groups. See Hoffman, *Inside Terrorism*.

45. For an overview of problems and research questions in the study of suicide attacks, see Crenshaw, "Explaining Suicide Terrorism: A Review Essay."

46. Ibid., 160.

47. Assaf Moghadam, "Suicide Terrorism, Occuption, and the Globalization of Martyrdom: A Critique of *Dying to Win*," *Studies in Conflict and Terrorism* 29, no. 8 (2006): 713. Pape argues it is closer to 50 percent. See Robert A. Pape, *Dying to Win: The Strategic Logic of Suicide Terrorism* (New York: Random House, 2006).

48. Hoffman, *Inside Terrorism*, 133.

49. Ibid., 132–34.

50. Robert Pape has been criticized for aggregating suicide attacks against combatants and noncombatants. See Moghadam, "Suicide Terrorism, Occuption, and the Globalization of Martyrdom: A Critique of *Dying to Win*."

51. Hoffman, *Inside Terrorism*, 131. This may be a product of the "globalization of martyrdom," whereby Islamic movements are transnational, possess international goals, operate beyond the traditional local area of conflict, and have successfully transmitted their message across the internet. See Moghadam, "Suicide Terrorism, Occuption, and the Globalization of Martyrdom: A Critique of *Dying to Win*," 720–23.

52. Hoffman, *Inside Terrorism*, 132, 35.

53. John Mueller, *Overblown: How Politicians and the Terrorism Industry Inflate National Security Threats, and Why We Believe Them* (New York: Free Press, 2009).

54. Keir A. Lieber and Daryl G. Press, "Why States Won't Give Nuclear Weapons to Terrorists," *International Security* 38, no. 1 (2013): 83.

55. Tim Sweijs and Jaakko Kooroshy, *The Future of CBRN*, Future Issue No. 12 | 03 | 10 (The Hague, Netherlands: The Hague Centre for Strategic Studies, 2010).

56. Smith, *The Utility of Force: The Art of War in the Modern World*.

57. Fox News, "Zetas Drug Cartel Threatens Violence in Peten, Guatemala," *Fox News Latino*, March 21, 2012, http://latino.foxnews.com/latino/news/2012/03/21/zetas-drug-cartel-threatens-violence-in-peten-guatemala/.

58. Brigitte L. Nacos, *Mass-Mediated Terrorism: The Central Role of the Media in Terrorism and Counterterrorism* (Lanham, MD: Rowman and Littlefield Publishers, 2007).

59. http://www.almanar.com.lb/english/main.php. See also Avi Jorisch, *Beacon of Hatred: Inside Hizballah's Al-Manar Television* (Washington, DC: Washington Institute for Near East Policy, 2004).

60. http://www.moqawama.org.

61. Gabriel Weimann, *Terror on the Internet: The New Arena, the New Challenges* (Washington, DC: United States Institute of Peace Press, 2006), 25.

62. For a discussion of Hezbollah's media use as a force multiplier, see Frederic M. Wehrey, "A Clash of Wills: Hizballah's Psychological Campaign against Israel in South Lebanon," *Small Wars and Insurgencies* 13, no. 3 (2002): 53–74.

63. Steven Metz, "The Internet, New Media, and the Evolution of Insurgency," *Parameters* 42, no. 3 (2012): 80–90.

64. Marc Sageman, *Understanding Terror Networks* (Philadelphia, PA: University of Pennsylvania Press, 2004), 163.

65. For microtargeting in the context of American political campaigning, see Allison Brennan, "Microtargeting: How Campaigns Know You Better Than You Know Yourself," CNN.com, http://www.cnn.com/2012/11/05/politics/voters-microtargeting.

66. See Will Oremus, "The Militant Group Behind the Kenya Mall Attack Is Live-Tweeting the Massacre," Slate.com, September 21, 2013, http://www.slate.com/blogs/future_tense/2013/09/21/al_shabaab_on_twitter_hsmpress_tries_to_justify_nairobi_kenya_mall_shooting.html. See also Alexander Meleagrou-Hitchens, Shiraz Maher, and James Sheehan, *Lights, Camera, Jihad: Al-Shabaab's Western Media Strategy* (London: International Centre for the Study of Radicalisation and Political Violence [ICSR], 2012).

67. This draws from Gabriel Weimann, *Www.Terror.Net: How Modern Terrorism Uses the Internet*, Special Report No. 116 (Washington, DC: United States Instittue of Peace, 2004), 6.

68. Mohammed M. Hafez, "Martyrdom Mythology in Iraq: How Jihadists Frame Suicide Terrorism in Videos and Biographies," *Terrorism and Political Violence* 19, no. 1 (2007): 95–115.

69. Marighella, *Manual of the Urban Guerrilla*, 84–85.

70. Successful operations may create a bandwagoning effect, wherein people may be more likely to support the "winning side." In addition, it helps the group overcome the coordination and free rider problems.

71. BBC News, "Senior Pakistani Taliban Leader 'Shocked' by Malala Attack," *BBC News Asia*, July 17, 2013, http://www.bbc.co.uk/news/world-middle-east-23347425.

72. Christopher Paul, Colin P. Clarke, and Beth Grill, *Victory Has a Thousand Fathers: Sources of Success in Counterinsurgency* (Santa Monica, CA: RAND Corporation, 2010).

73. Daniel Byman et al., *Trends in Outside Support for Insurgent Movement* (Santa Monica, CA: RAND Corporation, 2001).

74. On state's leveraging support to achieve objectives vis-à-vis the targeted state, see Belgin San Akca, "Supporting Non-State Armed Groups: A Resort to Illegality?," *The Journal of Strategic Studies* 32, no. 4 (2009): 589–613.

75. Smith, *The Utility of Force: The Art of War in the Modern World*.

76. See San Akca, "Supporting Non-State Armed Groups: A Resort to Illegality?," 591.

77. Collier argues "grievance" issues are easier to "sell" to an external audience than "greed" issues, no matter the group's true ideology or objectives. See Paul Collier, "Doing Well out of War: An Economic Perspective," in *Greed and Grievance: Economic Agendas in Civil Wars*, ed. Mats Berdal and David M. Malone (Boulder, CO: Lynne Rienner, 2000).

78. Daniel Byman, "Passive Supporters of Terrorism," *Survival* 47, no. 4 (2005–06): 132–33.

79. The United Nations is built on the foundation of state sovereignty. Despite recent challenges under the rubric of "Responsibility to Protect" (R2P), international law has traditionally discouraged intervention in a civil war until the outcome is clear. On R2P, see International Commission on Intervention and State Sovereignty, *The Responsibility to Protect* (Ottawa, Canada: International Development Research Centre, December 2001), http://responsibilitytoprotect.org/ICISS%20Report.pdf.

80. See Anne Gearan, "U.S. Warns Russia against Sending Missiles to Syria," *Washington Post*, May 31, 2013.

81. This section borrows from the excellent compilation found in Byman et al., *Trends in Outside Support for Insurgent Movement*, 83–102.

82. Robert J. Art, "The Fungibility of Force," in *The Use of Force*, ed. Robert J. Art and Kenneth N. Waltz (Lanham, MD: Rowman and Littlefield Publishers, 2004), 6.

83. Ibid., 7.

84. United States Department of State, Bureau of Counterterrorism, *Foreign Terrorist Organizations*, September 28, 2012, http://www.state.gov/j/ct/rls/other/des/123085.htm.

85. "Reagan Presses Contra Aid Case," *Pittsburgh Press*, Saturday, March 8, 1986, http://news.google.com/newspapers?id=XHIcAAAAIBAJ&sjid=0WIEAAAAIBAJ&pg=5701%2C4216162.

86. Ronald Reagan, "Radio Address to the Nation on the Situation in Nicaragua," September 12, 1987. Online by Gerhard Peters and John T. Woolley, The American Presidency Project, http://www.presidency.ucsb.edu/ws/index.php?pid=34788.

87. Ronald Reagan: "Remarks on Signing the Afghanistan Day Proclamation," March 10, 1982. Online by Gerhard Peters and John T. Woolley, The American Presidency Project. http://www.presidency.ucsb.edu/ws/?pid=42248.

88. Christopher M. Blanchard and Jim Zanotti, *Libya: Background and U.S. Relations*, CRS Report Rl33142 (Washington, DC: US Congressional Research Service, 2011), 6.

89. "Pakistan Taliban says its fighters in Syria," Al Jazeera, July 16, 2013, http://www.aljazeera.com/news/middleeast/2013/07/20137167916826540.html.

90. Ricardo Rene Laremont, "After the Fall of Qaddafi: Political, Economic, and Security Consequences for Libya, Mali, Niger, and Algeria," *Stability: International Journal of Security and Development* 2, no. 2 (2013): 29.

91. Piers Mackesy, *The War for America, 1775–1783* (Lincoln: Univeristy of Nebraska Press, 1992).

Chapter Seven

Combating Armed Groups

Contemporary conflicts are a complex mixture of "conventional" and "irregular" warfare, which require a combination of strategies to counter their primary actors: armed groups.[1] There is no one formula for a successful countering strategy. Violence may be used to both protect the population and eradicate armed groups, while diplomacy, economic, and political initiatives are key to a comprehensive countering strategy.[2] Additionally, every insurgent, terrorist, militia, or TCO has a unique set of characteristics and a specific context that must be addressed. Moreover, a state's counterstrategy must account for international and domestic military, political, economic, and legal constraints. As Clausewitz reminds us, strategy is an art, not a science, and even the best-devised strategies and tactics may be derailed in the fog of war.[3]

An armed group's use of violence brings with it one key advantage for the state—violence exposes the armed group and removes, if only briefly, the clandestine nature of the armed group. Pictures and names of the attackers may be widely disseminated in order to locate the responsible individuals, materials used in an attack can be analyzed to determine their origins, and the outcome of the attack may be used for political purposes. Once individual attackers are identified, additional members of a cell or group may be identified. By exposing themselves through violence, the group may remove the veil of secrecy and allow the government to further penetrate and combat an organization. The more acts of violence a group commits, the probability increases that it will provide the state with enough evidence to hunt down and capture, kill, or otherwise demobilize an armed group.

COMBATING GRIEVANCES AND THE ENVIRONMENT

States must recognize that armed groups are the symptoms of greater problems in today's political, economic, social, and military arenas. The underlying foundations that led to the increasing threat from armed groups after the Cold War—the transportation revolution, increased communication capabilities, and the prevalence of small arms in fragile and postconflict states—remain as factors that create increasingly complex international environments, increase incentives for illicit activities, and create distortions in the market for privatized violence. Governments, in order to combat armed groups, may harden their defenses, communicate deterrent policies, or remove systemic political, social, or economic inequalities or points of contention from which the armed group draws its grievances.

Combating armed groups takes two broad forms: combating the group itself and shaping the environment and context within which the group germinates and draws strength. Focusing on armed groups may fail for purely internal reasons, and while states may accelerate this process, they may provide a convenient, unifying enemy for the group. Removing an armed group leaves in place the political grievances and economic and social imbalance that spawns such groups. Additionally, many groups rely on popular support or exist through predation of both domestic and international populations. A group's defeat will be difficult, given the external funding, international recognition, or safe haven among densely populated urban settings they receive. Separating the group from this support is key to countering armed groups. Today's counterinsurgencies are 100 percent political, in Kilcullen's estimation.[4] The state must address these political objectives or fail to create a credible countering strategy. Conflicts today are not simply clashes between opposing militaries. They are conducted in the political and psychological realms using strategies and tactics of fear, legal constraints, economic warfare, and protracted, low-level military operations geared to erode the state's will and ultimately create exhaustion and an unwillingness to continue.

Permissive Roots

Several permissive factors—the end of the Cold War, globalization, failing states, and ineffective governance—were discussed in chapter 2. These geopolitical factors require a state and its neighbors to increase their control over their territory, while boosting internal development. Additional factors might entail removing income inequalities; increasing development; better provision of services, including security and the rule of law; and increasing trade, foreign investment, or official development aid. While these factors are easy to enumerate, successfully engaging the domestic and international communities in enacting policies to address these societal grievances are some of the most complex policy decisions. Addressing these foundational issues will go part of the way toward removing the environmental incentives and opportunities for conflict.

Complicating the environment is the argument that primary commodity exports fuel conflicts, as do geographic features such as mountainous terrain.[5] This makes it easier for armed groups to expropriate goods, engage in rent-seeking, or to engage illicit trade networks while providing safe havens. These two factors fuel the group's needs in all aspects of their formation, operations, and perpetuation.

These factors all indicate that targeting the armed groups is not sufficient. Policy reform, market corrections, income or land redistribution, reestablishment of the rule of law including functioning and impartial courts, and political channels for expression, development, and other policies to shape the environment are required to combat the political and economic nature of modern conflict. In many cases, the armed group is a symptom of greater, underlying structural deficiencies in the target state. Eliminating the symptom does not always cure the underlying disease and dysfunction.

US counterterrorism and counterinsurgency strategies demonstrate this need. The US government defines counterterrorism (CT) as "actions taken directly against terrorist networks and indirectly to influence and render global and regional environments inhospitable to terrorist networks."[6] While CT is the primary mission of US special operations forces, there are two main points to consider. The first is that while CT has primarily been viewed as offensive military operations "taken to prevent, deter, preempt, and respond to terrorism," US strategists recognize the need for nonviolent strategies to include increasing law-enforcement capabilities and diplomatic action.[7] Second, beyond direct offensive action against the terrorist group, current US strategy seeks to expand the mission to indirectly influence their environment. While this may be more of an offensive military mission aimed at creating deterrence, it recognizes there is more to armed groups than the actual group leader and active members. Deterring potential members, rupturing networks, and altering environments demonstrates the broader efforts needed beyond directly attacking the group.

US counterinsurgents "seek to defeat insurgents and address core grievances to prevent insurgency's expansion or regeneration."[8] This "political, security, legal, economic, development, and psychological activities to create a holistic approach aimed at weakening the insurgents while bolstering the government's legitimacy in the eyes of the population."[9] One of the key elements in any counterinsurgent campaign has been to separate the insurgent from the population from which it draws support. Defeating or containing a group is a step in the right direction, but failure to shape the environment in a way that either addresses core grievances or in some way creates an "inhospitable environment" for a group is bound to lead to a group's rebirth or spawn new groups.

This is exemplified in recent writing on actions to counter TCOs. Removing one TCO will not end drug trafficking; it will leave incentives for new groups to join. Instead, a multilayered approach, targeting the TCO, but also engaging state–community relations, economic and political inequalities, and engaging in development processes to strengthen state institutions, is required. Furthermore, because TCOs are transnational, operating in an international marketplace, the solutions must be regionally or globally based. State-specific actions will be unlikely to eradicate the problem.[10]

Counterinsurgency (COIN) is a broad category that today may conjure images of the military working closely with local forces and populations and attempting to win "hearts and minds" in a "population-centric" strategy designed to win over and protect local populations. This strategy may include development and reconstruction projects aimed at increasing the state's capabilities and legitimacy to the provision of services and addressing societal inequalities. "Enemy-centric" counterinsurgency applies selective or indiscriminate violence in punishing insurgents and their supporters and deterring passive supporters and neutrals. In the extreme, these strategies may target entire populations as the Soviets did in Afghanistan through "migratory genocide."[11] Enemy-centric counterinsurgency is more focused on degrading or eradicating enemy capability and legitimacy than in directly engaging the affected population.

US counterinsurgency should be focused on "quick and sustainable outcome which integrates most of the insurgents into the national power structure . . . Protracted conflict, not insurgent victory, is the threat" because it creates complex, unstable environment that incubates other threats, such as militias, criminal organizations, and terrorists.[12] If insurgencies and others tend to evolve into criminal organizations, then counterinsurgency or counterterrorism should evolve into counterorganized crime or countergang activity as the insurgency matures and the longer the conflict operates.[13]

Counterinsurgency becomes more complicated as leaders become more dependent on outside sources of funding and support than domestic sources of funding and support. Steven Metz argues external sources of funding and linkages to external groups allow insurgencies to bypass the creation of a mass base.[14] States and armed groups have little need to build domestic legitimacy or address local grievances. Instead, the state and armed groups seek legitimacy from international audiences and face different constraints on their actions. This complicates efforts to combat these groups.

The US institutes COIN in other countries through foreign internal defense (FID). This creates problems ranging from being able to collect local intelligence, institute and create legitimacy for a foreign backed regime in the target state, and maintain legitimacy and will back home. The United States may believe it is necessary to let the target state run the actual operations or run the risk of creating a moral hazard problem. For example, the International Security Assistance Force (ISAF) in Afghanistan may fear that if it runs all counterinsurgent operations, Afghan security units may become dependent on ISAF personnel and not develop the resources and ability to carry out their own operations.

States must guard against ignoring deep-seated political grievances and underestimating nationalism and wide variance of armed groups.[15] Armed groups may be the tip of the iceberg, the visible part of society-wide resentment, imbalances, or grievances that motivate wide swaths of the population. At the same time, nationalist motivations are present in many armed groups, whether or not they seek territory, and may provide motivation where other ideologies are merely superficial appendages. Short-run policies may not be useful in influencing their perception of the future.[16] Lastly, armed groups are not so unique as to defy categorization or generalization, but they are different enough in key ways—desire for territory, relationship to the local population, or their source of funding and support—that they must be taken as is and not shoehorned into politically expedient categories.

MILITARY, POLITICAL, LEGAL, AND ECONOMIC CONSTRAINTS ON GOVERNMENTS

States face various constraints when fighting armed groups and constructing countering strategies. Armed groups may try to exploit these by acting in ways that either goad the state into responding in a way that violates norms, or acting in ways that they believe will not lead to state response for fear of violating norms.[17] As part of their countering strategies, states need to make excellent use of public diplomacy and pubic relations to highlight their narrative, mobilize all audiences, and gain, or regain, political power and legitimacy.[18]

Armed-group labels—both political and legal—can constrain the policy choices available to governments. Furthermore, state leadership is constrained by their constituency, whether that is a small group composed of military leaders or business elites, or the state's domestic population. States are further constrained by international norms, law, and treaty obligations, as well as the "international community." States are economically constrained by their own resource base, capabilities, and ability to extract resources from the domestic and international populations. Lastly, states take armed-group tactics and strategies into consideration when creating their own strategies. Strategic behavior assumes actors create policies independently from others, but based on what it thinks the others will do. Conversely, armed groups' strategy creation and tactical decisions will be partly dependent on the government's countering strategy.[19] The interdependence of these policies means that the analyst should not only consider what the appropriate government response should be for its own citizens and the safety and security of its country, but also how these counterstrategies will affect the armed group's strategy and tactics.

Military Constraints

Modern militaries designed to fight conventional wars against state militaries suffer from four main problems. Today's military weaponry, tactics, and strategies are frequently unsuited to attack an armed group's "center of gravity"—its ideology. While it is useful for killing those with a differing ideology, it is unlikely to change minds, win over converts, or convince someone to change their ideology. Ideology is more likely to be countered through nonviolent means, including demonstrating that a group's ideology is incoherent, hypocritical, or contrary to commonly understood interpretations.[20] Furthermore, conventional weaponry is too indiscriminate in its effects and risks undermining the government's message and legitimacy among the population and generating armed-group sympathizers. For example, the Clinton administration cancelled missile strikes that lacked strong intelligence concerning the presence of al-Qaeda leadership, fearing indiscriminate attacks would strengthen al-Qaeda.[21] Drones may provide greater precision, but they are no less immune to miscalculations and potentially indiscriminate violence. Additionally, state bureaucracies and hierarchical organizations are too rigid to adapt to the increased flow of information and change in armed-group strategies and tactics.[22] Likewise, state armed forces are geared toward understanding threats from peer rivals and may be ill-prepared to fight, let alone understand, armed groups and the contest for legitimacy. Any one armed-group accomplishment may appear trivial to the state. Maintaining constant pressure on an armed group in order to forestall the achievement of long-term objectives may entail monetary, political, and social costs that states and leaders may be unwilling to endure.[23]

Despite these military constraints, states may face incentives to use military force. Military retaliation is a popular policy option in the immediate aftermath of an attack due to the underlying assumption that "force" is the ultimate arbiter in the international system. Additionally, military retaliation may be viewed as a "quick fix" or "magic bullet" in an environment lacking political will for protracted conflicts, may be preferable to costly reconstruction projects to shape the environment and address core grievances, and it is relatively easier in the complex legal environment surrounding today's irregular conflicts. This underdeveloped legal environment is evident in US debates concerning the appropriateness of using the US military base at Guantanamo Bay versus holding terrorist suspects and "enemy combatants" in

US-based maximum-security civilian prisons, debates over where or whether to try suspected terrorists, and debates over whether civilian or military courts are the most effective and appropriate venue. These incentives provide a powerful counterweight to the military constraints many states face.

Political and Legal Constraints

Labeling a group a terrorist group is often a politically tinged decision, as the term is pejorative and may spark heated debate.[24] Additionally, designation as a terrorist group may have specific legal connotations. Designation of a group as a "Foreign Terrorist Organization" (FTO) in the United States means that it is unlawful for a US citizen to provide the group material support or resources, members of the group are not allowed into the United States, the group's assets may be seized, and the United States engages with other countries toward those ends. By bringing attention to the group, the United States seeks to stigmatize and isolate the group internationally, deter economic aid to the group, and signal other states about US intentions in regard to the group.[25]

This is especially true in the post-9/11 world, where countries want to be counted as fighting "terrorism" at home and abroad, possibly with an eye toward receiving aid, military cooperation, or other assistance from the United States, its allies, and the international community. Furthermore, labeling a group a terrorist group may resonate domestically. Politicians may find it politically and legally expedient to label a group a terrorist or criminal group, as opposed to the potentially more "legitimate" label of "insurgent."

Politicians may benefit from labeling groups with the negative "terrorist" moniker, but many choose not to label groups in a way that would embarrass, hinder, or cast aspersions on a friendly regime. In 2010, Secretary of State Hillary Clinton indicated that various Mexican drug cartels were "morphing into an insurgency," as they controlled territory within the country and were escalating the level of violence.[26] Mexico quickly refuted this statement.[27] An insurgency implies the government is facing a crisis in political legitimacy, unable to fully exercise its monopoly over the legitimate use of force, or is in some other way weak or failing. The government may view "insurgency" as conveying a sense of legitimacy that "criminal organization" or "terrorist" does not.

Lastly, governments face economic constraints on combating armed groups. Governments seek outside aid and assistance for development or reconstruction projects, face pressures to focus on domestic service provision instead of military operations, and invite larger states to conduct training and operations on their behalf. Economic constraints not only shape decisions on whether to engage armed groups, but also the strategies available to do so.

James D. Fearon and David D. Laitin argue that the more underresourced the counterinsurgent forces are, the more these groups are likely to commit indiscriminate violence or act in ways contrary to the state's objectives. These corrupt or incompetent counterinsurgent forces may be given tacit consent to enrich themselves at the expense of the population. Alternatively, state leadership may be unable to enforce discipline on a predatory group. These actions move undecided members of the population toward supporting the armed group and solidify support from group loyalists. This ill-disciplined government response may be crucial to an armed group's provocation strategy. The lack of resources creates a principal–agent problem, where the government is either unwilling or incapable of controlling individuals in order to make up for economic deficiencies.[28]

"Media constraints" exacerbate the aforementioned issues. This is the degree to which media and communication have become globalized phenomena that are important in amplifying legitimizing messages, as well as publicizing missteps. Crucial to this new media-saturated environment is the importance of shaping a narrative. Governments seeking to bolster their legitimacy will be under constant attack from armed groups using violence and propaganda to create and disseminate a narrative of an evil, brutal, and inherently unpopular government. The government must be prepared to counter this and provide its own compelling story to both foreign and domestic audiences.

Government's Commitment Problems

The government faces a time-consistency problem in addressing these constraints. The government may guarantee a group greater political representation, inclusion in civic discourse, or monetary rewards; protection from armed-group retaliation; protection from legal prosecution; or provision of services and addressing of grievances. The sympathizer or armed-group member may have little reason to trust the government to deliver on their promises, especially since the government has previously failed to address the issues and because the government remains in a position to punish the armed-group members who lay down their weapons. Domestic or international pressure may compel the state to change its policies in the future.

If the government does deliver on the promised changes, the government may inadvertently create incentives for extortion. The government's attempts to provide services in order to reduce the opportunity for an armed group to exploit socioeconomic or political grievances create an incentive for armed groups to increase their level of violence. Armed groups have incentives to outbid each other in competition for government attention. Agreeing to address armed-group issues may encourage others to increase their violent actions in an attempt to secure further benefits for their groups.

GENERAL COUNTERING STRATEGIES

Many studies provide specific recommendations for a country's fight against a specific armed group, such as David Kilcullen's argument that the fight against al-Qaeda should be envisioned as a "global insurgency" with the need for a "disaggregation" countering strategy to separate local actors from the central al-Qaeda networks.[29] Daniel Byman argues that US options to combat al-Qaeda and terrorism include crushing the group, containing the group, defense, diverting the group to an alternative target, delegitimizing the group, or democracy promotion, ultimately recommending a multilateral containment strategy.[30] More broadly, Mariya Omelicheva argues state strategies will be shaped by their view of who the terrorists are and the threats they pose, which is informed by a domestic and international discourse on norms and treaties.[31] Arie Perliger, writing from the vantage point of democratic regimes, argues reactions will fall along both a legal and operative-violent dimension.[32] This section incorporates these differing ideas while discussing five broad strategies applicable across a range of armed groups: deterrence, defense, use of force, law enforcement, and negotiation and reconciliation.[33]

Deterrence

Glenn H. Snyder divided deterrence into deterrence by punishment and deterrence by denial.[34] Deterrence by punishment involves threatening your opponent with unacceptable costs if he takes a particular action, while deterrence by denial prevents the opponent from realizing the benefits from an attack. Three broad factors determine whether deterrence is successful: the threat must be clearly communicated, the threat must be credible, and the threatened outcome—whether punishment or denial—must come at a greater cost to the target than any anticipated benefit from the action being deterred. These factors are complicated when the target is an armed group.

Multiple authors and policies, including the 2002 US *National Security Strategy*, argue that terrorists cannot be deterred. Armed groups, especially terrorists, are said to be irrational, highly motivated and immune to punishments, do not have a "return address," and what they value may not be known to the state.[35] Many armed groups are clandestine and lack territory, providing no physical space to target. Groups may have a membership but lack a discernable "population" to threaten, in the same way states threatened cities during Cold War nuclear deterrence. A group's most important value or center of gravity is likely its ideology and political goals—intangible constructs. All of these reduce the state's ability to credibly threaten the target.

Matthew Kroenig and Barry Pavel recommend four forms of deterrence to counter terrorist threats.[36] Direct response threatens unacceptable retaliation on those perpetrating an attack, while an indirect response threatens unacceptable retaliation on something the perpetrators hold dear, such as family members. Former US Representative Tom Tancredo's (R-CO) suggestion to use nuclear weapons on Mecca and Medina if "Muslim fundamentalist terrorists" attack the United States with WMD demonstrates the great difficulties in credibly committing to an indirect response.[37] The United States might also employ tactical denial, which "deny terrorists the ability to successfully conduct an attack," while strategic denial prevents terrorists from realizing their ultimate goals or to abandon terrorism, even if individual attacks are successful.[38]

Successful deterrence requires a full understanding of armed-group characteristics. First, direct response is a viable policy, as armed-group members vary in their susceptibility to punishments.[39] Determining who is susceptible requires an understanding of an armed group's membership and ideology. While groups may not control territory or population in the traditional sense, they may utilize external safe havens. Second, successful indirect response and tactical and strategic denial require understanding a group's leadership, membership, ideology, objectives, tactics, and strategy, while the state must be able to communicate failures, convince terrorists that their actions are in vain, and publicize the state's resilience.[40]

Deterrent strategies rely on other general strategies for optimal success and signify the need to assemble comprehensive policies to combat armed groups. States demonstrating defense and resiliency improve their ability to deter by denial, while targeted law enforcement and the use of force create credible deterrence by punishment and denial. Lastly, negotiation and reconciliation bolsters strategic denial by demonstrating that there are alternatives available to those who relinquish violence.

Defense

Defense is "forcefully preventing an enemy from attaining his physical objectives."[41] Defense can mean not only passive barricades to prevent car bombers from reaching their targets, but also defending a state's values, traditions, or institutions. Defensive actions may take an offensive nature through preventive or preemptive measures. If a state believes that it is the target of an attack, it may try to strike the armed group before the group is able to carry out the attack. This reduces the threat even further, as the attack is countered or greatly reduced and may have the added advantage of being carried out on foreign soil, away from the media and domestic political or legal constraints. These "preemptive defensive" measures may also deter future groups from attacking the state.

Defensive measures, whether passive or active, require increased intelligence capability, law-enforcement investigations, and international cooperation. The state must understand not only the tactics and strategy of its enemies, but also their own vulnerabilities. As in the case of deterrence, defense against armed groups can be difficult based on the armed group's desire to attack and delegitimize the state, as well as credibly commit the state to defend its territory, people, and values. Spending cuts, loss of political will, or a shift in political priorities may lessen a state's defensive measures.

The US Department of Homeland Security was originally created with a "single, urgent mission: securing the homeland of America and protecting the American people from terrorism," and continues with its primary mission to "ensure a homeland that is safe, secure, and resilient against terrorism and other hazards."[42] Homeland Security's missions also include securing US borders, enforcing immigration laws, safeguarding cyberspace, and ensuring resiliency after disasters of all types.[43] All of these missions require intelligence sharing across federal, state, and local governments, as well as between the public and private sector, and with international partners.

The department acts as a massive intelligence clearinghouse, a place where numerous agencies charged with protecting the United States can share information and intelligence. This includes redirecting law enforcement to specifically address terrorist threats.[44]

The department protects the United States through "active" defense operations, namely, aggregating intelligence in order to identify threats and operations before they occur and stop them. Furthermore, the United States attempts to prevent terrorist attacks by deterring "all potential terrorists from attacking America through our uncompromising commitment to defeating terrorism wherever it appears."[45]

Finally, the first *National Strategy for Homeland Security* makes clear that both physical and nonphysical threats were to be the focus for the incipient Department of Homeland Security. It argues the United States should protect America's physical well-being; Americans' "way of life," focusing on democracy, liberties, security, economics, and culture; protect and advance science and technology research; and identify and share information on critical infrastructure and key assets.[46]

Law Enforcement

Law enforcement is integral to any attempt at combating armed groups and provides additional capability to a state's counterarmed group capabilities.[47] Many of the actions that armed groups are forced to take today to perpetuate their organizations are illegal and open to criminal prosecution by the state or international actors. Armed groups may fund themselves through organized crime or acquire small arms through smuggling. Law enforcement may be the only option for dealing with some armed groups, as their clandestine nature or urban setting may not lend themselves to military counterstrategies.

The nature of many "twenty-first-century security threats" such as "weapons proliferation, human trafficking, drug smuggling, and piracy . . . , none of which are particularly susceptible to military solutions" are best approached through law-enforcement practices.[48] Furthermore, for terrorist groups that are little more than loosely connected cells sharing an ideological foundation, criminalizing more common group actions, such as calls for violence and funding through illicit activities, may be the most effective means of disrupting organizations and their ability to commit violent acts.[49]

Anticorruption measures have been a primary tool in combating TCOs and reestablishing governance, but can be difficult to implement without the rule of law and the provision of security and alternative economic opportunities. The legal system may be unsuitable for prosecuting anticorruption laws and security forces that may be charged with enforcing the laws may be predatory and corrupt in their own right.[50] States need to accompany crackdowns on TCOs with community engagement and processes that demonstrate the application of reform and accountability practices.[51] Law-enforcement policies may focus exclusively on the armed group, but if they are not connected to broader attempts to address structural issues in society, may not adequately address the underlying problems.[52] A more inclusive approach might include creating legitimate business opportunities and jobs, engaging civil society and social networks, encouraging illicit networks toward legitimate behaviors, and addressing underlying policy inequalities. Likewise, statebuilding and development cannot effectively take place without a dialogue between the state and its population.[53]

Use of Force

Preemptive actions are those taken to stop an enemy who is about to strike.[54] The threat is imminent and the armed group is in the process of undertaking or about to launch an operation. Preventive actions are those taken to stop an enemy who is planning future attacks, but may not be currently mobilizing for an attack. Both preemptive and preventive actions are intended to prevent future, costly attacks by assuming some lesser cost now. Both of these "active" defensive measures require a high degree of confidence in intelligence and analysis, which may frequently be difficult to obtain due to the group's clandestine nature and the state's lack of local information. Furthermore, there may be legal, ethical, diplomatic, and military risks to carrying out these operations, especially in the case of preventive attacks, where there is no immediate threat from the armed group. States may find domestic and international resistance to policies that go beyond passive defense to assuming an active defense role.

Selective vs. Indiscriminate Violence

Security measures may be difficult to narrowly target, which may lead to harassing, abusing, or detaining innocent civilians. Increased security measures may also achieve permanent status and erode the rule of law and attempts to reach negotiated compromise. Although the government's desire to demonstrate resolve through the use of force may be a natural tendency, it can quickly spiral out of control and inadvertently delegitimize the government's policies while increasing the armed group's legitimacy.[55] Violence alone will not achieve success, as the state needs a mix to address the various aspects of political grievances and nationalism. Additionally, brutal or indiscriminate violence may not crush a group, generates new recruits, and may not be economically, politically, or legally sustainable by the state.[56]

Democratic states engaged in counterinsurgency today attempt to drive a wedge between the population and insurgents by means other than brutal repression. Historically, this restraint was often missing. This does not mean that these harsh measures were effective, as van Creveld notes "the 'counterinsurgency' forces failed in *every* case [of colonial powers attempting to maintain their empires after 1945]" and the colonial powers were frequently "utterly ruthless."[57]

States may consciously choose a policy of indiscriminate violence, but are also likely to resort to indiscriminate violence given two constraints. The first is the absence of local information, whether due to denial by the enemy, lack of state legitimacy among the population, or insufficient resources to secure this intelligence. This may lead to indiscriminate violence, as information discerning "friend from foe" and those supporting the armed group may be difficult to come by.[58] Second, as previously discussed, underresourced counterinsurgents are likely to perpetrate indiscriminate violence due to lack of control over their forces.[59]

States need to recognize the role of politics and the nature of the war they are fighting in order to counter it and its main protagonists.[60] States that lack ultimate political objectives create an open-ended and ultimately futile campaign.

If irregular warfare is about competition for influence over a population, it is questionable as to whether more "surgical strikes," such as from drones, are beneficial in the end. First, the local population facing the possibility of drone strikes resents collateral damage and is unlikely to help those operating the drones. Strikes may also generate new recruits. Second, the host country where the strike occurs may protest at this perceived violation of its sovereignty. Leaders in states friendly with, or purportedly working with, the country carrying out drone strikes may feel the need to publicly disavow the program, to claim that it is not occurring, or to generally respond to their constituents' negative reactions to drone strikes, even if the state's leadership privately supports the strikes.

Pakistan's population holds generally negative views on drone strikes, with only one in five supporting US strikes in Pakistan in conjunction with the Pakistani government.[61] This creates difficulty in securing the population's aid in combating armed groups, even when the groups targeted are responsible for violence committed against the Pakistani people and may be a greater threat to Pakistan than the United States. Furthermore, public opinion toward drone strikes in countries friendly to the United States is nearly universally negative. Disapproval outweighs approval of drone strikes in the United Kingdom, Germany, France, Italy, Spain, and Japan, while over 80 percent of those surveyed in Turkey, Egypt, and Jordan disapproved of US drone strikes.[62] Gaining support and aid from these countries is crucial to US counterterrorist and counterinsurgent operations, which are threatened if their leaders and populations are against the use of drone strikes.

Negotiation and Reconciliation

Governments may amplify voices of tolerance and moderation, freedom, or democracy within their society. Bringing forward victims of armed-group attacks, moderate religious or political figures who are working within the political system to find areas of accommodation and agreement, and generally seeking to portray the government as willing to work toward a compromise solution seek to paint the armed group as extremists who will never be satisfied. Creating alternatives to an extremist education system and demonstrating how integration into society provides for long-term benefits for an individual and his family may aid this. This may delegitimize extremist ideological leaders, while sowing doubt or dissension within the membership, supporters, or potential supporters, some of whom may desire a negotiated settlement and reintegration into society. An armed group turned political actor's failure to adhere to promises or represent their constituents may lead to the group's loss of power and delegitimization in the eyes of the population.[63]

Parties in an intrastate conflict may seek to bargain or negotiate, as the IRA did in the Good Friday Accords in 1998. The armed group, depending on its objectives and underlying grievances, may seek economic opportunity or profit to defect, the leadership may seek political positions or recognition of their group as a legitimate political party, or the group may call for policy change. The government may demand disarmament and intelligence, as well as public disavowal of past actions in order to convince group members and supporters to give up the fight.[64] If successful, these groups may be reintegrated into society in the form of political parties.

There are several difficulties inherent in state negotiation and reconciliation with armed groups. Negotiations are more likely if all sides agree there is a military stalemate.[65] In addition, political parties may not operate in a postconflict setting, such that alternative sources for political participation are needed when states lack strong institutions.[66] While domestic electoral incentives can impose discipline on a group, a group's transformation into a political party may not be accompanied by legitimacy or support.[67] Moreover, economically motivated groups may use their newfound political positions to improve their patronage networks and ignore political institution building.[68]

Governments also face threats from armed group spoilers. This creates principal–agent problems for both the armed group and state. The armed group is unable to control extremist factions that do not want peace, while the government is unable to rely on the moderates in the armed groups to corral the extremist spoilers.[69]

The government faces a time-consistency problem and may be unable to deliver on its promises. The government has an incentive to make peace with the armed group and then, once the armed group has negotiated and demobilized, retaliate or renege on promises. Armed groups will be uncertain as to whether the government can or will deliver on its promises for opportunities and reintegration of surrendering armed group members. Furthermore, former armed-group members may fear retaliation such as harassment, imprisonment, or worse from the government. Government actions taken prior to negotiations or as negotiations are ongoing may exacerbate these conditions. A US drone strike killed the Pakistani Taliban's second in command in May 2013, leading the group to end talks with Pakistan and renew calls for attacks in Pakistan.[70] The Pakistani Taliban faced a similar situation when their leader Hakimullah Mehsud, who claimed to be receptive to talks, was killed in November 2013. The Pakistani government stated this undermined proposed talks, and a Pakistani Taliban spokesman vowed revenge.[71] Armed groups have an incentive to continue fighting while the government attempts policy reforms, or in some other way credibly commits to changes that the armed group seeks.

These problems may be impossible for the armed group and government to credibly commit to on their own. They may need the help and enforcement power of an outside party.[72] Finding an "objective observer" may require the United Nations or regional organization, whose member nations may be reluctant to intervene unless they can guarantee some level of security for the peacekeepers or economic remuneration. Intrastate conflicts face many roadblocks to resolution and it should come as no surprise that these conflicts, and the armed groups that fight them, rarely reach decisive conclusions.

COMBATING THE ARMED GROUP

States need to understand not only the environment, but also the specific characteristics of the armed group in order to construct a comprehensive countering strategy. Armed groups may decline due to a variety of reasons, including international political changes, internal tensions, and government responses. Armed groups may suffer internal problems due to the principal–agent, free-rider, time-consistency, or coordination problems. Armed-group members and supporters may seek both "exit" from the group, or to "voice" their discontent and attempt to change a group in decline.[73] Both exit and voice can be destructive to the group, while loyalty—perhaps fostered by ideological indoctrination, economic incentives, or "severe initiation costs"—attempts to enforce cohesion and coordination and prevent free riders and the principal–agent problem.[74] Loyalty, however, may lead to group-think symptoms and greater group inflexibility and isolation from everyday events and reality.[75]

Government may try to leverage conflict within an armed group or between an armed group and its rivals. This may be difficult due to the need to infiltrate the armed group or obtain detailed intelligence on internal group dynamics. The government may attempt to create misinformation or a propaganda campaign aimed at countering the armed group, but this may create a broader problem of misperception and misunderstanding among the population and negatively shape the broader environment.[76]

A state's countering strategies may help in accelerating or enabling internal armed-group tensions, such as by offering select leaders or group members amnesty or incentives to participate in the political process. Armed groups may fracture and decline due to internal dynamics and not in response to state actions.[77] This may be due to their inability to achieve their objectives.[78] At the same time, state strategies should be geared to both the context and group, as armed groups are a product of their environment and may rely on support from the local population. The analyst should examine each element of the framework and understand the group's structure, changes, and dynamics.

Nevertheless, states have multiple options at their disposal. States can combat armed groups by engaging each aspect of the profile. At a broader level, states undertake operations that shape the environment within which armed groups operate by curbing armed-group opportunities and constraining incentives.[79] These countering strategies overlap, as efforts to prevent potential supporters from joining a group may rely on strategies specifically focused on increasing costs to joining through targeted police surveillance or imprisonment, while altering contextual incentives by opening opportunities for access to political channels or decreasing socioeconomic grievances.

Leadership

Targeting a group's leadership, whether through decapitation strikes or planting misinformation, may create or exploit tensions among the leadership. Planting false information and sowing discord concerning the "power plays" of various actors vying for leadership positions may exploit factional rivalries, jealousies, and competition. If the group is hierarchical, isolating or removing the leadership may lead to a break down in group governance and ideological motivation. Cutting off the nodes of a decentralized group, or isolating them such that they are unable to channel information up to the leadership or out to other nodes, may starve the organization of local, tactical information. In the end, isolating or removing the leadership may disrupt long-term strategic planning and vision, interrupt logistical operations including fundraising and coordination of group activities, and send a message that the group has been compromised, creating a negative psychological effect on members.

Decapitation Tactics

Decapitation operations, whether carried out by missile and drone strikes or conventional raids, are an increasing topic of discussion. Debates center on the effectiveness, legality, and ethical issues surrounding state attempts to kill an armed group's leaders in the hope of destroying, crippling, or severely impairing a group's ability to operate. This tactic has received attention in the past decade because of operations in Iraq, Afghanistan, and Yemen. While comprehensive studies of group decapitation have only recently been assembled, often with incomplete and uncertain data, we have some picture of the groups most susceptible to drone strikes: small, hierarchical, young armed groups led by a cult-of-personality-type figure.[80] While this is a tactical level response to armed groups, it can have a broader impact, due to the potentially indiscriminate casualties created from a drone strike. When others beyond the intended target are killed, or when the attack is launched in error against innocent groups, it can create blowback that erodes the government's legitimacy.

The utility of using drone strikes to remove an armed group's leadership has generated considerable debate in the United States and abroad.[81] From a policy efficacy standpoint, many al-Qaeda leaders and high-level operatives have been killed by strikes.[82] In addition, as bin Laden himself is purported to have remarked, while it can be difficult to find suitable replacements for those killed in drone strikes, those they do find to replace killed leaders are frequently inexperienced and prone to errors.[83]

Drone strikes likewise put pressure on the armed group to remain constantly on the move and not congregate in large numbers for fear of being targeted. Electronic communication is made more difficult due to surveillance, and training may be impossible without attracting attention. This is intensified with the US move toward "signature strikes," in which drone strikes are used against those exhibiting terrorist leader characteristics or those whom the United States believes may be terrorists, without actual knowledge that the targets are terrorists.

Simultaneously, drone strikes may possess a deterrent quality, whereby possible leaders are wary of accepting positions in an organization for fear of becoming a target. More broadly, the uncertainty of a future strike is enough to disrupt and deter armed-group operations.

Nevertheless, drone strikes may create several long-term costs that prevent them from remaining a useful tactic. Despite short-term success in removing al-Qaeda leaders, drone strikes may not be useful in the long term. The few studies of decapitation programs have shown that these programs are not applicable to al-Qaeda, which is an established, networked group with a strong ideological motivation. Leadership and internal degradation should be accompanied by a decrease in al-Qaeda's propaganda production, which requires access to al-Qaeda leaders and skill, experience, time, and opportunity to create and disseminate. All of these should be degraded through drone strikes, yet evidence indicates al-Qaeda's propaganda output appears unaffected.[84] While drone strikes may be effective in other situations, their long-term success against the United States' main armed-groups threat appears debatable.

Armed-group decapitation through capturing and interrogating suspects remains a better way to gather intelligence and may lead to greater long-term successes against armed groups. Additionally, US special operations forces raids that kill group leaders, such as the operation that killed bin Laden, may provide an opportunity to gather useful information. The recent defection and capture of al-Shabaab's leader Sheikh Hassan Dahir Aweys—pushed out by an internal power struggle—may provide previously unknown details of the Somali group's capabilities and operations.[85]

Membership

Membership may be exploited through creating or furthering fissures, factions, and rivalries; increasing costs to joining; or reducing costs to leaving the group. Governments may offer armed-group members monetary incentives not to join; transparent or effective communication channels for political expression; or opportunities to exit the group through amnesty. The government may attempt to promote internal dissent in an armed group and may increase the costs of joining an armed group.[86] Increasing the costs to joining will prevent some from joining the group, but generate loyalty and inhibit exit among members through "severe initiation costs."[87] In attempting to increase the costs of joining, states will have to identify the recruitment pool and go after supporters, rather than group members. Supporters have less invested, have little or no voice in the armed group, and will find it easier to exit the group, and the state may find it easier to lure the supporter away from the group. The main difficulty in increasing joining costs is in identifying supporter's incentives and credibly committing to addressing these.[88]

Due to the clandestine and networked nature of many armed groups, it may be difficult to verify this information. Cells may not know other members of their group, but may see their arrest, or hear that defectors have denounced the group, which leaves them wondering who can be trusted. Government attempts to sow confusion and discord within the group, or accelerate existing rivalries, introduces some fundamental principal–agent problems, as group members may refuse to take part in operations, fail to provide leaders with information, or refuse to meet with others in the group for fear that they are exposing themselves to government agents or informants.

Government may reduce the costs of leaving a group by providing monetary payouts, political appointments or opportunities, or amnesty. This may exploit and increase existing fissures, or identify group members, as "the greatest threat for terrorists is infiltration by informants, traitors, and information given to the authorities by third parties (e.g., former activists, neighbors, acquaintances)."[89]

Organization

Attacking the armed-group organization may involve cutting off its resources, exploiting the geographical distance between armed-group cells, and capitalizing on the clandestine nature of the organization. All groups require financing for their operations. Cutting off the organization's source of funding, whether individuals, the diaspora community, illicit activities, or donations from charitable organizations, decreases the group's ability to provide benefits and services to its members, as well as shuts down its operational capability.

Geographical distance between cells can lead to a basic lack of information and the need for communication. If the communication systems are basic—runners or individual couriers—they may be physically tracked or intercepted. As many armed groups have utilized advanced technology to communicate—whether satellite phones, email, websites and chat rooms, or prepaid cell phones—these open up new avenues of interception. Governments may track or intercept calls, monitor emails or websites, or shutdown communications on webpages. While these media channels may provide the armed groups with some manner of anonymity, they also allow anonymous and potentially undetectable monitoring. Intercepted communications can be used to anticipate and plan for impending attacks, gather information on developing divisions within the organization, or to attack other sections of the group, such as fundraising or ideological cells in the organization.

The clandestine nature of the organization presents both a problem and opportunity for combating them. Armed groups may isolate themselves from regular communication or interaction with group members, and supporters, and potential supporters. This creates an information gap, which may be exploited as the authorities take down parts of the group, or key nodes replaced by government agents. A lack of information may sow distrust and allow government disinformation campaigns, fostering principal–agent problems within the group.

Ideology

According to the US Department of Defense, extremist ideology is the center of gravity for terrorist networks and as such is a key, yet complex, avenue of vulnerability.[90] Governments may emphasize and play up differences within the group, whether due to regional, ethnic, racial, or national differences in the members. The government may point out ideological violations of international laws and norms, religious tenants, or cultural taboos from the local culture, especially if the group ideology is imported from an outside culture. Furthermore, governments may use covert political action, propaganda, or agents of influence to try to discredit, delegitimize, or in other ways degrade the armed group's ideology. Sebastian Gorka has suggested that one method of countering al-Qaeda's message has been to point out that the group has killed far more Muslims than Westerners since 9/11.[91]

Combating a group's ideology remains a difficult undertaking. The government may not have legitimacy with the local population, a counterideology may be dismissed out of hand, and foreign powers may not understand ideological nuances separating the armed group from the local population or commonly held interpretations. Nevertheless, the government can challenge the group's worldview, magnify divisions and inconsistencies in the group's ideology, or create a marketplace of ideas through the support of local civil society.[92] This requires intimate knowledge and local intelligence, or risk discrediting the government in the eyes of the domestic population and international audience.

Strategy and Tactics

Sun Tzu argued that attacking the enemy's strategy is preferable to having to fight the enemy.[93] Anticipating and reacting to an armed group's strategy may be difficult, as many targeted countries face both domestic and international pressure to retaliate, playing directly into an armed group's strategy. If an armed group pursues a strategy of provocation, the government will need to tailor its response so as to not generate an overwhelming and indiscriminate retaliation against the armed group and innocent civilians. There may, however, be domestic pressure to be seen as "tough on terrorists" or to "punish" those responsible. Furthermore, pressure from international financial institutions or states to establish stability may push the government into enacting counterproductive policies.

At a more fundamental level, governments may invest in defensive measures to protect against small-arms fire or IEDs, as the United States has done in Iraq and Afghanistan. Other global initiatives seek to detect, map, and ultimately remove landmines. Additionally, government agents may attempt to sabotage equipment and operations by preventing the delivery of military equipment and supplies. Governments may disrupt communications between the various cells in a group, or plant false information between the leadership and various active cells. As weapons and communication technology becomes more complex, there may be more opportunities to identify and neutralize operations, as weapon suppliers may be traced and advanced technology may be purchased from a limited number of sources. Although armed groups frequently employ basic small arms and communications equipment, those seeking advanced communication equipment or even WMD become more visible as they pursue these avenues.

Strategic Communication

The government may seek to prevent the armed group from effectively communicating its messages by taking down websites; banning the publication of books, pamphlets, or other printed material; or by punishing the promotion of certain inflammatory views. All of these actions, however, may run counter to a country's foundational laws, or prove impossible to enforce. The US Constitution provides a right to free speech and the freedom to publish potentially inflammatory or subversive tracts or ideas that challenge basic tenets of the US government. Other states may find that stopping the spread of printed material a fool's errand: documents posted on the Internet may be impossible to remove. Documents can exist on many different servers located in many different countries and no longer physically exist, except for when they are downloaded and printed. Destroying a hard drive is no guarantee that a particular file is unavailable online. Governments may attempt to censor content available to its citizens, but armed groups, and regular citizens, may, with varying degrees of success, defeat these measures and find other ways to present their information. From basic forms of communication such as Mexican drug cartels hanging sheets from bridges advertising jobs or deterring authorities to extremist groups relying on online anonymity to evade government restrictions, removing or preventing an armed group from publicizing its message is a challenging proposition for even the most advanced countries.

Governments may have more success publicizing an event in order to delegitimize an armed group. If a group detonates a bomb at a wedding, if an attack kills innocent women and children, or if an armed group's stated objectives would disenfranchise or harm other minority groups in society, publicizing these facts may help delegitimize the armed group and legitimize the government. Additionally, governments may provide political and moral support and encouragement to other governments facing armed group threats. The population in the threatened state may see this external support as a positive, legitimating step for the government and subsequently decrease the armed group's legitimacy and communications, especially if the armed group is attempting to portray the government as internationally isolated. This also recognizes the need for governments to counter an armed group's strategic communication and narrative with their own.

External Support

External support is key to many armed groups not just in the early stages of their formation, but also in their perpetuation. The state can attempt to both isolate the armed group from receiving external support and prevent the third party from providing the support. Strengthening border controls, interdicting supplies, or shutting down communications may prevent the armed group from receiving outside aid. The United States has attempted to prevent individuals from leaving the country to receive training in another state, or to engage in fighting against other governments as part of an armed group, such as Somali youth returning to fight for al-Shabaab. The United States has also launched legal challenges to NGOs that, acting in a supposed "charity function," funneled funds to al-Qaeda or other groups on the US State Department's FTO list.

Creating a "name and shame" campaign, whereby the state publicly accuses external sponsors of siding with and supporting terrorist groups, may decrease the third party's willingness to provide support. There is always the concern that heated rhetoric between states will escalate into violence, so operations targeting third-party states may be more difficult to achieve. Alternatively, calling out the diaspora as suppliers and enablers of brutally violent armed groups may pressure not just individuals to suspend their aid, but also indirectly pressure the state government to crack down on funds and supplies leaving their country.

If Geoffrey Blainey is correct that "a prominent cause of war can at times be a prominent cause of peace," then governments need to look transnationally to counter armed group threats.[94] Internal conflicts may be triggered by external events, motivated by external actors, or exist to address broad regional or global grievances, which must be taken into account when confronting and combating these groups. Furthermore, these conflicts persist in a globalized space, which is especially true given the importance of external support to armed groups. External support is a key component in a group's creation, survival, and success, and thus any government strategy of combating armed groups must confront the reality that a seemingly internal conflict against a nationalist-oriented armed group may likely be regional, if not global, in scope and not simply confined to one village, province, or even country.

CONCLUSION

No matter the manner by which states attempt to combat armed groups, there is no short-term, all-encompassing policy. The most fundamental aspect is to understand the armed group as thoroughly as possible, seeking to establish the group's incentives and internal dynamics, as well as the constraining environment and the group's relations with the people, the state, foreign powers, and potential rival armed groups, whether foreign or domestic. A mixture of policies that address the armed group, the population, and the underlying structural imbalances and inequalities over the medium and long term will best reduce the threat from armed groups.

DISCUSSION QUESTIONS

1. What is the role of other nonstate actors—including MNCs, international institutions, NGOs, and super-empowered individuals—in combating armed groups?
2. What complications arise for states combating domestic armed groups disconnected from the local population?
3. What advantages/disadvantages do states face when combating armed groups in foreign countries?
4. How can governments coordinate the complex strategies required to combat armed groups?

RECOMMENDED READINGS

Melanne Civic and Michael Miklaucic, eds., *The Monopoly of Force: The Nexus of DDR and SSR* (Washington, DC: NDU Press, 2011).

Audrey Kurth Cronin, *How Terrorism Ends: Understanding the Decline and Demise of Terrorist Campaigns* (Princeton, NJ: Princeton University Press, 2011).

Audrey Kurth Cronin and James M. Ludes, eds., *Attacking Terrorism: Elements of a Grand Strategy* (Washington, DC: Georgetown University Press, 2004).

David Galula, *Counterinsurgency Warfare: Theory and Practice* (Westport, CT: Praeger Security International, 2006. First published 1964).

Heather S. Gregg, "Fighting the Jihad of the Pen: Countering Revolutionary Islam's Ideology." *Terrorism and Political Violence* 22, no. 2 (2010): 292–314.

Idean Salehyan, *Rebels without Borders: Transnational Insurgencies in World Politics* (Ithaca, NY: Cornell University Press, 2011).

David H. Ucko, *The New Counterinsurgency Era: Transforming the U.S. Military for Modern Wars* (Washington, DC: Georgetown University Press, 2009).

Barbara F. Walter, *Committing to Peace: The Successful Settlement of Civil Wars* (Princeton, NJ: Princeton University Press, 2002).

World Bank, *World Development Report 2011: Conflict, Security, and Development* (Washington, DC: World Bank, 2011).

NOTES

1. David H. Ucko, "Whither Counterinsurgency: The Rise and Fall of a Divisive Concept," in *The Routledge Handbook of Insurgency and Counterinsurgency*, ed. Paul B. Rich and Isabelle Duyvesteyn (New York: Routledge, 2012).

2. Kelly M. Greenhill and Paul Staniland, "Ten Ways to Lose at Counterinsurgency," *Civil Wars* 9, no. 4 (2007): 402–19.

3. Carl von Clausewitz, *On War*, trans. Michael Howard and Peter Paret (Princeton, NJ: Princeton University Press, 1984).

4. David Kilcullen, "Counter-Insurgency *Redux*," *Survival* 48, no. 4 (2006–2007): 123.

5. Paul Collier, "Doing Well out of War: An Economic Perspective," in *Greed and Grievance: Economic Agendas in Civil Wars*, ed. Mats Berdal and David M. Malone (Boulder, CO: Lynne Rienner, 2000), 106 and James D. Fearon and David D. Laitin, "Ethnicity, Insurgency, and Civil War," *American Political Science Review* 97, no. 1 (2003): 75–90.

6. US Department of Defense, *Antiterrorism*, Joint Publication 3-07.2, p. vii, November 24, 2010, http://www.bits.de/NRANEU/others/jp-doctrine/JP3_07.2(10).pdf.

7. US Department of Defense, *Counterterrorism*, Joint Publication 3-26, p. v, November 13, 2009, http://www.dtic.mil/doctrine/new_pubs/jp3_26.pdf.

8. US Department of Defense, *Counterinsurgency Operations*, Joint Publication 3-24, p. x, October 5, 2009, http://www.dtic.mil/doctrine/new_pubs/jp3_24.pdf.

9. CIA, *Guide to the Analysis of Insurgency* (Washington, DC: US Government, 2012), 1, https://www.hsdl.org/?view&did=713599.

10. United Nations Office on Drugs and Crime, *The Globalization of Crime: A Transnational Organized Crime Threat Assessment* (Vienna, Austria: UNODC, 2010).

11. Edward Girardet, *Afghanistan: The Soviet War* (New York: St. Martin's Press, 1985).

12. Steven Metz, *Rethinking Insurgency* (Carlisle, PA: Strategic Studies Institute, US Army War College, 2007), 50.

13. Ibid., 52.

14. Ibid. See also William Reno, *Warlord Politics and African States* (Boulder, CO: Lynne Rienner, 1999) and Patrick Chabal and Jean-Pascal Daloz, *Africa Works: Disorder as Political Instrument* (Bloomington: Indiana University Press, 1999).

15. Greenhill and Staniland, "Ten Ways to Lose at Counterinsurgency," 414.

16. Ibid.

17. Ibid., 408.

18. Ibid., 409–10.

19. See Bard E. O'Neill, *Insurgency and Terrorism: From Revolution to Apocalypse* (Washington, DC: Potomac Books, 2005), chap. 8.

20. The conundrum between militarization of US policy and US COIN doctrine is discussed in Roland Marchal, "Warlordism and Terrorism: How to Obscure an Already Confusing Crisis? The Case of Somalia," *International Affairs* 83, no. 6 (2007): 1102.

21. Steve Coll, *Ghost Wars: The Secret History of the CIA, Afghanistan, and Bin Laden, from the Soviet Invasion to September 10, 2001* (New York: Penguin, 2004), 422–23.

22. Martin van Creveld, *The Transformation of War* (New York: Free Press, 1991), 30.

23. Gil Merom, *How Democracies Lose Small Wars: State, Society, and the Failures of France in Algeria, Israel in Lebanon, and the United States in Vietnam* (Cambridge: Cambridge University Press, 2003).

24. Eric Chase, "Defining Terrorism: A Strategic Imperative," *Small Wars Journal*, January 24, 2013, http://smallwarsjournal.com/print/13722.

25. US Department of State, *Foreign Terrorist Organizations*, Bureau of Counterterrorism. September 28, 2012, http://www.state.gov/j/ct/rls/other/des/123085.htm.

26. Andrew Quinn, Adriana Barrera, and Mica Rosenberg, "Clinton Sees Drug 'Insurgency' in Mexico and Central America," Reuters, September 8, 2010, http://www.reuters.com/article/2010/09/08/us-usa-mexico-clinton-idUSTRE68758820100908. See also Paul Richter and Ken Dilanian, "Clinton Says Mexico Drug Wars Starting to Look Like Insurgency," *Los Angeles Times*, September 9, 2010, http://articles.latimes.com/2010/sep/09/world/la-fg-mexico-insurgency-20100909. This echoes Manwaring's argument that gangs have evolved into a twenty-first-century form of insurgency. See Max G. Manwaring, *A Contemporary Challenge to State Sovereignty: Gangs and Other Illicit Transnational Criminal Organizations in Central America, El Salvador, Mexico, Jamaica, and Brazil* (Carlisle, PA: Strategic Studies Institute, US Army War College, 2007).

27. Tom A. Peter, "Mexico Denies Hillary Clinton's 'Insurgency' Comparison," *The Christian Science Monitor*, September 9, 2010. http://www.csmonitor.com/World/terrorism-security/2010/0909/Mexico-denies-Hillary-Clinton-s-insurgency-comparison.

28. Fearon and Laitin, "Ethnicity, Insurgency, and Civil War," 80.

29. David J. Kilcullen, "Countering Global Insurgency," *The Journal of Strategic Studies* 28, no. 4 (2005): 597–617.

30. Daniel Byman, "US Counter-Terrorism Options: A Taxonomy," *Survival* 49, no. 3 (2007): 121–50.

31. Mariya Omelicheva, "Combating Terrorism in Central Asia: Explaining Differences in States' Responses to Terror," *Terrorism and Political Violence* 19, no. 3 (2007): 369–93.

32. Arie Perliger, "How Democracies Respond to Terrorism: Regime Characteristics, Symbolic Power and Counterterrorism," *Security Studies* 21, no. 3 (2012): 490–528.

33. These are adopted from Jeffry A. Frieden, David A. Lake, and Kenneth A. Schultz, *World Politics: Interests, Interactions, Institutions* (New York: Norton, 2010), 397-402.

34. Glenn H. Snyder, *Deterrence and Defense: Toward a Theory of National Security* (Princeton, NJ: Princeton University Press, 1961).

35. Robert F. Trager and Dessislava P. Zagorcheva, "Deterring Terrorism: It Can Be Done," *International Security* 30, no. 1 (2005): 87 and Matthew Kroenig and Barry Pavel, "How to Deter Terrorism," *The Washington Quarterly* 35, no. 2 (2012): 21.

36. "How to Deter Terrorism," 25-33.

37. Associated Press, "Tancredo: If They Nuke Us, Bomb Mecca," July 18, 2005, http://www.foxnews.com/story/0,2933,162795,00.html.

38. Kroenig and Pavel, "How to Deter Terrorism," 28, 31.

39. Trager and Zagorcheva, "Deterring Terrorism: It Can Be Done," 98 and Kroenig and Pavel, "How to Deter Terrorism," 26.

40. "How to Deter Terrorism," 30.

41. Glenn Snyder, as quoted from Martha Crenshaw, "Theories of Terrorism: Instrumental and Organizational Approaches," in *Inside Terrorist Organizations*, ed. David C. Rapoport (New York: Columbia University Press, 1988), 16.

42. *National Strategy for Homeland Security*, p. 47, July 2002, Permanent.access.gpo.gov/lps20641/nat_strat_hls.pdf and US Department of Homeland Security, "Our Mission," www.dhs.gov/our-mission.

43. US Department of Homeland Security, "Our Mission."

44. *National Strategy for Homeland Security*.

45. Ibid., 2.

46. Ibid., 8, 9, 51.

47. See, for example, the increased calls for law enforcement capabilities in US Department of Defense, "Counterinsurgency Operations," Joint Publication 3-24. See also the overlay of

counterinsurgency and law enforcement in Elena Pokalova, "Terrorism: The Dilemma of Response," in *International Criminal Justice: Critical Persepctives and New Challenges*, ed. George Andreopoulos, Rosemary Barberet, and James P. Levine (New York: Springer, 2011).

48. Christopher J. Fettweis, *Dangerous Times?: The International Politics of Great Power Peace* (Washington, DC: Georgetown University Press, 2010), 191.

49. However, policing in a multiethnic society may see the police "captured" by local interests or exacerbate ethnic tensions. See, for example, Andrew Novo, "Friend or Foe? The Cyprus Police Force and the Eoka Insurgency," *Small Wars and Insurgencies* 23, no. 3 (2012): 414–31.

50. Rachel Locke, *Organized Crime, Conflict, and Fragility: A New Approach* (New York: International Peace Institute, 2012), 3.

51. Ibid.

52. United Nations Office on Drugs and Crime, *The Globalization of Crime: A Transnational Organized Crime Threat Assessment*.

53. Locke, *Organized Crime, Conflict, and Fragility: A New Approach*, 13–15.

54. Russell D. Howard, "Preemptive Military Doctrine: No Other Choice," in *Terrorism and Counterterrorism: Understanding the New Security Environment*, ed. Russell D. Howard, Bruce Hoffman, and Stacy Neal (New York: McGraw-Hill, 2012).

55. Audrey Kurth Cronin, "Ending Terrorism: Lessons for Defeating Al-Qaeda," *Adelphi Paper* 47, no. 394 (2007): chap. 2.

56. Greenhill and Staniland, "Ten Ways to Lose at Counterinsurgency."

57. Van Creveld, *The Transformation of War*, 22. Van Creveld acknowledges that only Britain in Malaysia "won." Ibid., 23.

58. Alexander B. Downes, "Draining the Sea by Filling the Graves: Investigating the Effectiveness of Indiscriminate Violence as a Counterinsurgency Strategy," *Civil Wars* 9, no. 4 (2007): 420–44.

59. Fearon and Laitin, "Ethnicity, Insurgency, and Civil War."

60. Ucko, "Whither Counterinsurgency: The Rise and Fall of a Divisive Concept."

61. Richard Wike, "What Pakistan Thinks," Pew Research Global Attitudes Project, May 10, 2013, www.pewglobal.org/2013/05/10/what-pakistan-thinks.

62. Pew Research Center, *Global Opinion of Obama Slips, International Policies Faulted: Drone Strikes Widely Opposed*, Pew Research Global Attitudes Project, June 13, 2012, www.pewglobal.org/files/2012/06/Pew-Global-Attitudes-U.S.-Image-Report-FINAL-June-13-20123.pdf.

63. Heather S. Gregg, "Setting a Place at the Table: Ending Insurgencies through the Political Process," *Small Wars and Insurgencies* 22, no. 4 (2011): 645.

64. Gregg argues disarmament should be the last, not first step. See ibid. On disarmament, demobilization, and reintegration (DDR) and security sector reform (SSR) more broadly, see Sean McFate, "There's a New Sheriff in Town: DDR-SSR and the Monopoly of Force," in *The Monopoly of Force: The Nexus of DDR and SSR*, ed. Melanne A. Civic and Michael Miklaucic (Washington, DC: NDU Press, 2011).

65. Gregg, "Setting a Place at the Table: Ending Inusrgencies through the Political Process."

66. Mats Berdal and David H. Ucko, "Introduction: The Political Reintegration of Armed Groups after War," in *Reintegrating Armed Groups after Conflict: Politics, Violence, and Transition*, ed. Mats Berdal and David H. Ucko (New York: Routledge, 2009), 6. On alternative avenues, see Alexandra Guaqueta, "The Way Back In: Reintegrating Illegal Armed Groups in Colombia Then and Now," ibid. On the need for strong state institutions, see Gregg, "Setting a Place at the Table: Ending Inusrgencies through the Political Process."

67. "Setting a Place at the Table: Ending Inusrgencies through the Political Process." On this "false process of political reintegration" in Iraq, see David H. Ucko, "Militias, Tribes and Insurgents: The Challenge of Political Reintegration in Iraq," in *Reintegrating Armed Groups after Conflict: Politics, Violence and Transition*, ed. Mats Berdal and David H. Ucko (New York: Routledge, 2009), 96.

68. Reno, *Warlord Politics and African States* and Zoë Marriage, "Flip-Flop Rebel, Dollar Soldier," in *Reintegrating Armed Groups after Conflict: Politics, Violence and Transition*, ed. Mats Berdal and David H. Ucko (New York: Routledge, 2009).

69. Stephen John Stedman, "Spoiler Problems in Peace Processes," *International Security* 22, no. 2 (1997): 5–53.

70. Tim Craig and Haq Nawaz Khan, "Pakistan's Taliban Rejects Peace Talks, Citing No. 2 Leader's Death in U.S. Drone Strike," *Washington Post*, May 30, 2013, http://articles.washingtonpost.com/2013-05-30/world/39621956_1_hakimullah-mehsud-taliban-s-pakistani-taliban.

71. BBC News, "Mehsud Death: US Says Pakistan-Taliban Talks 'Internal'" *BBC News Asia*, November 2, 2013, http://www.bbc.co.uk/news/world-asia-24792516.

72. Barbara F. Walter, *Committing to Peace: The Successful Settlement of Civil Wars* (Princeton, NJ: Princeton University Press, 2002).

73. Crenshaw, "Theories of Terrorism: Instrumental and Organizational Approaches." Crenshaw draws on Albert O. Hirschman, *Exit, Voice, and Loyalty: Responses to Decline in Firms, Organizations, and States* (Cambridge, MA: Harvard University Press, 1970).

74. Crenshaw, "Theories of Terrorism: Instrumental and Organizational Approaches," 22–23.

75. Ibid., 23. This is similar to the isolating effects arising from the armed group's clandestine nature. See Gordon H. McCormick, "Terrorist Decision Making," *Annual Review of Political Science* 6, no. 1 (2003): 473–507.

76. Crenshaw, "Theories of Terrorism: Instrumental and Organizational Approaches," 26.

77. Cronin, "Ending Terrorism: Lessons for Defeating Al-Qaeda," chap. 2.

78. Crenshaw, "Theories of Terrorism: Instrumental and Organizational Approaches," 16 discusses this in relation to terrorist groups failing.

79. For a related view tackling al-Qaeda, see Reid Sawyer and Jodi M. Vittori, "The Uncontested Battles: The Role of Actions, Networks, and Ideas in the Fight against Al Qaeda," in *Terrorism and Counterterrorism: Understanding the New Security Environment*, ed. Russell D. Howard, Bruce Hoffman, and Stacy Neal (New York: McGraw-Hill, 2012).

80. Jenna Jordan, "When Heads Roll: Assessing the Effectiveness of Leadership Decapitation," *Security Studies* 18, no. 4 (2009): 719–55.

81. This section draws on issues discussed in Daniel Byman, "Why Drones Work," *Foreign Affairs* 92, no. 4 (2013): 32–43 and Audrey Kurth Cronin, "Why Drones Fail," ibid.

82. The discussion focuses on al-Qaeda, as the first *National Strategy for Homeland Security* in 2002 noted al-Qaeda was the foremost threat to the United States.

83. Byman, "Why Drones Work."

84. Megan Smith and James Igoe Walsh, "Do Drone Strikes Degrade Al Qaeda?: Evidence from Propaganda Output," *Terrorism and Political Violence* 25, no. 2 (2013): 311–27.

85. Farouk Chothia, "Will Somali Islamist Purge Strengthen Al-Shabab?," BBC News, July 3, 2013, http://www.bbc.co.uk/news/world-africa-23146744.

86. Crenshaw, "Theories of Terrorism: Instrumental and Organizational Approaches," 22–26. Economic incentives and opportunities may be key for militia members. See Chris Alden, Monika Thakur, and Matthew Arnold, *Militias and the Challenges of Post-Conlict Peace* (New York: Zed Books, 2011), 36–37.

87. Crenshaw, "Theories of Terrorism: Instrumental and Organizational Approaches," 26.

88. Ibid.

89. Anthony Oberschall, "Explaining Terorrism: The Contribution of Collective Action Theory," *Sociological Theory* 22, no. 1 (2004): 29–30.

90. Chairman of the Joint Chiefs of Staff, *National Military Strategic Plan for the War on Terrorism* (Washington, DC: Government Printing Office, 2006), 7.

91. Sebastian L. v. Gorka, "Ten Years Later: Are We Winning the War?," *CTX: Combating Terrorism Exchange* 1, no. 2 (2011): 23–24.

92. Heather S. Gregg, "Fighting the Jihad of the Pen: Countering Revolutionary Islam's Ideology," *Terrorism and Political Violence* 22, no. 2 (2010): 307–08.

93. Sun Tzu, *The Art of War*, trans. Samuel B. Griffith (Oxford: Oxford University Press, 1963).

94. Geoffrey Blainey, *The Causes of War* (New York: The Free Press, 1988), 122. However, conflict outcomes may be the result of bargaining over both changing information and objectives. See Dan Reiter, *How Wars End* (Princeton, NJ: Princeton University Press, 2009).

Chapter Eight

Conclusion

This book first examined the environment within which armed groups flourish—a globalized world filled with weak and failed states, bereft of Cold War management, and awash in small arms. Intrastate conflicts with armed groups as their central players have dominated the landscape since 1945. Today, a variety of factors work against the reappearance of interstate conflicts while creating incentives for intrastate conflicts and armed groups.

Economic interdependence, the end of the superpowers' ideological struggles, the US preponderance of power, the prevalence of laws and norms against territorial conquest, and nuclear weapons' deterrent effects have reduced the occurrence and future prospects of interstate conflicts, at least among the larger powers.

At the same time, the opportunities for engaging in insurgency, terrorism, or criminal activities have never been greater. At the systemic level, changes in the international environment brought advantages to armed groups seeking to survive in a postbipolar international system. These transformations include globalization, which brought a communication, transportation, and technological revolution to the masses; the retreat of the superpowers, who monitored and suppressed conflict that threatened to destabilize the system; the removal of superpower funding, which forced armed groups to seek new, illicit profits; and the disintegration of the Soviet Union and Warsaw Pact, which flooded markets with small arms, military supplies, and unemployed security forces.

At the state level, weak states' inability or unwillingness to monitor their borders translates into ungoverned spaces and safe havens. Demographic shifts such as urbanization, population growth, and youth bulges provide vast pools of potential members. Individual alienation occurs due to the resurgence of identity politics and the skillful application of extremist ideological narratives, dissatisfaction over modernization, and the growing recognition that corruption and inequality have never been greater, nor advancement more out of reach for so many. Opportunities to exploit rapidly globalizing economic networks provide added incentive and opportunity for armed groups to grow and provide new identities and opportunities for their members. Given these opportunities and pressures, individuals are easily mobilized to fight real or perceived grievances. Armed groups today provide more than the possibility of economic and political change—they provide a livelihood, a sense of belonging, and a sense of power.

Additionally, changes in US military doctrine increases the potential for future US engagement in irregular warfare missions. As one report demonstrated, the number of missions that fell under the heading "irregular warfare" tripled over a two-year span.[1] US forces will continue to be engaged in irregular warfare missions and by extension, intrastate conflicts.

Warfare is a product of its environment and there may be no greater impact on the environment than the relationships between great powers. Future study of armed groups must begin with an understanding of the international state system. A new "cold war" between states may lead to a resurgence of armed groups benefiting from great power largesse. Regional states checked by their neighbors may support armed-group proxies. Economic globalization has transformed the world economy, providing a more open, target-rich environment for armed groups. Whether or not future armed groups are a part of state competition, or fighting on their own behalf, they may be able to strike at more sensitive, vulnerable, and ultimately costly targets. The study of armed groups is clearly one of concern to theorists and practitioners of international security and understanding individual groups is the first step in understanding the contemporary security environment.

ARMED-GROUP ADAPTATION AND EVOLUTION

This book surveyed armed-group archetypes, as if armed groups were unitary actors holding to an exact template. We quickly relented and realized that, whether due to lack of funding, changes in leadership, inability to achieve their goals, government response, or a myriad of other factors both internal and external to the armed groups, archetypical boundaries blurred and groups appear to change over time. Evolution may imply a unidirectional movement toward more complex organisms, but that is not necessarily true. Armed-group evolution is simply the transformation, over time, of an organization to adopt characteristics and policies that enable its survival. These could be creating more complicated hierarchical organization in order to ensure leadership accession in the event of decapitation strikes, or the dispersal of the armed-group membership, connected only by the Internet and an ideological narrative, in order to avoid imprisonment or mass execution at the hands of a state's security forces. When confronted with government pressure, the LRA in Uganda split its forces and fled into the jungles. While this may ultimately bring great difficulty to the group as it is unable to communicate or coordinate its operations, it has also enabled it to survive for longer than if it had remained a single, cohesive organization.

Armed groups challenge the legitimacy of the state, the region, and even the state system itself. States, with the goal of protecting their own regimes and privileged positions as sovereign actors in international relations, seek to root out these groups. The state enters the conflict with greater resources by almost any measure than the armed group. Armed groups are forced to adopt not only asymmetric warfare to fight against militarily stronger opponents, but to adopt any tactic or strategy that will allow them to prevail in a clash over gaining or securing influence among a target population. The group's survival, and possibly the survival of their "cause," requires staying one step ahead of the state and international forces arrayed against them.

Armed groups are, by necessity, better organized than states to carry out the necessary changes. They are in many cases small, decentralized networks, which allows for local factors to take precedence over centrally planned policies. Armed groups frequently benefit from a socially networked membership adhering to a common ideology and bound by the shared experience of oppression and violence. Their prime motivations—challenging the state to achieve their political and economic goals, backed by an ever-present concern with personal and group survival and cohesion—push them to innovate. While states can and do innovate, they are not challenged by armed groups in the same way that armed groups are challenged by states. For most conflicts, the asymmetry extends to the issues at stake—the state may not feel that its very existence is at stake, but the members of an armed group may have joined together precisely because of this concern.

Adaptation and evolution also do not always mean that the group has become more successful, lethal, or larger. A group such as the FARC in Colombia may adapt to the current geopolitical context by engaging in illicit activities in order to fund their activities.[2] They have not changed to become strictly a transnational criminal organization, any more than they have given up their desire to replace the Colombian government and achieve their political objectives. What they have done is adapt to the lack of funding and popular support they once commanded. The FARC has also engaged in negotiations with the Colombian government, which may signal a change of strategy or tactics, but does not necessarily indicate their political objectives have changed. They have simply adapted to their current situation in order to achieve their objectives.[3]

Armed groups may adapt new measures or characteristics in the short term, or they may permanently evolve into a different type of group. It may be difficult, in the moment, to know whether the group is making a funda-mental pivot away from being an insurgent group to a terrorist group, or whether their forays into organized crime are simply to fund their next wave of atrocities or because they have lost the ability or interest to effect political change. Adding to the complexity, armed groups may increasingly behave in multiple ways, never renouncing political objectives and occasionally acting to achieve those objectives, while carrying out day-to-day criminal opera-tions to ensure their continued funding. This reinforces the point from chap-ter 4 that many armed groups today have, as a common denominator, the need to acquire greater resources through crime. This does not indicate that all conflicts today are motivated by "greed," but that securing additional resources is a commonality to all conflicts today. Armed groups are becom-ing hybrids and as such, the demarcations between groups grow weaker.

While legal and heuristic purposes may preclude abolishing armed-group archetypes, these archetypes may be too rigid to ultimately understand to-day's complex security environment. Crenshaw notes that the "new terror-ism" literature may be driven, in part, by the desire for simplicity by policy makers, who are looking for short cuts to decision making. Furthermore, those pushing specific policies and looking for justifications for US govern-ment actions after the 9/11 attacks may find the concept of "new" terrorism appealing. Lastly, many may find monetary benefits by peddling a new form of an old concept.[4] As the environment changes, and as groups react to these changes, the language of "terrorist" and "insurgent," "criminal organization" and "militia" may become so broad, while ultimately explaining so little, as to warrant a return to the basic foundations upon which groups are created. Additionally, as armed-groups analysis embraces some of the theoretical concepts examined here—the principal–agent, coordination, time-consisten-cy, and free-rider problems—it may move in a direction characterized by state analyses in international relations. Instead of assuming that every state is unique, analyses in comparative politics seek crosscutting tools, such as examining state institutions using rigorous methodologies. Broad, compara-tive analyses of voting or legal systems and economic institutions are charac-teristic of state analysis today. Likewise, the aggregation of factors inside of armed groups—similar to corporations' internalization of processes in order to reduce costs and increase efficiency—is a hallmark of a dynamic and evolving armed-group threat that crosses analytical and archetypical boun-daries.

Relationship with Population

As the strict delineation between archetypes recedes, one factor that should be considered is the relationship that armed groups have with the population, both at home and abroad. While Ulrich Schneckener and others explicitly discuss this relationship—running the gamut from coordinated and agreeable to predatory—examining armed groups on this variable may yield significant information on the tactics, strategies, and other aspects of an armed group.[5] While all of the characteristics under consideration influence each other and should thus be considered as a whole, the issue of a group's relationship to the population may be an outcome of all of these factors, as well as a cause of these factors and transcend the simple analysis positing that indiscriminate attacks are due to, or a cause of, fewer linkages with the population. Jeremy M. Weinstein follows Stathis N. Kalyvas in arguing violence is shaped by the armed group's strategic attempts to secure support from noncombatants.[6] The situation within an armed group, the fluidity of the environment within which it operates, and the strategic competition involving armed groups, their rivals, the government, and relevant populations may lead groups to seek simultaneous and different relationships with different population groups. This increased complexity is not fully captured by the characteristics discussed here, nor can it be considered as its own variable without the input of the other factors discussed in chapters 5 and 6. Armed groups, like any social organization or group, are complex, in that the "output" of the group is not always easily measured by the "inputs" or individual characteristics of the group. As other authors have noted, a group's organizational structure, which itself may be based on the ability to secure resources or shaped by ideological demands, will play a key role in determining a group's strategy, tactics, or ability to secure external funding.[7] But it is not a variable that can be considered in isolation from the group's relationship with the population.

Criminal Activity

Armed groups frequently pursue external funding through criminal activities. As groups engage in more criminal activities, they may move toward becoming purely criminal organizations and give up their political pursuits. As discussed in chapter 5, a group may avoid the time-consistency problem by paying out immediate monetary benefits to its members instead of promising future wealth or political appointments. The need for funding, and the incentives it provides for membership retention, may change a group such that it may not renounce its political objectives, but may simply focus on criminal activities and profit maximization.

Groups engaged in crime may find it easier to satisfy the time-consistency problem, but may suffer from free-rider or principal–agent problems. With imperfect information, the group's leadership may be unable to keep track of all of its members, the amount of money collected, and control over all aspects of its various trafficking operations. In order to satisfy these problems, armed groups may, despite current thinking, move toward more hierarchical organizational structures. While flat, decentralized networks of cells

are harder for law enforcement and intelligence agencies to detect and monitor, the organizational demands of a TCO may create pressure to evolve more
hierarchical and complex organizational structures to solve the free-rider and
principal–agent problems.[8]

Overall, armed groups are a moving target and clear distinctions between
them will continue to erode. Some have argued that the common denominator among all armed groups is that they engage in crime. But even TCOs,
with an explicitly economic motive, exhibit some political tendencies, even if
they are to elect compliant politicians, maintain existing laws, and reduce
government attention. This mixture of political and economic objectives may
be the common denominator that creates future armed groups that resemble
militias more than any other armed-group archetype—proto-political units
that, unlike groups in early modern Europe that sought to carve out new
states, have no desire to challenge the state, but with economic and political
objectives that nevertheless constitute an indirect challenge to state sovereignty.

Transnational Funding and Domestic Population Disconnect

The search for outside funding, spurred by the withdrawal of support by the
super powers and the ending of a half-century of ideological conflict, could
potentially spur a new cycle of conflict as groups thought to be on the decline
fight for survival in an increasingly competitive international marketplace.
The transnational search for funding may be coupled with the decreasing
importance of the domestic audience. In turn, this may lead both the state and
armed groups to increasing violence against the domestic audience. Instead
of winning hearts and minds, indiscriminate violence and predatory behavior—in short, the increased adoption of terrorist tactics—may be the result.[9]

Despite the leadership's potential recognition that terrorist tactics are self-
defeating in the long run, groups may have internal pressures to increase the
number or severity of attacks against civilian targets. Organizational constraints, ideological predisposition, leadership, membership pressures, and
strategic communication abilities all play a role in a group's strategies and
tactics. These internal pressures, when combined with environmental incentives and the time-consistency problem, determine whether or not an armed
group will adopt and maintain terrorist tactics. The complex mixture of factors creates incentives to engage in short-term behavior that ultimately constrains and potentially upends an armed group's long-term objectives and
commitment to victory.

Public vs. Private

States and armed groups develop hazy boundaries between the public and private use of force, with states employing or supporting progovernment militias, private military and security companies, or rival insurgent groups in order to surreptitiously combat their armed-group challengers. Armed groups, by contrast, may use public resources, draw on the state's transportation, commercial, or legal infrastructure in order to arm themselves, supply their supporters, or carry out attacks against the governing regime in alternative ways.

The breakdown in the government's ability to provide services—namely security and the rule of law—leads to security privatization, depending on the individual's or community's ability to pay. These private security actors may work at odds with the state, providing security, not human rights or justice; competing for skilled personnel; and withholding evidence or refusing to cooperate with law enforcement. The state may not admit that these groups are operating domestically, nor is the state always able to provide "effective control" over the armed group, which creates a principal–agent problem. The very presence of these groups, as with TCOs, militias, or others, delegitimizes the state by demonstrating its weakness and inability to provide security.[10]

Combatants vs. Noncombatants

The ambiguous divide between public and private spills over into the discussion of who is a combatant. In a fluid political environment where crime and war are often simultaneous events and clandestine armed groups purposefully target the population as a strategy to force government acquiescence, it should come as no surprise that "noncombatants" are simultaneously armed-group targets, supporters, and members. In addition, law-enforcement figures who may be neither prepared nor capable of combating armed group threats are often thrust into duties emanating from today's "crime-war battlefield."[11]

Political vs. Economic Objectives

Lastly, armed groups today may primarily seek political or economic objectives, but the overlap between the two and ultimate objectives sought may create further confusion. Many historical armed groups, acting with political objectives, sought the creation of their own states. This remains true today among some insurgent, militia, or even terrorist groups. Nevertheless, many groups, such as al-Qaeda, may aspire to a political objective that encompasses the overthrow of the state system and the creation of a new political unit, such as the caliphate. Furthermore, militias or TCOs may control territory in some manner but have no desire to govern the territory or to replace the existing national government. As long as they are left alone, they are happy to maintain an ambiguous economic and political status quo.

FUTURE ARMED-GROUP THREATS

Armed-group evolution and hybridization create new threats to a variety of actors and make it more difficult to understand and combat these threats. Human security is now a pressing concern for many countries, as armed groups destabilize states and regions, creating forced migration, the spread of disease, resource conflicts, and food and water scarcity. The armed group's ability to react quickly in providing services to a population after a natural disaster establishes credibility and supporters. An armed group's global strategic communication provides a legitimating ideological narrative to its violent challenge to the state. Additionally, states may find it more difficult to react to armed groups' adoption of terrorist tactics. Lastly, the overlap of crime and security threats complicates the state's counterinsurgent or counterterrorist missions and provides the armed groups with the ability to sidestep traditional state sponsors.

History may have demonstrated the extent to which proxies are a useful, yet troublesome, tool, but today's proliferation of armed groups may nonetheless create incentives to project power through these relatively inexpensive and unofficial tools.[12] This increases uncertainty and misperception in the system and in interstate relations, while also weakening state power in the long run. This creates a moral hazard problem, as states will have little incentive to build up their legitimate, official diplomatic, military, or economic capabilities if they are able to rely on the services and opportunities armed groups create. An extreme version, evident in patrimonial, "warlord politics" in many African countries, may remove state leadership from obligations to its population and diminish human security within a country, all while weakening state governance and legitimacy even further and fraying the fabric of the international society of states. As these disemboweled states retreat into their isolated existence where services, security, and diplomatic and economic relationships become the purview of armed-group relationships with corrupt and complicit politicians, societal breakdown increases the likelihood of greater state erosion, regional spillovers and disruptions, and stagnant zones of instability and insecurity.

The issue of states using armed groups as proxies, along with the threat that states perceive from armed groups, will also be a function of international structural changes. During the Cold War, the bipolar distribution of power led the superpowers to avoid direct confrontation. While arguments vary as to whether the current system is unipolar or multipolar or a hybrid, the structure may impact the view of armed-group threats and the role armed groups play in state foreign policy. A growing China may lead to a great power challenge to US hegemony through indirect means, including using armed groups as proxies to strike US national and commercial interests in Africa or Latin America, or disrupt US attempts to rebalance toward Asia.[13] Continued US hegemony may lead to attempts to reassert a balance of power. Since they cannot challenge the United States directly, smaller states seeking to balance the United States may use armed groups. The same case may be made in a multipolar system, where uncertainty and threat misperception are already rampant and no state is powerful enough to take on its rivals.[14]

COMBATING ARMED GROUPS

States face several challenges as they combat today's armed groups. As more groups take up crime, this may create legal and political ramifications as governments seek appropriate and authorized tools to combat these groups. While military and law-enforcement tools can be used in conjunction, they are frequently seen as alternative approaches. This means the government will continue to seek political cover and justification for using one or the other approach, while not acknowledging the complexity of the threat.

The international community may be at a loss given armed groups' challenges to sovereignty and the confusion generated within the legal community. While international law argues for international audiences to allow civil wars to play out, there is a growing call under the R2P movement to intervene in the name of human security. While the United Nations was founded on the notion of state sovereignty, it also has reacted favorably to recent calls for humanitarian intervention in cases of complex emergencies involving natural disasters in unstable and insecure areas.[15] Additionally, there has been a push for intervention following human rights abuses, whether perpetrated by local or regional governments or armed groups. These cases have divided international opinion and lack clear grounding in international law.

Intrastate conflicts may become increasingly transnational in nature, as both armed groups and states receive external funding. Armed groups need external support to succeed because they cannot match the initial resource endowment of the state. States will increasingly rely on external support because conflicts are largely occurring in weak and failing states, which lack large initial resource endowments, are adversely affected by globalization, and will be unable to extract resources to fight armed groups, which further erode their legitimacy and resources. As a consequence, neither armed groups nor states will be reliant on winning the support of the domestic population that they once were. Legitimacy may become more depend on externally driven identities and appealing to an international audience.

James D. Fearon and David D. Laitin have argued that states are likely to have corrupt or inept counterinsurgent efforts when they lack the resources to recruit, train, and finance top-tier counterinsurgent forces. They note the difficulty of counterinsurgency even for the strongest, most well-financed countries, including the United States, France, and the UK.[16] As more countries find themselves in the weak or failing categories, or as more countries are unable to move out of those categories, their inept and corrupt counterinsurgent forces may precipitate and prolong more conflicts. Armed groups of all varieties benefit from a provocation strategy, whereby the armed group tries to provoke the government into indiscriminate retaliation against the population. This, in turn, may push the population into the arms of the armed group and reinforce group loyalists. It may be easier for armed groups to pursue a provocation strategy if counterinsurgent forces remain at a substandard level. There is clearly a need for increased partnership and training capability between countries with the resources to fund these efforts and those most adversely affected. The host states' lack of resources, however, complicates any foreign internal defense operations and may limit options to training or direct action by the foreign partner.

THREE QUESTIONS

Are Armed-Group Threats Analogous to State Threats?

The brief scenarios outlined above create a paradoxical situation. On one hand, no matter the international structure, armed groups will remain state tools and conflict instigators. On the other hand, the degree to which states treat armed groups as threats needing military attention will vary based on the other threats in the system. While China's continued rise may lead it to rely on armed groups, given its weak power projection capability, the United States is far more likely to be concerned with an assertive China's conventional and nuclear military forces and pay less attention to any armed groups China might support.[17] This is natural, given the bias in IR theory, traditional ideas concerning threat perception, and the findings of prospect theory, where highly unlikely but greater threats—great power war—are viewed with greater trepidation and worthy of attention than more likely but smaller threats, such as armed groups challenging commercial and diplomatic interests in a vast number of countries. Nevertheless, the threat from China, Iran, or any state may lie in its use of armed proxies.

Should the United States Transform Its Forces to Address Armed-Group Threats?

The United States and other states are in an era of reductions and budgetary constraints on their use of economic, diplomatic, and military power. As Michael J. Mazarr notes, "Continually trying to do too much will create more risk—risk of demands unmet, requests unfulfilled, and a growing sense of the absurdity of the U.S. posture."[18] What is needed is a reformatting of US strategic doctrines and to recalibrate our interests and the threats the United States faces. Mazarr's argument that counterinsurgency's heyday has "come and gone" does not mean that armed groups will not remain a threat, nor that the United States must always go after every armed group that pops up in a game of global "whack-a-mole."[19] Understanding the armed group threats the United States and its allies face is the first step in constructing a force to combat the threat.

Second, international cooperation is greatly magnified given the transnational nature of these groups. The United States and others need not shoulder the burden alone, nor will attempts to do so be successful. Third, intelligence, training, and education as to the nature, source, and successful means of combating armed groups are key. Fourth, while military force plays a role, influence over populations may be gained by addressing economic and political inequalities that defy military solutions. Governments that use violence to crackdown on domestic opposition shorten their tenure in office.[20] While both democracies and dictatorships face pressure to crack down on social movements and armed groups for fear of appearing weak and setting a precedent for future action, those who can resist the call solidify their legitimacy and maintain a greater level of popular support.

Should the "Pivot to Asia" Include a Greater Irregular Warfare Component?

Finally, US policy is undergoing a "pivot to Asia" to rebalance US forces after more than a decade at war in Central Asia. As discussed above, this frequently envisions a more traditional approach to deterring an aggressive China using conventional and nuclear military forces. However, China's ability to project power is limited, which increases its incentives to employ armed groups in a harassing or distracting manner. Furthermore, rising great powers may seek other avenues to challenge a hegemon in order to avoid direct confrontation.[21] The United States should address the potential for China, or any other rising power, to include a substantial irregular warfare component into their strategic considerations. Whether operating separately from regular state armed forces or in conjunction with state forces, armed-group proxies may draw attention away from more severe threats.

The complex nature of the contemporary security environment poses a related question: are armed group threats of a substantial nature that the United States should not be pivoting to East Asia, but should instead be focusing on some other region? The Maghreb and Sahel regions of Africa are rife with ungoverned spaces and porous borders, drug and arms traffickers, insurgents, militias, and terrorists. These destabilizing forces enjoy freedom of movement across wide swaths of territory and have created networks between insurgents, terrorists, TCOs, and militias. Drug traffickers have transformed Guinea-Bissau into a transit point for South American drugs to enter Europe. Mali, Algeria, Nigeria, Sudan, and Somalia, among others, are flooded with arms following the disintegration of Libya, which fuel overlapping local insurgencies with extremist global ideologies. US interests in many parts of Africa may appear limited, until the costs of unstable oil and gas production from Nigeria, Libya, Algeria, and South Sudan are considered. Furthermore, natural resources from around the continent fuel the global economy. Qaddafi's overthrow led to fears of migrants overwhelming Italy and human security catastrophes within Libya.

Are these regularly occurring, yet less severe, armed-group-fueled conflicts of greater importance than the potentially catastrophic, but relatively unlikely event of interstate war in East Asia? This is, at its base, a political question, complicated by questions concerning China's domestic stability, US political leverage over regional Asian powers, or the actions of an insurgent-terrorist hybrid group in Mali. US geostrategic concerns are complicated by its apparent ability to project its power worldwide. As with any other state, however, the United States is limited in the extent of its reach and capabilities and must rectify its interests and objectives with its means. US policy makers will have the final word on US military force deployments. This text is a first step in ensuring that they attain a thorough and rigorous understanding of the primary actors in today's complex security environment. As long as the opportunities and incentives for a "market for security" remain, whether due to globalization, state weakness, or lack of international cooperation to enforce laws and norms, armed groups will remain the twenty-first-century security threat.

RECOMMENDED READINGS

Daron Acemoglu and James Robinson, *Why Nations Fail: The Origins of Power, Prosperity, and Poverty* (New York: Crown Business, 2013).

John Arquilla, "The New Rules of War," *Foreign Policy*, March/April 2010, http://www.foreignpolicy.com/articles/2010/02/22/the_new_rules_of_war..

Colin S. Gray, *Another Bloody Century: Future Warfare* (London: Weidenfeld and Nicolson, 2005).

Parag Khanna, *The Second World: How Emerging Powers Are Redefining Global Competition in the Twenty-first Century* (New York: Random House, 2009).

Steven Metz, *Rethinking Insurgency* (Carlisle, PA: Strategic Studies Institute, 2007).

Stewart Patrick, *Weak Links: Fragile States, Global Threats, and International Security* (Oxford: Oxford University Press, 2011).

NOTES

1. Eric V. Larson et al., *Assessing Irregular Warfare: A Framework for Intelligence Analysis* (Santa Monica, CA: RAND Corporation, 2008), 10.

2. Robert Beckhusen, "Colombia's Rebels Switch from Cocaine to Cattle," Wired.com Danger Room (Blog), January 18, 2012, www.wired.com/dangerroom/2012/01/colombias-rebels-switch-from-cocaine-to-cattle.

3. BBC News. "Colombia Agrees FARC Political Participation," *BBC News: Latin America and Caribbean*, November 6, 2013, www.bbc.co.uk/news/world-latin-america-24842432..

4. Martha Crenshaw, "The Debate over 'New' vs. 'Old' Terrorism," in *Terrorism and Counterterorrism: Understanding the New Security Environment*, ed. Russell D. Howard and Bruce Hoffman (New York: McGraw-Hill, 2012), 175-76.

5. Ulrich Schneckener, *Spoilers or Governance Actors?: Engaging Armed Non-State Groups in Areas of Limited Statehood*, Sfb-Governance Working Paper Series No. 21 (Berlin, Germany: Freie Universität Berlin, 2009).

6. Jeremy M. Weinstein, *Inside Rebellion: The Politics of Insurgent Violence* (Cambridge: Cambridge University Press, 2007), 45.

7. For different reasons, see ibid. and Marc Sageman, *Understanding Terror Networks* (Philadelphia: University of Pennsylvania Press, 2004).

8. Similarly, O'Neill observed that as an insurgent's strategy increased in complexity, it developed a more hierarchical organization. See Bard E. O'Neill, *Insurgency and Terrorism: From Revolution to Apocalypse* (Washington, DC: Potomac Books, 2005).

9. Steven Metz, *Rethinking Insurgency* (Carlisle, PA: Strategic Studies Institute, US Army War College, 2007).

10. DCAF and Geneva Call, *Armed Non-State Actors: Current Trends & Future Challenges*, DCAF Horizon 2015 Working Paper No. 5 (Geneva, Switzerland: Geneva Centre for the Democratic Control of Armed Forces (DCAF), 2011), 8, 15–16.

11. Vanda Felbab-Brown, "The Crime-War Battlefield," *Survival* 55, no. 3 (2013): 147–66.

12. See Janice E. Thomson, *Mercenaries, Pirates, and Sovereigns* (Princeton, NJ: Princeton University Press, 1994); Ariel I. Ahram, *Proxy Warriors: The Rise and Fall of State-Sponsored Militias* (Stanford, CA: Stanford University Press, 2011); and Ethan Corbin, "Principals and Agents: Syria and the Dilemma of Its Armed Groups Allies," *The Fletcher Forum of World Affairs* 35, no. 2 (2011): 25–46.

13. Seth G. Jones and Patrick B. Johnston, "The Future of Insurgency," *Studies in Conflict and Terrorism* 36, no. 1 (2013): 1–25.

14. On instability in a multipolar system, see Kenneth N. Waltz, *Theory of International Politics* (Reading, MA: Addison-Wesley, 1979).

15. On complex emergencies, see David Keen, *Complex Emergencies* (Malden, MA: Polity Press, 2008).

16. James D. Fearon and David D. Laitin, "Ethnicity, Insurgency, and Civil War," *American Political Science Review* 97, no. 1 (2003): 75–90.

17. Jones and Johnston, "The Future of Insurgency."

18. Michael J. Mazarr, "The Risks of Ignoring Strategic Insolvency," *The Washington Quarterly* 35, no. 4 (2012): 15.

19. Ibid., 14.

20. *The Economist*, "Street Protests: The Weapon of Choice," September 28, 2013, http://www.economist.com/news/international/21586842-bloodshed-sometimes-helps-autocrats-stay-power-it-rarely-benefits-protesters-weapon.

21. Jones and Johnston, "The Future of Insurgency."

Bibliography

Abrahms, Max. "Why Terrorism Does Not Work." *International Security* 31, no. 2 (2006): 42–78.

Acharya, Amitav, and Barry Buzan. *Non-Western International Relations Theory: Perspectives on and Beyond Asia.* New York: Routledge, 2010.

Adamsky, Dima. "Jihadi Operational Art: The Comig Wave of Jihadi Strategic Studies." *Studies in Conflict and Terrorism* 33, no. 1 (2009): 1–19.

Ahram, Ariel I. *Proxy Warriors: The Rise and Fall of State-Sponsored Militias.* Stanford, CA: Stanford University Press, 2011.

Airports Council International. "Preliminary 2012 World Airport Traffic and Rankings." March 26, 2013. http://www.aci.aero/media/afc782a2-a258-4c49-a700-fea9047d15fb/News/Releases/2013/PR_260313_Prelim_2012_World_Traffic_Rankings-final_pdf.

Alden, Chris, Monika Thakur, and Matthew Arnold. *Militias and the Challenges of Post-Conlict Peace.* New York: Zed Books, 2011.

Aly Sergie, Mohammed, and Toni Johnson. "Boko Haram." Backgrounder: Council on Foreign Relations. February 26, 2014. http://www.cfr.org/nigeria/boko-haram/p25739.

Amstutz, J. Bruce. *Afghanistan: The First Five Years of Soviet Occupation.* Washington, DC: National Defense University Press, 1986.

Angell, Norman. *The Great Illusion: A Study of the Relation of Military Power to National Advantage.* New York: G. P. Putnam's Sons, 1913.

Arquilla, John, and David Ronfeldt. "The Advent of Netwar (Revisited)." In *Networks and Netwar: The Future of Terror, Crime, and Militancy,* edited by John Arquilla and David Ronfeldt, 1–25. Santa Monica, CA: RAND, 2001.

Art, Robert J. "The Fungibility of Force." In *The Use of Force,* edited by Robert J. Art and Kenneth N. Waltz, 3–22. Lanham, MD: Rowman and Littlefield Publishers, 2004.

Asal, Victor, and R. Karl Rethemeyer. "The Nature of the Beast: Organizational Structures and the Lethality of Terrorist Attacks." *Journal of Politics* 70, no. 2 (2008): 437–49.

Asprey, Robert B. *War in the Shadows: The Guerrilla in History.* New York: William Morrow and Company, 1994.

Associated Press. "Tancredo: If They Nuke Us, Bomb Mecca." July 18, 2005. http://www.foxnews.com/story/0,2933,162795,00.html.

Avant, Deborah D. *The Market for Force: The Consequences of Privatizing Security.* Cambridge: Cambridge University Press, 2005.

Bangerter, Olivier. "Regulating Armed Groups from Within: A Typology." *Small Arms Survey Research Notes,* no. 13 (2012): 1–4.

BBC News. "Colombia Agrees FARC Political Participation." *BBC News: Latin America and Caribbean.* November 6, 2013. www.bbc.co.uk/news/world-latin-america-24842432.

———. "Mehsud Death: US Says Pakistan-Taliban Talks 'Internal.'" *BBC News Asia*. November 2, 2013. http://www.bbc.co.uk/news/world-asia-24792516.

———. "Palestinians Get Saddam Funds." *BBC News*. March 13, 2003. http://news.bbc.co.uk/2/hi/middle_east/2846365.stm.

———. "Senior Pakistani Taliban Leader 'Shocked' by Malala Attack." *BBC News Asia*. July 17, 2013. http://www.bbc.co.uk/news/world-middle-east-23347425.

Beckett, Ian. "The Future of Insurgency." *Small Wars and Insurgencies* 16, no. 1 (2005): 22–36.

Beckhusen, Robert. "Colombia's Rebels Switch from Cocaine to Cattle." Wired.com *Danger Room* (Blog). January 18, 2012. www.wired.com/dangerroom/2012/01/colombias-rebels-switch-from-cocaine-to-cattle.

Beittel, June S. *Mexico's Drug Trafficking Organizations: Source and Scope of the Violence*. CRS Report R41576. Washington, DC: US Congressional Research Service, April 15, 2013.

Berdal, Mats, and David H. Ucko. "Introduction: The Political Reintegration of Armed Groups after War." In *Reintegrating Armed Groups after Conflict: Politics, Violence, and Transition*, edited by Mats Berdal and David H. Ucko, 1–9. New York: Routledge, 2009.

Bergeron, James. "Transnational Organised Crime and International Security: A Primer." *The RUSI Journal* 158, no. 2 (2013): 6–9.

Bhatia, Michael V. "Fighting Words: Naming Terrorists, Bandits, Rebels and Other Violent Actors." *Third World Quarterly* 26, no. 1 (2005): 5–22.

Blainey, Geoffrey. *The Causes of War*. New York: The Free Press, 1988.

Blanchard, Christopher M., and Jim Zanotti. *Libya: Background and U.S. Relations*. CRS Report RI33142. Washington, DC: US Congressional Research Service, 2011.

Blattman, Christopher, and Jeannie Annan. "On the Nature and Causes of LRA Abduction: What the Abductees Say." In *Lord's Resistance Army: Myth and Reality*, edited by Tim Allen and Koen Vlassenroot. London: Zed Books, 2010.

Bolanos, Alejandra. "Yes: The 'New Terrorism' or the 'Newness' of Context and Change." In *Contemporary Debates on Terrorism*, edited by Richard Jackson and Samuel Justin Sinclair, 30–35. New York: Routledge, 2012.

Boot, Max. *Invisible Armies: An Epic History of Guerrilla Warfare from Ancient Times to the Present*. New York: Liveright, 2013.

———. *Small Wars and the Rise of American Power*. New York: Basic Books, 2002.

Brennan, Allison. "Microtargeting: How Campaigns Know You Better Than You Know Yourself." CNN.com. http://www.cnn.com/2012/11/05/politics/voters-microtargeting.

Bull, Hedley. *The Anarchical Society: A Study of Order in World Politics*. New York: Columbia University Press, 1977.

Bundy, McGeorge. "The Unimpressive Record of Atomic Diplomacy." In *The Use of Force: Military Power and International Politics*, edited by Robert J. Art and Kenneth N. Waltz, 99–107. Lanham, MD: Rowman and Littlefield, 2009.

Bunker, Robert J. "Strategic Threat: Narcos and Narcotics Overview." *Small Wars and Insurgencies* 21, no. 1 (2010): 8–29.

Buzan, Barry. *People, States, and Fear: An Agenda for International Security Studies in the Post–Cold War Era*. 2nd ed. Colchester, UK: European Consortium for Political Research Press, 2008.

Buzan, Barry, and Lene Hansen. *The Evolution of International Security Studies*. Cambridge: Cambridge Univeristy Press, 2009.

Buzan, Barry, Ole Waever, and Jaap de Wilde. *Security: A New Framework for Analysis*. Boulder, CO: Lynne Rienner, 1998.

Byman, Daniel. "Passive Supporters of Terrorism." *Survival* 47, no. 4 (2005–06): 117–44.

———. "US Counter-Terrorism Options: A Taxonomy." *Survival* 49, no. 3 (2007): 121–50.

———. "Why Drones Work." *Foreign Affairs* 92, no. 4 (2013): 32–43.

Byman, Daniel, Peter Chalk, Bruce Hoffman, William Rosenau, and David Brannan. *Trends in Outside Support for Insurgent Movement*. Santa Monica, CA: RAND Corporation, 2001.

Callwell, C. E. *Small Wars: Their Principles and Practice*. 3rd ed. Lincoln: University of Nebraska Press, 1996. 1906.

Campana, Paolo, and Federico Varese. "Cooperation in Criminal Organizations: Kinship and Violence as Credible Commitments." *Rationality and Society* 25, no. 3 (2013): 263–89.

Carey, Sabine C., Neil J. Mitchell, and Will Lowe. "States, the Security Sector, and the Monopoly of Violence: A New Database on Pro-Government Militias." *Journal of Peace Research* 50, no. 2 (2013): 249–58.

Cerny, Philip G. "Neomedievalism, Civil War and the New Security Dilemma: Globalisation as Durable Disorder." *Civil Wars* 1, no. 1 (1998): 36–64.

Cha, Victor D. "Globalization and the Study of International Security." *Journal of Peace Research* 37, no. 3 (2000): 391–403.

Chabal, Patrick, and Jean-Pascal Daloz. *Africa Works: Disorder as Political Instrument.* Bloomington: Indiana University Press, 1999.

Chairman of the Joint Chiefs of Staff. *National Military Strategic Plan for the War on Terrorism.* Washington, DC: Government Printing Office, 2006.

Chase, Eric. "Defining Terrorism: A Strategic Imperative." *Small Wars Journal.* January 24, 2013. http://smallwarsjournal.com/print/13722.

Chothia, Farouk. "Will Somali Islamist Purge Strengthen Al-Shabab?" *BBC News.* Published electronically July 3, 2013. http://www.bbc.co.uk/news/world-africa-23146744.

CIA. *Guide to the Analysis of Insurgency.* Washington, DC: US Government, 2012. https://http://www.hsdl.org/?view&did=713599.

Clark, Kate. "Continuing Conflict Is Not Victory: What the 2013 UNAMA Civilian Casualties Report Tells Us About the War." *Afghanistan Analysts Network.* Published electronically February 11, 2014. http://www.afghanistan-analysts.org/continuing-conflict-isnt-victory-what-the-2013-unama-civilian-casualties-report-tells-us-about-the-war.

Clausewitz, Carl von. *On War.* Translated by Michael Howard and Peter Paret. Princeton, NJ: Princeton University Press, 1984.

Cohen, Dara Kay. "Female Combatants and the Perpetration of Violence: Wartime Rape in the Sierra Leone Civil War." *World Politics* 65, no. 3 (2013): 383–415.

Coll, Steve. *Ghost Wars: The Secret History of the Cia, Afghanistan, and Bin Laden, from the Soviet Invasion to September 10, 2001.* New York: Penguin, 2004.

Collier, Paul. "Doing Well out of War: An Economic Perspective." In *Greed and Grievance: Economic Agendas in Civil Wars,* edited by Mats Berdal and David M. Malone, 91–112. Boulder, CO: Lynne Rienner, 2000.

Collins, John M., Frederick Hamerman, and James P. Seevers. *U.S. Low-Intensity Conflicts: 1899–1990.* Washington, DC: Congressional Research Service, 1990.

Corbin, Ethan. "Principals and Agents: Syria and the Dilemma of Its Armed Groups Allies." *The Fletcher Forum of World Affairs* 35, no. 2 (2011): 25–46.

Craig, Tim, and Haq Nawaz Khan. "Pakistan's Taliban Rejects Peace Talks, Citing No. 2 Leader's Death in U.S. Drone Strike." *Washington Post.* May 30, 2013. http://articles.washingtonpost.com/2013-05-30/world/39621956_1_hakimullah-mehsud-taliban-s-pakistani-taliban.

Crenshaw, Martha. "The Debate over "New" Vs. "Old" Terrorism." In *Terrorism and Counterterrorism: Understanding the New Security Environment,* edited by Russell D. Howard and Bruce Hoffman, 165–82. New York: McGraw-Hill, 2012.

———. "Explaining Suicide Terrorism: A Review Essay." *Security Studies* 16, no. 1 (2007): 133–62.

———. "Theories of Terrorism: Instrumental and Organizational Approaches." In *Inside Terrorist Organizations,* edited by David C. Rapoport. New York: Columbia University Press, 1988.

Cronin, Audrey Kurth. "Ending Terrorism: Lessons for Defeating Al-Qaeda." *Adelphi Paper* 47, no. 394 (2007).

———. "Why Drones Fail." *Foreign Affairs* 92, no. 4 (2013): 44–54.

Daboné, Zakaria. "International Law: Armed Groups in a State-Centric System." *International Review of the Red Cross* 93, no. 882 (2011): 395–424.

DCAF, and Geneva Call. *Armed Non-State Actors: Current Trends and Future Challenges.* DCAF Horizon 2015 Working Paper No. 5. Geneva, Switzerland: Geneva Centre for the Democratic Control of Armed Forces (DCAF), 2011.

Deibel, Terry L. *Foreign Affairs Strategy: Logic for American Statecraft.* Cambridge: Cambridge University Press, 2007.

della Porta, Donatella. *Social Movements, Political Violence, and the State: A Comparative Analysis of Italy and Germany.* Cambridge: Cambridge University Press, 1995.

Downes, Alexander B. "Draining the Sea by Filling the Graves: Investigating the Effectiveness of Indiscriminate Violence as a Counterinsurgency Strategy." *Civil Wars* 9, no. 4 (2007): 420–44.

Drazen, Allan. *Political Economy in Macroeconomics.* Princeton, NJ: Princeton University Press, 2000.

Drezner, Daniel W. *Theories of International Politics and Zombies.* Princeton, NJ: Princeton University Press, 2011.

Dunn, Kevin C. "The Lord's Resistance Army and African International Relations." *African Security* 3, no. 1 (2010): 46–63.

Duyvesteyn, Isabelle, and Leena Malkki. "No: The Fallacy of the New Terrorism Thesis." In *Contemporary Debates on Terrorism*, edited by Richard Jackson and Samuel Justin Sinclair, 35–41. New York: Routledge, 2012.

Economist, The. "Street Protests: The Weapon of Choice." September 28, 2013. http://www.economist.com/news/international/21586842-bloodshed-sometimes-helps-autocrats-stay-power-it-rarely-benefits-protesters-weapon.

Farah, Douglas. "Terrorist-Criminal Pipelines and Criminalized States: Emerging Alliances." *PRISM* 2, no. 3 (2011): 15–32.

Farnham, Barbara, ed. *Avoiding Losses, Taking Risks: Prospect Theory and International Conflict.* Ann Arbor: University of Michigan, 1994.

Fearon, James D., and David D. Laitin. "Ethnicity, Insurgency, and Civil War." *American Political Science Review* 97, no. 1 (2003): 75–90.

Felbab-Brown, Vanda. "The Crime-War Battlefield." *Survival* 55, no. 3 (2013): 147–66.

Fernandes, Edna. "Face to Face with General Butt Naked—'The Most Evil Man in the World.'" *Daily Mail.* November 27, 2010. http://www.dailymail.co.uk/news/article-1333465/Liberias-General-Butt-Naked-The-evil-man-world.html.

Fettweis, Christopher J. *Dangerous Times?: The International Politics of Great Power Peace.* Washington, DC: Georgetown University Press, 2010.

Fisher, Max. "Report: North Korea Ordered Its Foreign Diplomats to Become Drug Dealers." *WorldViews-The Washington Post.* Published electronically March 22, 2013. http://www.washingtonpost.com/blogs/worldviews/wp/2013/03/22/report-north-korea-ordered-its-foreign-diplomats-to-become-drug-dealers/.

Fleming, Colin M. "New or Old Wars? Debating a Clausewitzian Future." *Journal of Strategic Studies* 32, no. 2 (2009): 213–41.

Forest, James J. F. "Global Trends in Kidnapping by Terrorist Groups." *Global Change, Peace and Security* 24, no. 3 (2012): 311–30.

Fox News. "Zetas Drug Cartel Threatens Violence in Peten, Guatemala." *Fox News Latino.* March 21, 2012. http://latino.foxnews.com/latino/news/2012/03/21/zetas-drug-cartel-threatens-violence-in-peten-guatemala/.

Frieden, Jeffry A., David A. Lake, and Kenneth A. Schultz. *World Politics: Interests, Interactions, Institutions.* New York: Norton, 2010.

Gearan, Anne. "U.S. Warns Russia against Sending Missiles to Syria." *Washington Post*, May 31, 2013.

George, Alexander L. *Bridging the Gap: Theory and Practice in Foreign Policy.* Washington, DC: United States Institute of Peace, 1993.

Girardet, Edward. *Afghanistan: The Soviet War.* New York: St. Martin's Press, 1985.

Godson, Roy, ed. *Menace to Society: Political-Criminal Collaboration around the World.* Piscataway, NJ: Transaction Publishers, 2003.

Godson, Roy, and William J. Olson. "International Organized Crime." *Society* 32, no. 2 (1995): 18–29.

Goldstein, Judith, and Robert O. Keohane, eds. *Ideas and Foreign Policy.* Ithaca, NY: Cornell University Press, 1993.

Gorka, Sebastian L. v. "Ten Years Later: Are We Winning the War?". *CTX: Combating Terrorism Exchange* 1, no. 2 (2011): 22–32.

Greenhill, Kelly M., and Paul Staniland. "Ten Ways to Lose at Counterinsurgency." *Civil Wars* 9, no. 4 (2007): 402–19.

Gregg, Heather S. "Fighting the Jihad of the Pen: Countering Revolutionary Islam's Ideology." *Terrorism and Political Violence* 22, no. 2 (2010): 292–314.

———. "Setting a Place at the Table: Ending Insurgencies through the Political Process." *Small Wars and Insurgencies* 22, no. 4 (2011): 644–68.

Guaqueta, Alexandra. "The Way Back In: Reintegrating Illegal Armed Groups in Colombia Then and Now." In *Reintegrating Armed Groups after Conflict: Politics, Violence, and Transition*, edited by Mats Berdal and David H. Ucko, 10–46. New York: Routledge, 2009.

Gupta, Dipak K., John Horgan, and Alex P. Schmid. "Terrorism and Organized Crime: A Theoretical Perspective." In *Faces of Terrorism: Multidisciplinary Perspectives*, edited by David Canter, 123–36. Hoboken, NJ: Wiley, 2009.

Gurr, Ted Robert. *Why Men Rebel*. Princeton, NJ: Princeton University Press, 1970.

Hafez, Mohammed M. "Martyrdom Mythology in Iraq: How Jihadists Frame Suicide Terrorism in Videos and Biographies." *Terrorism and Political Violence* 19, no. 1 (2007): 95–115.

Haftendorn, Helga. "The Security Puzzle: Theory-Building and Discipline-Building in International Security." *International Studies Quarterly* 35, no. 1 (1991): 3–17.

Hammes, Thomas X. "Armed Groups: Changing the Rules." In *Armed Groups: Studies in National Security, Counterterrorism, and Counterinsurgency*, edited by Jeffrey H. Norwitz, 447–56. Newport, RI: US Naval War College Press, 2008.

———. *The Sling and the Stone*. St. Paul, MN: Zenith Press, 2006.

Hanlon, Querine H. "Globalization and the Transformation of Armed Groups." In *Armed Groups: Studies in National Security, Counterterrorism, and Counterinsurgency*, 137–47. Newport, RI: US Naval War College Press, 2008.

Hansen, John Mark. "The Political Economy of Group Membership." *American Political Science Review* 79, no. 1 (1985): 79–96.

Hardin, Russell. *One for All: The Logic of Group Conflict*. Princeton, NJ: Princeton University Press, 1995.

Hazen, Jennifer M. "Force Multiplier: Pro-Government Armed Groups." In *Small Arms Survey 2010: Gangs, Groups, and Guns*, edited by Eric G. Berman, Keith Krause, Emile LeBrun and Glenn McDonald, 255–75. Cambridge: Cambridge University Press, 2010.

———. "Gangs, Groups, and Guns: An Overview." In *Small Arms Survey 2010: Gangs, Groups, and Guns*, edited by Eric G. Berman, Keith Krause, Emile LeBrun and Glenn McDonald, 85–99. Cambridge: Cambridge University Press, 2010.

———. "Understanding Gangs as Armed Groups." *International Review of the Red Cross* 92, no. 878 (2010): 369–86.

Henriksen, Rune, and Anthony Vinci. "Combat Motivation in Non-State Armed Groups." *Terrorism and Political Violence* 20, no. 1 (2007): 87–109.

Hewitt, J. Joseph. "Trends in Global Conflict, 1946–2007." In *Peace and Conflict 2010*, edited by J. Joseph Hewitt, Jonathan Wilkenfeld and Ted Robert Gurr, 27–32. Boulder, CO: Paradigm Publishers, 2010.

Hewitt, J. Joseph, Jonathan Wilkenfeld, and Ted Robert Gurr. *Peace and Conflict 2010*. Boulder, CO: Paradigm Publishers, 2010.

Hirschman, Albert O. *Exit, Voice, and Loyalty: Responses to Decline in Firms, Organizations, and States*. Cambridge, MA: Harvard University Press, 1970.

Hodes, Cyrus, and Mark Sedra. "The Search for Security in Post-Taliban Afghanistan." *Adelphi Paper* 47, no. 391 (2007): 17–33.

Hoffman, Bruce. *Inside Terrorism*. New York: Columbia University Press, 2006.

Hoffman, Frank G. *Conflict in the 21st Century: The Rise of Hybrid Wars*. Arlington, VA: Potomac Institute for Policy Studies, 2007.

Hofmann, Claudia, and Ulrich Schneckener. "Engaging Non-State Armed Actors in State- and Peace-Building: Options and Strategies." *International Review of the Red Cross* 93, no. 883 (2011): 603–21.

Horwitz, Sari. "Cigarette Smuggling Linked to Terrorism." *Washington Post*, June 8, 2004.

Howard, Russell D. "Preemptive Military Doctrine: No Other Choice." In *Terrorism and Counterterrorism: Understanding the New Security Environment*, edited by Russell D. Howard, Bruce Hoffman and Stacy Neal, 612–23. New York: McGraw-Hill, 2012.

Howard, Russell D., and Margaret J. Nencheck. "The New Terrorism." In *Terrorism and Counterterrorism: Understanding the New Security Environment*, edited by Russell D. Howard and Bruce Hoffman. New York: McGraw-Hill, 2012.

Huntington, Samuel. *The Clash of Civilizations and the Remaking of World Order*. New York: Touchstone, 1997.

IISS Armed Conflict Database. "Background: Philippines (ASG)." https://acd.iiss.org/en/conflicts/philippines--asg-f55d?as=E12DFD99A21F45CEBF1903733FDB7D3E.

International Commission on Intervention and State Sovereignty. *The Responsibility to Protect: Report of the International Commission on Intervention and State Sovereignty*. Ottawa, Canada: International Development Research Centre. 2001. http://responsibilitytoprotect.org/ICISS Report.pdf.

Janis, Irving L. *Groupthink*. 2nd ed. Boston: Houghton Mifflin, 1982.

Johnson, Thomas H. "Taliban Adaptations and Innovations." *Small Wars and Insurgencies* 24, no. 1 (2013): 3–27.

Jones, Seth G., and Patrick B. Johnston. "The Future of Insurgency." *Studies in Conflict and Terrorism* 36, no. 1 (2013): 1–25.

Jordan, Jenna. "When Heads Roll: Assessing the Effectiveness of Leadership Decapitation." *Security Studies* 18, no. 4 (2009): 719–55.

Jorisch, Avi. *Beacon of Hatred: Inside Hizballah's Al-Manar Television*. Washington, DC: Washington Institute for Near East Policy, 2004.

Juergensmeyer, Mark. "Understanding the New Terrorism." *Current History* 99, no. 636 (2000): 158–63.

Jung, Dietrich. "A Political Economy of Intra-State War: Confronting a Paradox." In *Shadow Globalization, Ethnic Conflicts and New Wars: A Political Economy of Intra-State War*, 9–26. New York: Routledge, 2003.

Kaldor, Mary. "In Defence of New Wars." *Stability: International Journal of Security and Development* 2, no. 1 (2013): 1–16.

———. *New and Old Wars: Organized Violence in a Global Era*. Stanford, CA: Stanford University Press, 2007.

Kalyvas, Stathis N. *The Logic of Violence in Civil Wars*. Cambridge: Cambridge University Press, 2006.

Kang, David C. "Getting Asia Wrong." *International Security* 27, no. 4 (2003): 57–85.

Kaplan, Robert D. *The Coming Anarchy: Shattering the Dreams of the Post Cold War*. New York: Random House, 2001.

Karnowski, Steve. "Somalis Still Leaving Minn. to Join Terror Group." *USA Today*, September 26, 2013.

Katzenstein, Peter J. *The Culture of National Security*. New York: Columbia University Press, 1996.

Kaysen, Carl. "Is War Obsolete?: A Review Essay." *International Security* 14, no. 4 (Spring 1990): 42–64.

Keen, David. *Complex Emergencies*. Malden, MA: Polity Press, 2008.

———. "The Economic Functions of Violence in Civil Wars." *Adelphi Paper*, no. 320 (1998).

Khalil, James. "Know Your Enemy: On the Futility of Distinguishing between Terrorists and Insurgents." *Studies in Conflict and Terrorism* 36, no. 5 (2013): 419–30.

Kilcullen, David. "Counter-Insurgency *Redux*." *Survival* 48, no. 4 (2006–07): 111–30.

Kilcullen, David J. "Countering Global Insurgency." *The Journal of Strategic Studies* 28, no. 4 (2005): 597–617.

Killebrew, Bob, and Jennifer Bernal. *Crime Wars: Gangs, Cartels and U.S. National Security*. Washington, DC: Center for a New American Security, 2010.

Kobrin, Stephen J. "Back to the Future: Neomedievalism and the Postmodern Digital World Economy." *The Journal of International Affairs* 51, no. 2 (1998): 361–86.

Krasner, Stephen D. *Sovereignty: Organized Hypocrisy*. Princeton, NJ: Princeton University Press, 1999.

Krause, Keith, and Jennifer Milliken. "Introduction: The Challenge of Non-State Armed Groups." *Contemporary Security Policy* 30, no. 2 (2009): 202–20.

Kroenig, Matthew, and Barry Pavel. "How to Deter Terrorism." *The Washington Quarterly* 35, no. 2 (2012): 21–36.

Kydd, Andrew, and Barbara Walter. "The Strategies of Terrorism." *International Security* 31, no. 1 (2006): 49–80.

LaFree, Gary, Laura Dugan, and R. Kim Cragin. "Trends in Global Terrorism, 1970–2007." In *Peace and Conflict 2010*, edited by J. Joseph Hewitt, Jonathan Wilkenfeld and Ted Robert Gurr, 51–64. Boulder, CO: Paradigm, 2010.

Lake, David A. "Why 'Isms' Are Evil: Theory, Epistemology, and Academic Sects as Impediments to Understanding and Progress." *International Studies Quarterly* 55, no. 2 (2011): 465–80.

Lake, David A., and Robert Powell, eds. *Strategic Choice and International Relations*. Princeton, NJ: Princeton University Press, 1999.

Laremont, Ricardo Rene. "After the Fall of Qaddafi: Political, Economic, and Security Consequences for Libya, Mali, Niger, and Algeria." *Stability: International Journal of Security and Development* 2, no. 2 (2013): 29. doi:http://dx.doi.org/10.5334/sta.bq.

Larson, Eric V., Derek Eaton, Brian Nichiporuk, and Thomas S. Szayna. *Assessing Irregular Warfare: A Framework for Intelligence Analysis*. Santa Monica, CA: RAND Corporation, 2008.

Lasswell, Harold D. *Politics: Who Gets What, When, How*. New York: Peter Smith Publishing, 1936.

LeBrun, Emile, Glenn McDonald, Anna Alvazzi del Frate, Eric G. Berman, and Keith Krause, eds. *Small Arms Survey 2013: Everyday Dangers*. Cambridge: Cambridge University Press, 2013.

Lia, Brynjar, and Thomas Hegghammer. "Jihadi Strategic Studies: The Alleged Al Qaida Policy Study Preceding the Madrid Bombing." *Studies in Conflict and Terrorism* 27, no. 5 (2004): 355–75.

Lieber, Keir A., and Daryl G. Press. "Why States Won't Give Nuclear Weapons to Terrorists." *International Security* 38, no. 1 (2013): 80–104.

Locke, Rachel. *Organized Crime, Conflict, and Fragility: A New Approach*. New York: International Peace Institute, 2012.

Lyall, Jason. "Does Indiscriminate Violence Incite Insurgent Attacks? Evidence from Chechnya." *Journal of Conflict Resolution* 53, no. 3 (2009): 331–62.

Mackesy, Piers. *The War for America, 1775–1783*. Lincoln: Univeristy of Nebraska Press, 1992.

Makarenko, Tamara. "The Crime-Terror Continuum: Tracing the Interplay Bewteen Transnational Organised Crime and Terrorism." *Global Crime* 6, no. 1 (2004): 129–45.

Manwaring, Max G. *A Contemporary Challenge to State Sovereignty: Gangs and Other Illicit Transnational Criminal Organizations in Central America, El Salvador, Mexico, Jamaica, and Brazil*. Carlisle, PA: Strategic Studies Institute, US Army War College, 2007.

———. *Street Gangs: The New Urban Insurgency*. Carlisle, PA: Strategic Studies Institute, US Army War College, 2005.

Mao Tse-tung. "The Three Stages of the Protracted War." In *The Guerrilla Reader: A Historical Anthology*, edited by Walter Laqueur, 189–97. Philadelphia, PA: Temple University Press, 1977.

March, James G., and Herbert A. Simon. *Organizations*. Cambridge, MA: Blackwell, 1993.

Marchal, Roland. "Warlordism and Terrorism: How to Obscure an Already Confusing Crisis? The Case of Somalia." *International Affairs* 83, no. 6 (2007): 1091–106.

Marighella, Carlos. *Manual of the Urban Guerrilla*. Translated by Gene Hanrahan. Chapel Hill, NC: Documentary Publications, 1985.

———. "The Seven Sins of the Urban Guerrilla." *Minimanual of the Urban Guerrilla*. http://www.marxists.org/archive/marighella-carlos/1969/06/minimanual-urban-guerrilla/ch37.htm.

Marks, Thomas A. "Ideology of Insurgency: New Ethic Focus or Old Cold War Distortions?" *Small Wars and Insurgencies* 15, no. 1 (2004): 107–28.

Marriage, Zoë. "Flip-Flop Rebel, Dollar Soldier." In *Reintegrating Armed Groups after Conflict: Politics, Violence and Transition*, edited by Mats Berdal and David H. Ucko, 119–43. New York: Routledge, 2009.

Marten, Kimberly. *Warlords: Strong-Arm Brokers in Weak States*. Ithaca, NY: Cornell University Press, 2012.

Mazarr, Michael J. "The Risks of Ignoring Strategic Insolvency." *The Washington Quarterly* 35, no. 4 (2012): 7–22.

Mazzitelli, Antoni L. "Transnational Organized Crime in West Africa: The Additional Challenge." *International Affairs* 83, no. 6 (2007): 1071–90.

Mc Hugh, Gerard, and Manuel Bessler. *Humanitarian Negotiations with Armed Groups: A Manual for Practitioners*. New York: United Nations Office for the Coordination of Humanitarian Affairs, 2006.

McCormick, Gordon H. "Terrorist Decision Making." *Annual Review of Political Science* 6 (2003): 473–507.

McCubbins, Mathew D., and Thomas Schwartz. "Congressional Oversight Overlooked: Police Patrols Versus Fire Alarms." *American Journal of Political Science* 28, no. 1 (1984): 165–79.

McElroy, Damien. "Al-Qaeda's Scathing Letter to Troublesome Employee Mokhtar Belmokhtar Reveals Inner Workings of Terrorist Group." *The Telegraph* (UK). May 29, 2013. http://www.telegraph.co.uk/news/worldnews/al-qaeda/10085716/Al-Qaedas-scathing-letter-to-troublesome-employee-Mokhtar-Belmokhtar-reveals-inner-workings-of-terrorist-group.html.

McFate, Sean. *The Modern Mercenary: Private Armies and What They Mean for World Order*. Oxford: Oxford University Press, Forthcoming.

———. "There's a New Sheriff in Town: DDR-SSR and the Monopoly of Force." In *The Monopoly of Force: The Nexus of DDR and SSR*, edited by Melanne A. Civic and Michael Miklaucic, 213–31. Washington, DC: NDU Press, 2011.

McQuinn, Brian. "Armed Groups in Libya: Typologies and Roles." *Small Arms Survey Research Notes*, no. 18 (2012).

Mearsheimer, John J. "Back to the Future: Instability in Europe after the Cold War." *International Security* 15, no. 1 (1990): 5–56.

Meleagrou-Hitchens, Alexander, Shiraz Maher, and James Sheehan. *Lights, Camera, Jihad: Al-Shabaab's Western Media Strategy*. London: International Centre for the Study of Radicalisation and Political Violence (ICSR), 2012.

Merom, Gil. *How Democracies Lose Small Wars: State, Society, and the Failures of France in Algeria, Israel in Lebanon, and the United States in Vietnam*. Cambridge: Cambridge University Press, 2003.

Metz, Steven. "The Internet, New Media, and the Evolution of Insurgency." *Parameters* 42, no. 3 (2012): 80–90.

———. *Rethinking Insurgency*. Carlisle, PA: Strategic Studies Institute, US Army War College, 2007.

Moghadam, Assaf. "Suicide Terrorism, Occuption, and the Globalization of Martyrdom: A Critique of *Dying to Win*." *Studies in Conflict and Terrorism* 29, no. 8 (2006): 707–29.

Moriarty, J. Thomas. "The Vanguard's Dilemma: Understanding and Exploiting Insurgent Strategies." *Small Wars and Insurgencies* 21, no. 3 (2010): 476–97.

Mueller, John. *Atomic Obsession: Nuclear Alarmism from Hiroshima to Al-Qaeda*. Oxford: Oxford University Press, 2010.

———. *Overblown: How Politicians and the Terrorism Industry Inflate National Security Threats, and Why We Believe Them*. New York: Free Press, 2009.

———. *The Remnants of War*. Ithaca, NY: Cornell University Press, 2007.

———. "War Has Almost Ceased to Exist: An Assessment." *Political Science Quarterly* 124, no. 2 (2009): 297–321.

Münkler, Herfried. *The New Wars*. Malden, MA: Polity Press, 2004.

Murray, Williamson. "The American Revolution: Hybrid War in America's Past." In *Hybrid Warfare: Fighting Complex Opponents from the Ancient World to the Present*, edited by

Williamson Murray and Peter R. Mansoor, 72–103. Cambridge: Cambridge University Press, 2013.

Murray, Williamson, and Peter R. Mansoor, eds. *Hybrid Warfare: Fighting Complex Opponents from the Ancient World to the Present*. Cambridge: Cambridge University Press, 2013.

Musil, Steven. "Anonymous Targets Israel in Another Cyberattack." CNET.com. http://news.cnet.com/8301-1009_3-57578331-83/anonymous-targets-israel-in-another-cyberattack/.

Nacos, Brigitte L. *Mass-Mediated Terrorism: The Central Role of the Media in Terrorism and Counterterrorism*. Lanham, MD: Rowman and Littlefield Publishers, 2007.

National Security Council. "Strategy to Combat Transnational Organized Crime: Definition." July 25, 2011. http://www.whitehouse.gov/administration/eop/nsc/transnational-crime/definition.

National Strategy for Homeland Security. July 2002. Permanent.access.gpo.gov/lps20641/nat_strat_hls.pdf.

Neumann, Vanessa. "Grievance to Greed: The Global Convergence of the Crime-Terror Threat." *Orbis* 57, no. 2 (2013): 251–67.

Noricks, Darcy M. E. "The Root Causes of Terrorism." In *Social Science for Counterterrorism: Putting the Pieces Together*, edited by Paul K. Davis and Kim Cragin, 11–70. Santa Monica, CA: RAND, 2009.

Novo, Andrew. "Friend or Foe? The Cyprus Police Force and the Eoka Insurgency." *Small Wars and Insurgencies* 23, no. 3 (2012): 414–31.

O'Neill, Bard E. *Insurgency and Terrorism: From Revolution to Apocalypse*. Washington, DC: Potomac Books, 2005.

Oberschall, Anthony. "Explaining Terorrism: The Contribution of Collective Action Theory." *Sociological Theory* 22, no. 1 (2004): 26–37.

Olson, Mancur. *The Logic of Collective Action: Public Goods and the Theory of Groups*. Camrbidge, MA: Harvard University Press, 1965.

———. *Power and Prosperity*. New York: Basic Books, 2000.

Olson, Parmy. *We Are Anonymous: Inside the Hacker World of Lulzsec, Anonymous, and the Global Cyber Insurgency*. New York: Back Bay Books, 2013.

Omelicheva, Mariya. "Combating Terrorism in Central Asia: Explaining Differences in States' Responses to Terror." *Terrorism and Political Violence* 19, no. 3 (2007): 369–93.

Oremus, Will. "The Militant Group Behind the Kenya Mall Attack Is Live-Tweeting the Massacre." Slate.com. September 21, 2013. http://www.slate.com/blogs/future_tense/2013/09/21/al_shabaab_on_twitter_hsmpress_tries_to_justify_nairobi_kenya_mall_shooting.html.

Osumah, Oarhe, and Iro Aghedo. "Who Wants to Be a Millionaire? Nigerian Youths and the Commodification of Kidnapping." *Review of African Political Economy* 38, no. 128 (2011): 277–87.

Padgett, Tim. "Guatemala's Kaibiles: A Notorious Commando Unit Wrapped Up in Central America's Drug War." *Time World*. July 14, 2011. world.time.com/2011/07/14/guatemalas-kaibil-terror-from-dictators-to-drug-cartels.

Pape, Robert A. *Dying to Win: The Strategic Logic of Suicide Terrorism*. New York: Random House, 2006.

Paul, Christopher, Colin P. Clarke, and Beth Grill. *Victory Has a Thousand Fathers: Sources of Success in Counterinsurgency*. Santa Monica, CA: RAND Corporation, 2010.

Percy, Sarah. "Introduction." *Civil Wars* 11, no. 1 (2009): 1–4.

Perliger, Arie. "How Democracies Respond to Terrorism: Regime Characteristics, Symbolic Power and Counterterrorism." *Security Studies* 21, no. 3 (2012): 490–528.

Peter, Tom A. "Mexico Denies Hillary Clinton's 'Insurgency' Comparison." *The Christian Science Monitor*. September 9, 2010. http://www.csmonitor.com/World/terrorism-security/2010/0909/Mexico-denies-Hillary-Clinton-s-insurgency-comparison.

Pew Research Center. *Global Opinion of Obama Slips, International Policies Faulted: Drone Strikes Widely Opposed*. Pew Research Global Attitudes Project. June 13, 2012. www.pewglobal.org/files/2012/06/Pew-Global-Attitudes-U.S.-Image-Report-FINAL-June-13-20123.pdf.

Pfanner, Toni. "Military Uniforms and the Law of War." *International Review of the Red Cross* 86, no. 853 (2004): 93–124.

Phillips, Andrew. "How Al Qaeda Lost Iraq." *Australian Journal of International Affairs* 63, no. 1 (2009): 64–84.

Picard, Justin. "Can We Estimate the Global Scale and Impact of Illicit Trade?". In *Convergence: Illicit Networks and National Security in the Age of Globalization*, edited by Michael Miklaucic and Jacqueline Brewer, 37–60. Washington, DC: National Defense University Press, 2013.

Pierskalla, Jan H., and Florian M. Hollenbach. "Technology and Collective Action: The Effect of Cell Phone Coverage on Poltical Violence in Africa." *American Political Science Review* 107, no. 2 (2013): 207–24.

Pike, John. "Liberation Movements, Terrorist Organizations, Substance Cartels, and Other Para-State Entities." FAS Intelligence Resource Program. https://www.fas.org/irp/world/para/.

———. "Para-States—Scope Note." FAS Intelligence Resource Program. https://www.fas.org/irp/world/para/scope.htm.

Pokalova, Elena. "Terrorism: The Dilemma of Response." In *International Criminal Justice: Critical Persepctives and New Challenges*, edited by George Andreopoulos, Rosemary Barberet and James P. Levine, 109–27. New York: Springer, 2011.

Qasem, Islam, Anna Michalkova, and Marjolein de Ridder. *Drugs, Crime and Terror: A Thriving Business*. WFF Issue Brief No. 09. The Hague, Netherlands: World Foresight Forum, 2011.

Quinn, Andrew, Adriana Barrera, and Mica Rosenberg. "Clinton Sees Drug 'Insurgency' in Mexico and Central America." Reuters. September 8, 2010. http://www.reuters.com/article/2010/09/08/us-usa-mexico-clinton-idUSTRE68758820100908.

Rapoport, David C. "The Four Waves of Modern Terrorism." In *Attacking Terrorism: Elements of a Grand Strategy*, edited by Audrey Cronin and James Ludes, 46–73. Washington, DC: Georgetown University Press, 2004.

Reagan, Ronald "Radio Address to the Nation on the Situation in Nicaragua." September 12, 1987. Online by Gerhard Peters and John T. Woolley, The American Presidency Project. http://www.presidency.ucsb.edu/ws/index.php?pid=34788.

———. "Remarks on Signing the Afghanistan Day Proclamation." March 10, 1982. Online by Gerhard Peters and John T. Woolley, The American Presidency Project. http://www.presidency.ucsb.edu/ws/?pid=42248.

Reiter, Dan. *How Wars End*. Princeton, NJ: Princeton University Press, 2009.

Reno, William. *Warlord Politics and African States*. Boulder, CO: Lynne Rienner, 1999.

Richter, Paul, and Ken Dilanian. "Clinton Says Mexico Drug Wars Starting to Look Like Insurgency." *Los Angeles Times*. September 9, 2010. http://articles.latimes.com/2010/sep/09/world/la-fg-mexico-insurgency-20100909.

Ripsman, Norrin M., and T. V. Paul. *Globalization and the National Security State*. New York: Oxford University Press, 2010.

Rittner, Carol, and John K. Roth, eds. *Rape: Weapon of War and Genocide*. St. Paul, MN: Paragon House, 2012.

Roberts, J. A. G. "Warlordism in China." *Review of African Political Economy*, no. 45/46 (1989): 26–33.

Rosecrance, Richard. *The Rise of the Trading State: Commerce and Conquest in the Modern World*. New York: Basic Books, 1986.

———. *The Rise of the Virtual State: Wealth and Power in the Coming Century*. New York: Basic Books, 1999.

Rosecrance, Richard, and Peter Thompson. "Trade, Foreign Investment, and Security." *Annual Review of Political Science* 6, no. 1 (June 2003): 377–98.

Rucht, Dieter. "Leadership in Social and Political Movements: A Comparative Exploration." In *Comparative Political Leadership*, edited by Ludger Helms, 99–118. New York: Palgrave Macmillan, 2012.

Sagan, Scott D., and Kenneth N. Waltz. *The Spread of Nuclear Weapons: A Debate Renewed*. New York: Norton, 2003.

Sageman, Marc. *Understanding Terror Networks*. Philadelphia: University of Pennsylvania Press, 2004.

Salehyan, Idean. "Transnational Rebels: Neighboring States as Sanctuary for Rebel Groups." *World Politics* 59, no. 2 (2007): 217–42.

San Akca, Belgin. "Supporting Non-State Armed Groups: A Resort to Illegality?". *The Journal of Strategic Studies* 32, no. 4 (2009): 589–613.

Sawyer, Reid, and Jodi M. Vittori. "The Uncontested Battles: The Role of Actions, Networks, and Ideas in the Fight against Al Qaeda." In *Terrorism and Counterterrorism: Understanding the New Security Environment*, edited by Russell D. Howard, Bruce Hoffman and Stacy Neal, 652–73. New York: McGraw-Hill, 2012.

Schelling, Thomas C. *Arms and Influence*. New Haven, CT: Yale University Press, 1966.

Schmid, Alex P., and Albert J. Jongman. *Political Terrorism: A New Guide to Actors, Authors, Concepts, Data, Bases, Theories, and Literature*. New Brunswick, NJ: Transaction Publishers, 2005.

Schneckener, Ulrich. *Spoilers or Governance Actors?: Engaging Armed Non-State Groups in Areas of Limited Statehood*. Sfb-Governance Working Paper Series No. 21. Berlin, Germany: Freie Universität Berlin, 2009.

Shultz, Richard H., and Andrea J. Dew. *Insurgents, Terrorists, and Militias: The Warriors of Contemporary Combat*. New York: Columbia University Press, 2006.

Shultz, Richard H., Douglas Farah, and Itamara V. Lochard. *Armed Groups: A Tier-One Security Priority*. Inss Occasional Paper 57. Colorado Springs, CO: USAF Institute for National Security Studies, 2004.

Silberglitt, Richard, Philip S. Antón, David R. Howell, Anny Wong, Natalie Gassman, Brian A. Jackson, Eric Landree, et al. *The Global Technology Revolution 2020, In-Depth Analyses: Bio/Nano/Materials/Information Trends, Drivers, Barriers, and Social Implications*. Santa Monica, CA: RAND Corporation, 2006.

Simpson, Emile. *War from the Ground Up: Twenty-First-Century Combat as Politics*. New York: Columbia University Press, 2012.

Singer, P. W. *Children at War*. Berkeley and Los Angeles: University of California Press, 2006.

———. *Corporate Warriors: The Rise of the Privatized Military Industry*. Ithaca, NY: Cornell University Press, 2007.

Siskin, Alison, and Liana Sun Wyler. *Trafficking in Persons: U.S. Policy and Issues for Congress*. CRS Report R134317. Washington, DC: US Congressional Research Service, February 19, 2013.

Smith, Megan, and James Igoe Walsh. "Do Drone Strikes Degrade Al Qaeda?: Evidence from Propaganda Output." *Terrorism and Political Violence* 25, no. 2 (2013): 311–27.

Smith, Rupert. *The Utility of Force: The Art of War in the Modern World*. New York: Vintage Books, 2008.

Smoltczyk, Alexander. "Africa's Cocaine Hub: Guinea-Bissau a 'Drug Trafficker's Dream.'" *Spiegel Online International*. Published electronically March 8, 2013. http://www.spiegel.de/international/world/violence-plagues-african-hub-of-cocaine-trafficking-a-887306.html.

Snyder, Glenn H. *Deterrence and Defense: Toward a Theory of National Security*. Princeton, NJ: Princeton University Press, 1961.

Spruyt, Hendrik. *The Sovereign State and Its Competitors*. Princeton, NJ: Princeton University Press, 1994.

Stedman, Stephen John. "Spoiler Problems in Peace Processes." *International Security* 22, no. 2 (1997): 5–53.

Stein, Arthur A. *Why Nations Cooperate: Circumstance and Choice in International Relations*. Ithaca, NY: Cornell University Press, 1990.

Stock, Jonathan. "The Penitant [*sic*] Warlord: Atoning for 20,000 War Crimes." Spiegel Online International. October 30, 2013. http://www.spiegel.de/international/world/general-butt-naked-warlord-blahyi-seeks-forgiveness-in-liberia-a-930688.html.

Stout, Mark E., Jessica M. Huckabey, John R. Schindler, and Jim Lacey, eds. *The Terrorist Perspectives Project: Strategic and Operational Views of Al Qaida and Associated Movements*. Annapolis, MD: Naval Institute Press, 2008.

Sullivan, John P. "Counter-Supply and Counter-Violence Approaches to Narcotics Trafficking." *Small Wars and Insurgencies* 21, no. 1 (2010): 179–95.

Sun Tzu. *The Art of War*. Translated by Samuel B. Griffith. Oxford: Oxford University Press, 1963.

Sweijs, Tim, and Jaakko Kooroshy. *The Future of CBRN*. Future Issue No. 12 | 03 | 10. The Hague, Netherlands: The Hague Centre for Strategic Studies, 2010.

Tannenwald, Nina. *The Nuclear Taboo: The United States and the Non-Use of Nuclear Weapons since 1945*. Cambridge: Cambridge University Press, 2006.

Tetlock, Philip E. *Expert Political Judgement: How Good Is It? How Can We Know?* Princeton, NJ: Princeton University Press, 2006.

Thaler, Kai M. "Ideology and Violence in Civil Wars: Theory and Evidence from Mozambique and Angola." *Civil Wars* 14, no. 4 (2012): 546–67.

Themnér, Lotta, and Peter Wallensteen. "Armed Conflict, 1946–2012." *Journal of Peace Research* 50, no. 4 (2013): 509–21.

Thomson, Janice E. *Mercenaries, Pirates, and Sovereigns*. Princeton, NJ: Princeton University Press, 1994.

Tiefenbrun, Susan W. "Semiotic Definition of 'Lawfare.'" *Case Western Reserve Journal of International Law* 43, nos. 1 and 2 (2011): 29–60.

Tilly, Charles. *The Politics of Collective Violence*. Cambridge: Cambridge University Press, 2003.

Trager, Robert F., and Dessislava P. Zagorcheva. "Deterring Terrorism: It Can Be Done." *International Security* 30, no. 1 (2005): 87–123.

Ucko, David H. "Militias, Tribes and Insurgents: The Challenge of Political Reintegration in Iraq." In *Reintegrating Armed Groups after Conflict: Politics, Violence and Transition*, edited by Mats Berdal and David H. Ucko, 89–118. New York: Routledge, 2009.

———. "Whither Counterinsurgency: The Rise and Fall of a Divisive Concept." In *The Routledge Handbook of Insurgency and Counterinsurgency*, edited by Paul B. Rich and Isabelle Duyvesteyn, 67–79. New York: Routledge, 2012.

Ugarriza, Juan E. "Ideologies and Conflict in the Post-Cold War." *International Journal of Conflict Management* 20, no. 1 (2009): 82–104.

Ugarriza, Juan E., and Matthew J. Craig. "The Relevance of Ideology to Contemporary Armed Conflicts: A Quantitative Analysis of Former Combatants in Colombia." *Journal of Conflict Resolution* 57, no. 3 (2012): 445–77.

United Nations. "Charter of the United Nations." http://www.un.org/en/documents/charter/.

United Nations Office on Drugs and Crime. *The Globalization of Crime: A Transnational Organized Crime Threat Assessment*. Vienna, Austria: UNODC, 2010.

———. *United Nations Convention against Transnational Organized Crime and the Protocols Thereto*. New York: United Nations, 2004.

United States Code. Title 22, Chapter 38, § 2656f(d)(2). Legal Information Institute, Cornell University Law School. "22 USC § 2656f—Annual Country Reports on Terrorism." http://www.law.cornell.edu/uscode/text/22/2656f.

United States Department of Defense. *Antiterrorism*. Joint Publication 3-07.2. November 24, 2010. http://www.bits.de/NRANEU/others/jp-doctrine/JP3_07.2(10).pdf.

———. *Counterinsurgency Operations*. Joint Publication 3-24. October 5, 2009. http://www.dtic.mil/doctrine/new_pubs/jp3_24.pdf.

———. *Counterterrorism*. Joint Publication 3-26. November 13, 2009. http://www.dtic.mil/doctrine/new_pubs/jp3_26.pdf.

———. *Irregular Warfare: Countering Irregular Threats: Joint Operating Concept (IW JOC)*, V 2.0. May 17, 2010.

United States Department of Homeland Security. "Our Mission." www.dhs.gov/our-mission.

United States Department of State. "Terrorist Designations of Boko Haram and Ansaru." Media Note. Washington, DC: US Department of State. November 13, 2013. http://www.state.gov/r/pa/prs/ps/2013/11/217509.htm#.

United States Department of State, Bureau of Counterterrorism. *Foreign Terrorist Organizations*. September 28, 2012. http://www.state.gov/j/ct/rls/other/des/123085.htm.

United States House of Representatives. Report of the Majority Staff. Rep. John F. Tierney (Chair), Subcommittee on National Security and Foreign Affairs, Committee on Oversight and Government Reform. *Warlord, Inc.: Extortion and Corruption Along the U.S. Supply Chain in Afghanistan*. June 2010. http://www.cbsnews.com/htdocs/pdf/HNT_Report.pdf.

Uppsala Conflict Data Program. UCDP Conflict Encyclopedia: India. CPI-Maoist, Uppsala University. July 26, 2013. http://www.ucdp.uu.se/gpdatabase/gpcountry.php?id=74&region-Select=6-Central_and_Southern_Asia#.

van Creveld, Martin. *The Rise and Decline of the State*. Cambridge: Cambridge University Press, 1999.

———. *The Transformation of War*. New York: Free Press, 1991.

Vinci, Anthony. *Armed Groups and the Balance of Power*. London: Routledge, 2008.

———. "'Like Worms in the Entrails of a Natural Man': A Conceptual Analysis of Warlords." *Review of African Political Economy* 34, no. 112 (2007): 313–31.

———. "The 'Problems of Mobilization' and the Analysis of Armed Groups." *Parameters* 36, no. 1 (2006): 49–62.

———. "The Strategic Use of Fear by the Lord's Resistance Army." *Small Wars and Insurgencies* 16, no. 3 (2005): 360–81.

Vriens, Lauren. *Backgrounder: Armed Islamic Group*. Council on Foreign Relations. May 27, 2009. http://www.cfr.org/algeria/armed-islamic-group-algeria-islamists/p9154.

Walter, Barbara F. *Committing to Peace: The Successful Settlement of Civil Wars*. Princeton, NJ: Princeton University Press, 2002.

Waltz, Kenneth N. *Theory of International Politics*. Reading, MA: Addison-Wesley, 1979.

Weber, Max. "Politics as a Vocation." Translated by H. H. Gerth and C. Wright Mills. In *From Max Weber: Essays in Sociology*, edited by H. H. Gerth and C. Wright Mills, 77–128. New York: Oxford University Press, 1958.

Wehrey, Frederic M. "A Clash of Wills: Hizballah's Psychological Campaign against Israel in South Lebanon." *Small Wars and Insurgencies* 13, no. 3 (2002): 53–74.

Weimann, Gabriel. *Terror on the Internet: The New Arena, the New Challenges*. Washington, DC: United States Institute of Peace Press, 2006.

———. http://www.Terror.Net: *How Modern Terrorism Uses the Internet*. Special Report No. 116. Washington, DC: United States Institute of Peace, 2004.

Weinstein, Jeremy M. *Inside Rebellion: The Politics of Insurgent Violence*. Cambridge: Cambridge University Press, 2007.

White House, The. Office of the Press Secretary. "Fact Sheet: Overview of the Foreign Narcotics Kingpin Designation." April 15, 2009. http://www.whitehouse.gov/the_press_office/Fact-Sheet-Overview-of-the-Foreign-Narcotics-Kingpin-Designation-Act.

Wike, Richard. "What Pakistan Thinks." Pew Research Global Attitudes Project. May 10, 2013. www.pewglobal.org/2013/05/10/what-pakistan-thinks.

Williams, Phil. "Transnational Criminal Organisations and International Security." In *In Athena's Camp: Preparing for Conflict in the Information Age*, edited by John Arquilla and David Ronfeldt, 315–37. Santa Monica, CA: RAND, 1997.

———. *Violent Non-State Actors and National and International Security*. Zurich: Swiss Federal Institute of Technology Zurich, International Relations and Security Network, 2008.

Wolfers, Arnold. *Discord and Collaboration: Essays on International Politics*. Baltimore, MD: The John Hopkins Press, 1962.

Wolff, Stefan. *Ethnic Conflict: A Global Perspective*. Oxford: Oxford University Press, 2006.

Wooster, Robert. *The Military and United States Indian Policy, 1865–1903*. Lincoln: University of Nebraska Press, 1995.

World Shipping Council. "Top 50 World Container Ports." http://www.worldshipping.org/about-the-industry/global-trade/top-50-world-container-ports.

Wyler, Liana Sun. *Weak and Failing States: Evolving Security Threats and U.S. Policy*. CRS Report RL34253. Washington, DC: US Congressional Research Service, August 28, 2008.

Index

Abu Sayyaf Group (ASG), 149
Afghanistan, 19–20, 47, 49n15, 80, 100n66, 110, 145, 148, 164, 166, 168n22, 176–177, 189, 193
Al-Aqsa Martyrs Brigade, 145
Al-Nusra Front, 165
Al-Shabaab, 1, 83, 115, 138n49, 156, 190, 194
Al-Qaeda, 4, 5, 38, 64, 81–82, 83–84, 98n28, 109, 117–118, 123, 124, 130, 132, 137n34, 138n49, 147, 154, 165, 178, 181, 189, 190, 192, 194, 199n82
Al-Qaeda in the Arabian Peninsula (AQAP), 83
Al-Qaeda in the Islamic Maghreb (AQIM), 15, 26n31, 83, 117–118, 149, 169n37
Algeria, 138n50, 157, 212
Anarchists, 84, 131, 169n44
Anonymous, 62, 65–66
Armed Islamic Group (GIA), 138n50, 157
Art, Robert J., 162
AQAP. *See* Al Qaeda in the Arabian Peninsula
AQIM. *See* Al Qaeda in the Islamic Maghreb
armed groups: archetypes, 75–96; as proxy actors, 17, 18, 29, 31, 38, 70, 71, 93–94, 159, 208–209; characteristics, 26n35, 55–59; combating, 173–196; "commercial," 93–94, 131; evolution, 94, 104, 202–204; external

characteristics, 139–166; factions, 65, 138n49; formation, 66–69; funding, 1, 17, 18, 33, 35–36, 38–39, 43, 55–56, 68, 69, 72, 79, 83–84, 94–95, 96, 109, 111, 113–114, 122, 142, 158, 159, 165, 169n37, 174, 176, 177, 183–184, 191, 205–206; hybridization, 21, 76, 76–77, 89, 94–96, 128; internal characteristics, 103–135; legitimacy, 5, 35–36, 45, 53, 55, 57–58, 61–62, 69, 70–71, 106, 122, 128, 129, 131, 145–146, 149, 152, 153, 155, 156, 157, 160, 162, 165, 166, 176, 185, 187, 194; rationality, 62–64; relationship with the population, 204, 206; threat to the state, 59–62, 208–209, 210

Belmokhtar, Mokhtar, 15, 26n31, 117
Blainey, Geoffrey, 194, 199n94
Boko Haram, 83
Bull, Hedley, 23, 24
Byman, Daniel, 158, 167, 170n81, 181, 199n81

Campana, Paolo, 124
casualty avoidance, 31, 32–33, 159
CBRN. *See* weapons of mass destruction
Che Guevara, 122, 140
child soldiers, 3, 89, 92, 121–122, 137n38, 149

About the Author

Peter G. Thompson is an associate professor of International Security Studies at the College of International Security Affairs at National Defense University in Washington, D.C. He has developed and taught a wide range of International Relations and International Security courses at the undergraduate and graduate level. Prior to joining the faculty at NDU, Peter taught at UCLA, Loyola Marymount University, and Michigan State University. His research has been published in *Security Studies* and the *Annual Review of Political Science*. He holds a bachelor's degree from the University of Texas at Austin and earned his PhD at the University of California, Los Angeles. Peter resides in Falls Church, Virginia with his wife and two children.

CPSIA information can be obtained at www.ICGtesting.com
Printed in the USA
BVOW05s2016060814

361907BV00003B/7/P